NEGOTIATE GOOD
NEGOTIATE WELL
THE POWER OF AMBIDEXTERITY

D1574547

NEGOTIATE GOOD
NEGOTIATE WELL
THE POWER OF AMBIDEXTERITY

KANDARP H. MEHTA
GUIDO STEIN

Mc Graw Hill

Madrid · Milán · Londres · México D.F. · Sídney · Singapur · Taipéi · Shanghái
Seúl · Beijing · Hong Kong · Kuala Lumpur · Bangkok · Nueva York · Chicago
Dubuque · Los Ángeles · Columbus · Bogotá · Nueva Delhi · Toronto · Dubái

NEGOTIATE GOOD, NEGOTIATE WELL
THE POWER OF AMBIDEXTERITY

No part of this publication may be reproduced or distributed in any form or by any means, or Stored in a database or retrieval system, without the prior written consent of copyright proprietor, including, but not limited to, any network or other electronic storage or Transmission, or broadcast for distance learning.

Copyright reserved © 2021 by:

McGraw-Hill/Interamericana de España, S.L.
Edificio Oasis, 1.ª planta
Basauri, 17
28023 Aravaca (Madrid)

ISBN (print) 978-84-486-2537-5
ISBN (digital-ebook) 978-84-486-2539-9
ISBN (digital-VS) 978-84-486-2538-2
ISBN (bundle print-ebook) 978-84-486-2540-5

Legal Deposit: M-23313-2021

Editor: Cristina Sánchez Sainz-Trápaga
Higher Education Sales Manager: Pere Campanario Oliver
General Director South Europe: Álvaro García Tejeda
Cover Design: Mar Nieto Novoa
Interior Design: Noufront, S.L.
Printer: Pulmen, S.L.L.

0412356789 - 2625242322

IMPRESO EN ESPAÑA - PRINTED IN SPAIN

Dedicated to my parents,
Harsiddh Dinanath Mehta and Bhavna Mehta,
for successfully negotiating many hardships throughout
their lives and making us believe, everything is possible.

KANDARP H. MEHTA

To my beloved Luisa,
who does - Negotiate Good and Negotiate well,
and to Jaime, Alicia, Luisa, José Otto,
Guido and Juan, who are still "in process".

GUIDO STEIN

CONTENTS

Introduction: A way of life 13
    1. An attitude 14
    2. Ambidexterity 14

SECTION I Preparing to Negotiate: Situation and Process

CHAPTER 1: The Negotiation Challenge 19
    1. Management of Expectation 23
    2. Measurement of performance 24
    3. Summary 24

CHAPTER 2: Determining Expectations 25
    1. Analysis of Expectations 27
    2. The other side of the story 30
    3. Negotiation Analysis 32
    4. Zone of Possible Agreement (ZOPA) 33
    5. Summary 33

CHAPTER 3: Negotiation Preparation 35
    1. Situation Analysis 36
    2. Framework for analyzing the situation 41
    3. Summary 42

CHAPTER 4: Negotiation Process: Initiation 43
    1. Expectations and Process 43
    2. Approaches for determining the negotiation process 44
    3. Stage I: Preparation 46
    4. Stage - II Interaction Stage 47
        4.1. Exploration 47
    5. Summary 51

CHAPTER 5: Framing 53
    1. Understanding the counterpart's framing 56

    2. Construction of framing 60
    3. Summary 62

CHAPTER 6: Offers and concessions 63
    1. Advantages of making the first offer 63
    2. Disadvantages of making the first offer 65
    3. Strategies for making the first offer 68
    4. Concessions 70
        4.1. Impatience 72
        4.2. Irrationality 72
        4.3. Types of Concessions 73
    5. Strategies for Concessions 73
        5.1. Concession order 73
        5.2. Justification 74
        5.3. No Free Meals 74
        5.4. Hitch-hiking 74
    6. Multi-Issue Offers 74
        6.1. Risk of Deadlock 77
        6.2. Overshadowing 77
        6.3. Strategy 77
    7. Factors inhibiting Multi-issue Offers 78
    8. Principles of Multi-issue Offers 79
        8.1. Offer a negotiable package 79
        8.2. Build trust 79
        8.3. Discover priorities 79
        8.4. Create an evaluation system 79
        8.5. Always close the package 81

CHAPTER 7: Closing the Negotiation 83
    1. Reaching an Agreement 83
    2. Maintaining Calm 84
    3. Checklist for Closing a Negotiation 84
        3.1. Needs 85
        3.2. Agreement 85
        3.3. Time 85
        3.4. Allocation of Tasks 85
        3.5. Precision 85
        3.6. Measurability 85
        3.7. Dispute Resolution Mechanism 86
    4. Stage III Post-Negotiation 86

CHAPTER 8: Six Tenets of Ambidexterity 87

1. Focus on Multiple Needs	89
2. Do Your Homework	90
3. Listen Carefully to the Other Side	91
4. Use Offers Strategically	91
5. Always Seek the Common Ground	92
6. Don't Ignore the Music	93
7. Summary	94

SECTION II Negotiation in Special Contexts

CHAPTER 9: Negotiating in a Team 97
1. Impact of Team Negotiations on Outcomes 97
2. Challenges in a Team Negotiation 98
   2.1. Lack of Coordination 98
   2.2. Poor Control of the Process 99
3. Role-Assignment for Management of Information 100
4. Collective Preparation 100
5. Caucus 101
6. Conflict During the Negotiation 101
7. Leadership 102
8. Preparation Guides 102
9. Essential Information Sheet 103

CHAPTER 10: Multiparty Negotiation 105
1. Identifying Other's Interests 105
2. Power and Alliance 106
3. Affinity Map 106
4. Listening to Others and Showing You Listen 108
5. Making Suggestions about the Process 108
6. Reaching agreement and making alliances 109
7. Establishing the core 111
8. Circular Logrolling 112
9. Understanding Others 113
10. Fighting a Hostile Alliance 114

CHAPTER 11: Negotiating in Dire Straits 117
1. The Kidnapping 117
   1.1. Academic Break I - Where there is no negotiation, create one 118
   1.2. Whatever can go wrong 118
   1.3. Academic Break II - Determine Alternatives and Agreements 119
   1.4. Zone of Possible Agreements 120
2. What can I do? 121

  2.1. Who is the leader? 121
  2.2. Academic Break III - Avoid a play of positions 121
 3. Exploring options 122
  3.1. Academic Break IV - Analyze relative power and overcome imbalance of power 123
 4. Growing Trust 124
  4.1. Academic Break V - Trust and Empathy 125
 5. Creating an Agreement 125
 6. Epilogue - Process of Negotiation 126

CHAPTER 12: Negotiating Across Cultures 129
 1. Negotiation Situations and Style 129
 2. Keys to Understanding Culture 129
 3. Individualism Vs Collectivism 130
 4. How do individualistic and collectivist cultures affect negotiations? 131
 5. Egalitarian and Hierarchical Cultures 132
  5.1. How do hierarchical and egalitarian cultures affect negotiations? 132
 6. Low-Context vs High-Context Cultures 132
  6.1. Impact on Negotiation 132
 7. Cultural Prototypes and Impact on Negotiation 133
 8. False Affiliations 133
  8.1. Cultural Adaptation 134
 9. East vs. West and Beyond 135
 10. Dignity Culture 136
 11. Face Culture 136
 12. Honor Culture 136
  12.1. Mindset and Trust 137
  12.2. Trust and culture 137
  12.3. Social Motivation 137
 13. Final Advice: Do Not Overlook the Individual 138
 14. Recommendations for Negotiating with a Different Culture 139

CHAPTER 13: Negotiating Your Job Offer 141
 1. An Approach to Driving Negotiations 141
 2. The Question of Salary During Negotiations 143
 3. How Should You Approach a Job Interview? 145
  3.1. Help Them Help You 145
  3.2. Understanding the Other Parties: Sharing Their Criteria and Constraints 145
 4. The Trees Are Not the Whole Forest 146
 5. Anchoring in the Negotiation 146
 6. It's Not Personal—It's Negotiation 147

CHAPTER 14: Negotiating in a Virtual World 151
1. How do Space and Time Influence Negotiations? 151
2. The Social Distance Model 153
3. The Online Negotiation Process 154
4. Approach 155
5. Exploratory Phase 156
6. Options and Concessions 157
   6.1. Closing 157
7. Strategies for Successful Online Negotiations 158
   7.1. Preparation 158

CHAPTER 15: A Peep into the Future: Automated Negotiations 167
1. Introduction 167
2. Negotiation Support Systems 168
3. How do NSS Operate to Complement and Improve the Negotiation? 168
4. Facilitation and Communication Support 169
5. Decision Analysis Support 170
6. Negotiation Analysis Support 170
   6.1. NSS and the Negotiation Process 170
   6.2. Preparation of the Negotiation 171
   6.3. Examination of the Information 171
   6.4. Offers and Concessions 172
   6.5. Post-Negotiation 172
7. The Automation of Negotiation 172
8. Negotiation Preparation 173
   8.1. Negotiation Process 173
   8.2. Post-Negotiation 174
9. Final Reflection 174

SECTION III Cases and Self-Practice

Bagheera 177
1. Bagheera Buyer 178
2. Bagheera Seller 179

Kushphal Conundrum 180
1. Representative of Nutrison 181
   1.1. About Nutrison 181
   1.2. About You 181
   1.3. About Sanuter and Kushphal 181
   1.4. The procurement procedure of Kushphal 182
   1.5. Post-Purchase Processing 182
   1.6. Estimates 183

- 1.7. Emergency 183
- 1.8. Meeting with the boss 183
- 1.9. Today 184
- 2. Representative of Brin 185
  - 2.1. About Medicinal Research Lab, Brin University 185
  - 2.2. About SkinShield 185
  - 2.3. About You 185
  - 2.4. About SkinShield and Ramphal 186
  - 2.5. The procurement procedure of Kushphal 186
  - 2.6. Post-Purchase Processing 186
  - 2.7. Emergency 186
  - 2.8. Decision 187
  - 2.9. Today 187

The Apartment 188
- 1. The Role of Tenant 189
- 2. The Role of Owner 191

Style Biz 193
- 1. Style Biz - General Information 194
- 2. Style Biz Company - Role of Digital Director 197
- 3. Style Biz - Role of Director of Operations 201
- 4. Letter from the digital director to the director of operations (A) 202
- 5. Letter From the Chief Strategy Officer to the Director of Operations (B) 203
- 6. Style Biz - Role of Director of Strategy 205
- 7. Style Biz - The Final Outcome 209

Continental Insurance Vs. Alpaca Hotels 210
- 1. The chief investment officer of Continental Insurance 211
- 2. Continental Insurance versus. Alpaca Hotels 214

Yaris versus Zilan 217
- 1. Representative of Yaris, from Yaristan 217
  - 1.1. Micro-Drones 217
- 2. Representative of Zilan Ltd., from Ziland 221
  - 2.1. Micro-Drones 222
  - 2.2. Primary issues already agreed 223

Epilogue: Never stop learning 225
Bibliography and intellectual influences 227

> "Efficiency is doing things right;
> effectiveness is doing the right things."
>
> Peter Drucker

INTRODUCTION: A WAY OF LIFE

In your daily life, you make many decisions, both in your personal as well as professional space. For many decisions, you need consent, approval or contribution of some sort from others. *Negotiate Good, Negotiate Well* is a book to invite you to be more ambitious in those situations. Whenever you need the cooperation of others to obtain what you want or need, negotiation becomes the most effective tool and very often the shortest path to do it. The dichotomy is only theoretical, because, negotiating good, effectively, demands negotiating well, efficiently.

Prof. Juan Roure, at IESE Business School, started offering negotiation courses in the latter half of the 80s. The unique proposition of Juan Roure's negotiation philosophy was that, instead of focusing on a singular approach of negotiation, he showed that negotiation is a skill, and it is important to adapt to the situation. In this book, we have expanded the basic model introduced by Juan Roure and Richard Pascale to a situation-based negotiation model with ambidexterity as the primary element of the negotiation skill.

The authors want the reader to know from the very beginning that their intensive research, together with their teaching, and extensive practice under a rich array of circumstances over the last thirty years showed them that the best outcome of all kinds of negotiations always creates value for all parties involved by satisfying their real needs.

Effective negotiators know that the only good negotiation is the one that ends in a win-win solution, except in the case that one party strives to win twice. The name of the first step, or necessary condition, is thorough preparation, to which we will devote a large part. The second step is building trust towards cooperation; negotiation without cooperation is a mirage. The journey in search of mutual trust aims to be the thread to lead the reader through the labyrinth of real conflicts, present in every negotiation. Most negotiators believe that they are deceived on average 40-50% of the time. However, these same people admit to using deception in about 25% of their negotiations.

Like Ariadne in Crete, the reader might find some efficient and effective clues to get what they need, and even more.

1. AN ATTITUDE

Negotiating the positions of the involved parties might seem incompatible because they entail contradictory demands. Nevertheless, if they are ready to dig a bit deeper into the positions, preparing properly the questions to ask each other, then, after gathering the relevant information, they might discover that their goals, and therefore needs, were more complementary than what they had at first presumed.

Believing that one party has preferences that are directly opposed to the others on all the issues on the table constitutes initially a bias to be managed; the advisable attitude to negotiate good and well should avoid arguing over positions, but rather seek to explore underlying interests. The coming pages contain quite a few ideas and tools.

There is no valid substitute for preparation. Empirical studies and broad experience teach that there is a correlation between better preparation and richer performance. There are two kinds of preparation: the preparation that focuses on one side´s position, rehearsing its demands and figuring out a tough opening and a competitive framing, aiming at winning the other party over in every issue at stake; and the preparation that focuses firstly on identifying the most desirable set of terms for each of the issues. Secondly, on alternative courses of action, and, thirdly, on frames for the subsequent process as an open discussion, rather than a series of battles. In both cases, those who have not prepared themselves for the first offer should avoid starting a negotiation. In the book, you will discover that preparation does not mean just preparing for an outcome, but also preparing for the process of the negotiation.

Being the most prepared person in the room is a must: know the facts and the emotions involved, because facts provide information, and emotions provide the right interpretation; anticipate the arguments; understand your weaknesses.

2. AMBIDEXTERITY

The reader will face once and again situations where they have to make the right choice, either to compete or to explore the potential of collaboration to get what they want. We call ambidexterity the ability to negotiate good and well with both hands, so being competitive and collaborative depending on what the situation is demanding. In fact, negotiators who aim to become ambidextrous better realize that the only way to improve their outcomes is by improving the other party´s outcome.

The single-issue negotiations are fixed sum; it means that one side wins at the cost of the other side: whatever one gains, the other loses. If one can identify a new issue that at least one of the sides cares about, then this is the starting point for a win-win deal. The best way to overcome a fixed-sum negotiation (that means competitive) is by adding a new issue from outside the current negotiation's table; or by dividing the issue on the table into more than just one, for instance, by separating price from how to pay it: "name a price, I will give you a structure; name a structure and I will give you a price"; or distinguishing between now and the future; percentage versus total amount. So, one creates more opportunities for win-win tradeoffs. In order to squeeze this potential, it is key for a negotiator to handle several parts of a deal at the same time, instead of one after another.

A win-win negotiation generates an agreement that both parties cannot mutually improve upon. In general, this kind of positive relationship among parties is not the result of instrumental concessions, but an outcome of a satisfying social interaction.

As Leigh Thompson affirms: "The best state of affairs is to have a negotiator who is cooperative in working with the other party to understand and explore his issues and interests and competitive enough to claim valuable resources for himself". *Ambidexterity* is definitely the name of the game.

The authors want to express their gratitude first to IESE Business School for giving them the generous and unique opportunity to write this book and check their rigor and relevance with thousands of participants in all kinds of Programs at the School; also, their acknowledgement to the participants themselves for their outstanding contribution to the book, and to the colleagues of the Negotiation Unit.

We reserve our most special gratitude for Prof. Juan Roure who, for many years, apart from being the most inspirational intellectual leader, has been also the mentor for both authors. Juan Roure's teaching style and philosophy have greatly influenced not only the authors but almost all the colleagues at the Negotiation Unit at IESE Business School.

So, let's begin the journey!

SECTION I

PREPARING TO NEGOTIATE: SITUATION AND PROCESS

THE NEGOTIATION CHALLENGE

CHAPTER 1

1. WHAT ARE WE TALKING ABOUT?

One of our friends once recounted a funny anecdote. It was about his very first visit to India. Despite being on a business visit, he squeezed out some time to do some shopping. He went to a local market in the old quarter of the city and, while window-shopping at random, spotted an interesting t-shirt. It featured Mahatma Gandhi's picture and the inspirational adage, "Be the change!" Before buying the t-shirt, he remembered some of his friends' advice about the culture of bargaining prevalent in some markets in India. He decided to bargain for a better price. The seller asked for almost the equivalent of $25 in Indian Rupees (as per the exchange rate at the time), and our friend, after some heavy bargaining, ended up paying an equivalent of about $9. He felt triumphant. The next day at his local collaborator's office, he saw an intern wearing the same t-shirt with the same picture and adage. He asked the boy where he bought it. The boy said that he had got it from the market in the old quarter. Our friend was intrigued. He asked how much it cost him. The boy said 100 Indian Rupees, or a value of $2 (as per the exchange rate at the time). Our friend's self-image of a victorious bargainer started to melt. He later told us that what had troubled him was not the extra money he paid but the fact that he hadn't been as successful at negotiating as he'd thought.

Let's analyze this example a bit further. Think of our friend's dissatisfaction after learning about his negotiation failure. Two underlying factors made him unhappy: the realization that he had paid more than what he needed to and the false sense of adequacy he felt with his negotiation efforts. He thought he had negotiated well enough, but that was not the case.

There are two essential aspects to the evaluation of the result of a negotiation. One is the result itself (how much I have gained), and the other is the negotiation process and its impact (how I obtained it). The process and the result mutually affect each other. A very swift negotiation process may make a lousy negotiation result seem acceptable, and an awful and cumbersome negotiation experience may make a great outcome look bad. In the previous example, you could tell our friend felt good about the negotiation because he thought he had already achieved a great result. However, when he compared his transaction to another case, he realized the negotiation outcome was not as good. In our professional life, however, we seldom have the luxury of comparison. Consequently, we often don't know whether the result of our negotiation is fair.

In the following paragraph, we establish why it is so important to evaluate negotiation performance objectively.

1.1. Performance evaluation and confirmation bias

We negotiate because we want to achieve a certain outcome. Imagine you are selling your house. How would you determine what the property is worth? You would do some research. You would find some comparable properties in the same or a similar neighborhood which were put up for sale in the recent past. But what if you couldn't find this information? What if there were no comparable properties? Obviously it would be difficult for you to negotiate. When we are clear about what we want to achieve, it's easier to negotiate, and it's also easier to evaluate our negotiation performance. However, in negotiations where it's difficult to predetermine the result, any evaluation of the negotiation performance is difficult.

When we aren't sure about an objective result, confirmation bias kicks in. Confirmation bias is, primarily, wishful thinking. Sometimes in decision-making situations, we pick out bits of information that confirm our biases, prejudices, or theories. In other words, instead of doing research and then negotiating based on information, we do the opposite. First, we negotiate, and then we look for information to justify our actions.

An executive in one of our programs once shared a very interesting story. He was working for a chemical manufacturing company. One time, they made a mistake in the composition of ingredients in one of their shipments, and the customer demanded a complete replacement of the order. Since this was one of the company's biggest clients, the company agreed to this tall order. The biggest roadblock was a lack of raw material. Given the urgency of the situation, they decided to buy the raw material from their regular supplier. Let's say the supplier asked for $5 per ml of the ingredient. This would raise the cost to almost half a million dollars.

The company's internal calculations suggested that the cost of the ingredient should be no more than $2.25 per ml. Eventually, they settled for $3.50 per ml after a three-day negotiation. They could not afford to stretch the negotiation any longer. When they closed the deal, the entire negotiation team —our friend, his boss (the vice president), and the company's Chief Financial Officer— unanimously concluded that they couldn't have got a better price. They even had a little celebration after the final call from the supplier. After a couple of months, our friend met the Chief Marketing Officer of the same supplier organization. He had now retired from the job. Coincidentally, they became neighbors and good friends over time. One evening, about a year later, over a cup of coffee, they started talking about the aforementioned deal. The former Chief Marketing Officer shared that the deal they had reached was one of the best they had ever closed. The supplier was ready to sell for about $2 per ml as it had been a bad year for them and they badly needed to push their volumes up. When our friend asked him, "But if you were under pressure, why did you insist on a higher price? And why did you start so high?" the older gentleman replied, "Well, that's the way we always negotiated. You just didn't try enough!"

This is something that may happen to us as well. However, we don't have the luxury of our negotiation counterpart later on telling us how poorly we performed. In situations of high uncertainty, we tend to choose the information that confirms our assumptions. For example, how often have you told yourself, after a negotiation?, "I knew they couldn't have paid more." Or, "This was probably the best they could offer. It's good that I closed the deal." The tendency to be selective about information that only confirms our theories or opinions is known as confirmation bias. Due to confirmation bias, we don't see the situation in its entirety. Moreover, Confirmation bias becomes more relevant in multicultural negotiations. We have personally come across managers who confess they almost failed to land some potential deals just because they had severe misgivings about the cultural, national, or even professional background of their counterparts.

1.2. Agreement bias

Let's consider another example. Setu owns a family business for dry fruits and nuts in a city in western India. He once received an order from a big chain of restaurants to quickly supply a specific quantity of cashews and almonds. On the one hand, the chain needed someone urgently, so Setu didn't know if he should charge a slightly higher price than the market value, especially since, during the festive season, cashews and almonds were slightly in low supply, and he knew he might have to work extra hours to meet the order. He knew the restaurant chain had never bought from him before, and he wasn't sure who their leading suppliers were. However, he knew that his own main supplier would be out of stock. Setu's accountant told him that prices could rise in that season, and that he could charge a premium. However, Setu didn't want to lose a client with such a significant reputation. Nevertheless, when he started negotiating the order, the counterpart pressured him for a considerable discount. Setu tried to offer a long-term contract in return for a discount, to which the restaurant chain didn't agree. Setu did not want to budge. The restaurant was asking for at least a 15% discount on the market price. After two days of negotiation, Setu ended up asking for the market price and at least avoided any considerable discount.

Was this a good deal? Could Setu have charged more? When he discussed the agreement with his accountant, he said, "Well! At least we have closed the deal."

Have you ever been in a similar situation, when the only consolation you have is that at least you closed the deal? In other words, you measure the success of the negotiation based solely on whether the deal has been closed or not. This phenomenon is also known as agreement bias. An agreement bias occurs when a negotiator is not aware of any other rational yardstick by which to measure the outcome of the negotiation and assumes that any deal is always better than no deal. Agreement bias quite often makes a negotiator settle for a sub-optimal outcome.

Another problem with the agreement bias is that we end up overlooking the possibilities of creating more value. In the words of Leigh Thompson, "The agreement bias occurs when negotiators focus on reaching common ground with the other party and are reluctant to accept differences of interest, even when such acceptance might create viable options for joint gain."[1] In other words, having a different opinion or interest is not always bad for a negotiation.

1.3. Emotions

Furthermore, because of not having rational and comparable information during negotiation, we depend too much on how the process of negotiation 'feels' while we negotiate. Due to excessive emotional stress, a negotiator often gets unnecessarily personal, and emotions become obstacles to the process of rational decision making. Our experience has shown that when a negotiator deals with a very angry counterpart, regardless of how good the outcome may be for the negotiator, they perceive the process negatively and therefore aren't satisfied with the result.

This is why it is essential to analyze the negotiation situation rationally and overcome any individual biases before the negotiation begins.

2. MANAGEMENT OF EXPECTATION

The previous section shows us how important it is to manage expectations in a negotiation, in which the outcome is the most important factor. However, it's also vital to analyze our expectations before the negotiation to have a clearer idea of what we want to achieve.

- **Know which strategy to adopt:**

    In Lewis Carroll's masterpiece 'Alice in Wonderland', there is a very interesting conversation between the Cheshire cat and Alice. It goes like this:

    Alice: Cheshire Puss, would you tell me please, which way I ought to walk from here?
    Cat: That depends a good deal on where you want to get to.
    Alice: I don't much care where—
    Cat: Then, it doesn't matter which way you walk.
    Alice: So long as I get somewhere.
    Cat: Oh, you're sure to do that, if you only walk long enough.

    This little conversation is a very succinct example of why it is crucial to have a well-defined objective in a negotiation. Also, if we are not clear about what we wish to get in a negotiation, it will be even more challenging to know how to get it.

---

1   Thompson, Leigh, "The mind and heart of negotiator", sixth edition. Page 217.

- **Avoid agreement bias**
  As Alice says in the dialogue, when one doesn't know where to go, one just hopes "to get somewhere". As we have already learned, this might result in a dangerous agreement bias. Any negotiator who enters a negotiation thinking about going 'somewhere' ends up settling for something less than optimal. Negotiators should always do their best to know where they need or want to go.

3. MEASUREMENT OF PERFORMANCE

Finally, one of the main issues in negotiation is not being able to measure performance – not being able to gauge whether the negotiation has been a success or a failure. Ascertaining expectations before the negotiation helps understand how successful the negotiation has been as well.

4. SUMMARY

One of the main problems for a negotiator is the lack of clarity regarding the negotiation. The resulting issues are threefold: the lack of a defined result goal, falling victim to an agreement bias, and not adopting the optimum approach to the negotiation.

In the following chapter, we'll discuss how to ascertain expectations in a negotiation situation.

Food for Thought

Now that you've understood the importance of negotiation performance, take some time and write down your best and your worst negotiation so far. Try to write down what worked for you and what didn't.

CHAPTER 2

DETERMINING EXPECTATIONS

John left his job in sales on 31st December, the last day of the year. He had worked for the company for the past three years and had been studying computer programming at the same time. He recently finished his course and wanted to work for a company where he could put his programming skills to use. John sent his CVs to a total of three different companies, two of which had announced their openings on an employment portal. The third had not advertised any vacancy, but John had a friend who was working there, and he knew that soon the company would be hiring new programmers.

Let's take a closer look at the three positions John applied for. The first company that interviewed him was a small publishing house in need of back-office work, system maintenance, and occasional programming—primarily for web-page design for new publications. The bulk of the work, however, would involve back-office operations. The company offered him a salary of forty-one thousand US dollars ($41,000) which was about thirteen thousand US dollars ($13,000) more than the compensation provided by his previous employer.

The second company offered thirty-eight thousand US dollars ($38,000). This company was an automobile sales agency and needed someone with skills in computers and programming to work on their internal information systems that linked inventory and sales operations. The work involved a lot more intensive use of John's programming skills than the previous one. However, the position also entailed potentially longer work hours at the end of each quarter. Since the company office was located in an industrial area, far from the residential zone of the city where John lived, it would also involve at least a two-hour commute every day.

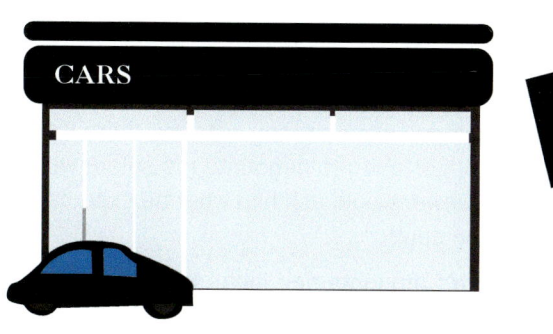

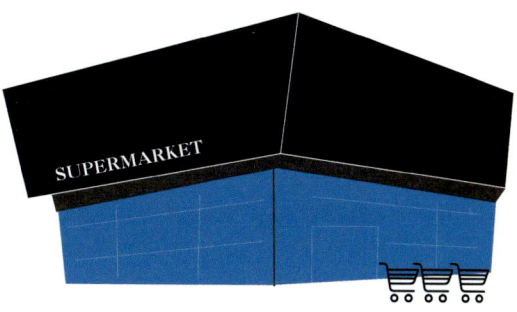

The third company was a supermarket chain that planned to open a new division for online shopping and was going to need programmers to design and execute a website for that purpose. Even though the company was going to hire external consultants to run the entire web-design operation, it wanted to encourage its staff to engage with the process so that future website updates and maintenance would be more affordable. That was the reason John's friend advised him to send his CV so that, when the position opened, his would be one of the first to be seen.

John interviewed for the first two companies on the same day, and both potential employers liked him and offered him the job. He had a week to decide. The next day his friend called him and said he should go in for an interview at the third company since they wanted to start screening potential candidates whose profiles were already in their system, instead of announcing the position on a portal and having to filter through hundreds of fresh applicants. John asked his friend about the expected salary. His friend said that this was a new position and online shopping was an entirely new line of business; as a result, there was no precedent. All he could tell John was that the company was looking for someone with a learning attitude and some programming skills as well as the ability to learn new skills on the job. This new line of business was likely to face many challenges. To make sure that the unit worked well, the company had decided to set up the online business division in a different premise altogether, removed from the central office. They wanted the online business division to function like a startup where employees worked as a team and adapted to new challenges at maximum efficiency. However, it was hard to say what the company would offer John. They scheduled an interview within a day, giving John about twenty-four hours to prepare.

John decided to approach a relative of his who happened to be a university professor of negotiation. He called the professor and described his situation. The first thing the professor asked was whether John had any alternatives, at which point John described his first two job offers. The professor asked, "So, how much money do you expect the third company to offer?" "At least $41,000," John immediately replied. "So if they offer anything less than that, you won't accept the offer," said the professor. "Probably not," said John off the bat, but he kept going over his answer. He suddenly realized there were a number of issues he hadn't stopped to consider. "Well, I don't know. It's not that straightforward," he amended. Noticing his hesitation, the professor asked him to write down his thoughts, specifically adding, "Write down your expectations, not only from this particular negotiation, but in general—from this entire interview process as well as life in general. Then we will discuss the matter."

John decided to write down his thoughts to prepare for the interview. In his interviews with the first two companies, the salaries were already set, and there was no room for negotiation. However, he saw an opportunity to negotiate his salary with the third company since he was sure the interviewer would ask him what he expected to be paid. What should he do? What should he say?

On the next page you will find a list of John's thoughts and ideas from his notes about his salary negotiation.

What to expect?
• I should at least be getting paid $41,000.
• However, the job that guarantees $41,000 doesn't offer as many opportunities to use my programming skills. Therefore, if this third company offers slightly less than $41,000, I should accept it because it's a much better learning opportunity.
• All the same, I shouldn't be getting paid below $38,000.
• Being part of a new team also means that I may get promoted faster, and if I stick around, I may end up with a more prominent role sooner than I would at the first two companies. • Furthermore, working IT in this third company means that, in the future, I can expect similar jobs, and I will be able to stay within the field of IT.
• Maybe something close to $35,000 would also be acceptable since I wouldn't have to commute very much for this job. The offices are closer. It's also a bigger company than the other two. • Some of my friends have told me that most programming jobs earn $35,000 to $40,000 in non-IT companies. In IT companies, programming jobs get more, but for a fresh programmer with no experience, it's complicated to get a foot in the door.
• I should push for more than $41,000 and not accept anything below $36,000.
• What if they offer something even lower? Can I demand a better salary? Well, if they offer something too low, I have two other options. Thank God for that!

1. ANALYSIS OF EXPECTATIONS

Now let's try to understand John's preparation.

1.1. Alternatives

John is basing his expectations on the available alternatives. Alternatives are a vital driver of expectations in many negotiations. The seminal book *Getting to Yes* introduced us to the concept of Best Alternative to Negotiated Agreement (BATNA). When a negotiator determines what to expect in a negotiation, the negotiator looks at different alternatives. Among all the alternatives, the best (BATNA) is the one that establishes the basic expectation of the negotiator. Look back at John's notes. The very first sentence he writes is that he shouldn't accept anything lower than forty-one thousand dollars. In strictly financial terms, his best alternative is the one that offers him the highest possible salary.

1.2. Power

Check the last sentence of John's notes. "Can I demand a better salary?" Let's rephrase that question as, "How can I demand a better salary?" What arguments would help John claim a better salary? There are two types of arguments he can use—self-promoting and self-positioning. Self-promoting arguments focus on the qualities and skills that a candidate possesses. Self-positioning arguments, on the other hand, show the candidate's position by highlighting how positively others have valued them. In a job interview candidates use both types of arguments. What kind of self-positioning argument can John present here? Of course, he already has two alternatives. According to the negotiation model elaborated by Pascal and Roure, negotiators in all types of negotiations use alternatives to emphasize how valuable their proposition is. Alternatives are the most significant source of power in a negotiation. What do you think John's expectations would be if he didn't have the two alternatives he has at present? In the absence of these two alternatives, John's expectations would be less precise and probably lower.

1.3. Needs

Let's consider John's notes once again. He starts with a rigorous financial analysis, but soon he mentions other issues as well. For instance, he makes note of three critical aspects that would convince him to accept a salary lower than the one already offered: (i) the opportunity to learn about programming, (ii) the possibility of faster promotions, and (iii) potential future jobs. His thinking clearly shows that it's not just money that matters to him. In other words, he isn't looking for a job that would pay him forty-one thousand dollars' salary only.

He's looking for a job that would offer him the opportunity to further develop his programming skills, chances to put those programming skills to good use, probable growth within the company, improved chances of getting a better IT job in the future, and a minimum salary of around thirty-five thousand dollars. It's imperative to understand and analyze one's needs before going into a negotiation. When one doesn't focus on their needs properly before going into a negotiation, there are two important risks involved.

Risks of not analyzing needs

- a) **Excessive influence of alternatives** It's important to consider potential alternatives when we negotiate. However, we shouldn't forget that alternatives are our safety nets, and they may not necessarily be the best choices in every situation. Think of John's scenario. What if he doesn't think beyond alternatives? He would never accept anything less than forty-one thousand dollars. Only when he analyzes his needs in greater detail does he realizes that it might be better to accept a lower salary and satisfy other essential needs instead.

- b) **Excessive influence of numerical positions** When a negotiator doesn't analyze their needs in sufficient detail, there's a greater chance of being influenced by numbers. Later we'll see how negotiating solely about positions may increase the risk of getting stuck in a deadlock or not reaching an agreement. Let's assume that John goes into the negotiation with his thoughts fixed only on those forty-one thousand dollars, but the company offers him thirty-six thousand dollars instead. John refuses to budge from his original figure and ends up missing out on the job altogether. A detailed analysis of needs before every negotiation helps a negotiator understand a wide range of issues to address during the negotiation and helps to have a more flexible negotiating approach, thus saving the negotiator from a potential deadlock.

1.4. References

Besides needs and alternatives, negotiators also use references in a negotiation. For example, we see in John's notes that he also mentions average salaries received by programmers in IT companies. This information can be a useful reference, but it can't provide a perfect basis for establishing expectations for the negotiation. A negotiator needs to have some relative references of value before going into a negotiation. For example, if you're buying a used car or a house, you would do some research and jot down comparable prices of similar assets. In a negotiation where there is no alternative, references can help a negotiator base their expectations.

1.5. Reservation Price

In the end, John concludes that he'll be satisfied as long as he gets thirty-six thousand dollars as his salary. In other words, to be satisfied with the deal, John expects to receive at least thirty-six thousand. He would most likely reject an offer of anything less than that. Quite often, negotiators set a limit for acceptability of the deal also known as a reservation price or walkaway price. Such a limit is slightly different from the BATNA. It shows additional value that the negotiator attaches to the negotiation at hand.

Here is a summary of our analysis of John's expectations.

	Understanding John's Expectations
Need	A job that offers good learning opportunities A job that opens better prospects in his chosen field in future A position with prospects of faster promotions
Alternative	$41,000 and $38,000 respectively
Reference	$35,000 – $40,000 average salary in the field
Reservation Price	Minimum $36,000

In summary, there are three crucial elements that negotiators use to determine what to expect from a negotiation. These three elements are **needs, alternatives, and references**. It is essential to understand each one of these factors in detail before every negotiation.

2. THE OTHER SIDE OF THE STORY

Here is the story of Michael. Michael is a general manager in the Human Resources department at a well-known supermarket chain. You guessed it right: the same supermarket chain where our friend from the previous section, John, applied for a job. Michael joined the company three months ago as a fresh MBA. Before his MBA, he was working in a software startup. During his MBA, Michael developed a keen interest in the management of talent and human capital in companies. He was surprised that a supermarket chain would show any interest in him, but he was told that he was hired primarily because of his experience in dealing with technical talent in a software startup. He was told he would eventually be needed to help manage human capital in a new division for an online business that the company was planning to start in about six months. Michael was still under training and was beginning to understand the complex operations of the company's human resource functions when, all of a sudden, he was asked to prepare for a transfer to the new division. He found out later that the company had decided to launch the online business much sooner than expected because some key competitors were likely to launch a similar business within the same timeframe. Michael had to set up a team of programmers and web designers to work on a beta version of the web page. He discussed the recruitment process with the senior vice president of human resources as well as the vice president of business development (who was slotted to be the Chief Operations Officer of the online business). They realized they didn't have enough time to approach universities to recruit fresh graduates since it was still January and new graduates wouldn't be available before May. They also discarded headhunters or recruitment agencies as those entities might charge a premium for working on such short notice. In the end, they decided to recruit junior programmers at this stage and invest more time and effort in recruiting senior executives at a later point in time.

Since they didn't have much time, Michael decided to have a look at some curriculum vitae they already had on file. He found two CVs that would suit the requirements for a junior programmer and called both of them for the interview. Both CVs had arrived through current company employees. Michael wished to hire both the candidates in order to save time and establish himself as an efficient recruiter. Before starting the interview process, he spoke with the Vice Presidents of Human Resources and Business Development about the salary structure of the candidates. Originally, it was arranged that the company would offer a base salary with a scale of $34,500 to $38,000, the same amount the company provided to junior executives with at least two years' work experience in other departments. With the base salary range of $34,500 to $38,000 and the addition of various adjustments and perquisites, candidates would end up receiving a net salary of about forty thousand ($40,000) dollars.

At the same time, Michael tried to investigate the salaries of programmers in information technology companies and software startups, and he noticed salaries went up to $45,000. For experienced programmers (about five years in the field), the number was as high as $50,000. After consulting a few friends who worked in similar companies, he presented the following arguments to his superiors.

1.	We need to make sure that the junior programmers who join stay on at least for a year.
2.	Given the high turnover in IT jobs, it would be crucial to offer them competitive salaries. Even though ours is not a software startup, we should provide similar salaries and an equivalent work environment. Otherwise, programmers will have too much incentive to find another job in any number of purely technological companies.
3.	Looking at the immediacy of the requirement, we should be prepared to offer up to $46,000 in salaries.
4.	However, if it becomes difficult to recruit a junior programmer at that level, then it would be better to invest more time and resources and hire more experienced programmer whom we would pay close to $50,000.

Both Michael's bosses liked his arguments, and they agreed to all his points except the last. They saw the sense in not paying more than the established limit, but they weren't sure if they could afford to wait for a more experienced programmer. The company would explore different options for temporarily outsourcing web design and maintenance if they couldn't put a team together right away. Either way, immediate programmer recruitment and the green light for an aggressive launch targets remained the top priorities.

Taking all this into consideration, let's follow the blueprint we developed in the previous section and try to understand Michael's expectations.

	Understanding Michael's Expectations
Need	Hiring a programmer or two Make sure that those programmers stay on at least a full year Make sure the programmers don't leave for pure IT startup companies
Alternative	To wait for at least three weeks, which his superiors may not approve.
Reference	$34,500 - $38,000 $45,000 $46,000
Reservation Price	$46,000

3. NEGOTIATION ANALYSIS

Now that we have the complete picture, let's go back to John. We know John will feel comfortable as long as he gets $36,000. However, now that we've read his counterpart's situation, we know John can ask for more. In most negotiations, negotiators leave value on the table or don't reach full potential because they don't either know or fail to recognize how much the other side is prepared to offer. Quite often, as we can gather from John's notes, negotiators approach a negotiation under the assumption that the other side won't be willing to meet their expectations. Negotiators often negotiate with one-sided information and fail to recognize the needs and interests of the other side.

Let's try to draw the complete picture now.

John's Expectations		Michael's Expectations
A job that offers good learning opportunities, a position that could lead to better prospects in his chosen field in the future, and a position with higher odds of quick promotion.	Need	Hire a programmer or two Make sure those programmers stay for at least a year Make sure they don't leave for pure IT startup companies
$41,000 and $38,000 respectively	Alternative	To wait for at least three weeks, although his superiors may not approve.
$35,000 to $40,000 average salary in the field	Reference	1. $34,500 to $38,000, the internal reference of the company 2. $45,000, the external reference of the software industry 3. $50,000, in reference to professionals with more experience
$36,000	Reservation Price	$46,000

When we consider the situation, we can see that John's position is a lot better than what he assumed; he could easily claim and create higher value for himself. In other words, it would help John to consider the following questions before negotiations begin.

1. What are the needs of the company? How might recruiting a programmer benefit the company strategically?
2. In the event he doesn't get recruited, how many alternatives might the company have?
3. What's the maximum salary the company is willing to pay for this position?

4. ZONE OF POSSIBLE AGREEMENT (ZOPA)

Another important concept to remember is something known as the Zone of Possible Agreement (ZOPA). In this case study, John would be willing to accept a salary of $36,000, while the company would be willing to pay a salary of about $46,000. In other words, the probabilities are high that the final agreement would land somewhere between those two figures.

$36,000 ←—————————————————————→ $46,000
Zone of Possible Agreement

A negotiator should always identify the ZOPA in order to have a better understanding of their potential creation of value. The zone of possible agreement would be determined either by the reservation price or by the respective BATNAs of the interested parties. It's essential to understand the zone of possible agreement not only to accurately assess potential value but also to establish better strategies for offers and concessions, as we'll observe later on.

5. SUMMARY

A proper analysis of needs is essential if a negotiator wants to avoid making mistakes—both one's own needs and the needs of any participating counterpart. One should also explore alternatives of each side. Alternatives are the fundamental source of power and control in a negotiation, and that's why neglecting alternatives may lead to errors. A negotiator often has to operate with a reservation price that sets their limit. The reservation price for both sides determines the ZOPA (Zone of Possible Agreement). A negotiator needs to assess the ZOPA in order to consider value creation potential.

> **Food for Thought**
>
> Take a negotiation you are going to engage in soon. Try to use the framework of analysis of expectations that we've developed and analyze your expectations as well as the expectations of your counterpart from the negotiation.

CHAPTER 3

PREPARING TO NEGOTIATE

In this chapter, we'll look at some of the different elements of negotiation preparation. Theoretically, there are three main issues that a negotiator should consider: expectations, situational analysis, and strategic response. In other words, before every negotiation, a series of questions need to be asked. What do I want? Where do I stand? How will I get what I want?

Preparation is the most crucial step in any negotiation process. We've already discussed the importance of understanding the expectations of both participating sides prior to the actual negotiation. To better understand the preparation stage, let's start with a list of questions and figure out how to respond to them. The following are the crucial points that a negotiator needs to consider before beginning a negotiation.

1. What result do I expect from this negotiation?
2. How much influence do I have over this negotiation?
3. What would the other side expect from this negotiation?
4. How much can the other side influence this negotiation?

In the previous chapter, we established that negotiation expectations depend on two crucial factors—needs and power. Needs are not just limited to a particular product or service; a negotiator must understand the underlying interests as well. For example, when you want to buy a book, the underlying interest is not the book itself but the desire for entertainment, information, etc. On the other hand, it's imperative to know how much influence one has in a negotiation. There are many sources of power and influence in a negotiation. Power in a negotiation could be situational or institutional or a combination of both. A supplier of vegetables to a big supermarket chain once complained that it was always difficult for him to negotiate prices because of the supermarket's substantial power over the suppliers during negotiations. When asked why, he said, "...Because they are what they are, a big organization." While negotiating with big corporations or prestigious institutions, negotiators often feel that the other side has more power by default. Power, however, can also be situational. A fresh university graduate without any substantial work experience feels that the recruiter has all the influence during an interview. Likewise, an entrepreneur competing for capital investment in their startup feels that the investor has all the power because they're the party with all the resources.

Nevertheless, we're still missing one important source of power. An entrepreneur with no investment proposals and an entrepreneur who has already acquired interest from an investor or two would negotiate their investments differently. Similarly, an unemployed graduate and a graduate with a job offer would negotiate their salaries differently. The reason for these differences is simple—a definite and reliable alternative to the deal is a significant source of power. As we observed in the previous chapter, BATNA (Best Alternative to Negotiated Agreement) has a powerful influence on the negotiator's expectations. However, negotiators often feel they don't have enough influence in the negotiation because they lack any alternatives. But what about the other side? What if they don't have other immediate options either? It's vital to explore the other side's BATNA and compare both sides' relative power. Without an alternative, the negotiator may have to work harder and even consider postponing talks altogether.

1. SITUATION ANALYSIS

In theory, negotiation situations range between competitive and collaborative, two terms that need a bit of explanation. Competitive negotiation situations are also known as distributive bargaining situations. These are the situations in which the objective of the negotiator is to get the maximum share of a fixed pie.

Here's a story that a supplier of dried fruits and nuts shared with me. One time, the supplier experienced a very tough negotiation with a supermarket chain. They supplied their product to the supermarket chain, which in turn sold the product under a private label. At one point, the supermarket had done some internal reshuffling and a new purchase manager had taken over procuring dried fruits and nuts. The supplier submitted a price, to which the new manager responded demanding a new quotation and claiming that the first one was impossible. The company revised the quotation with a more elaborate description of the product, highlighting the quality but without making any changes to the price. Once again, the supermarket chain responded negatively and gave the supplier an ultimatum of a few days. The supplier's sales director was already getting a bit anxious, so he called the procurement officer of the supermarket chain. He reminded him of their past relationship, as well as their excellent quality of service, and pleaded to accept the latest quotation. The supermarket chain's procurement officer argued that many suppliers were competing to sell, and that the supplier in question would only stand a chance if they reduced their quotation by forty percent (40%). The conversation continued the next day over the telephone, and in the end, the dry fruits supplier offered a final price which was almost twenty-five percent (25%) lower. The supermarket procurement officer still refused to budge, and the following day, the supermarket officer asked for a final offer. The supplier said no further discount was possible. The supermarket officer himself asked for a short discount of about 10% and made the final offer. The supplier made a final offer with a 30% discount and the supermarket accepted. Look at the graphic below to understand the entire chain of offers and counteroffers. This phenomenon happens all the time, albeit with variations to the percentages.

The Dried Fruits and Nuts Vendor	The Negotiation Process	The Supermarket Chain
	Step one	
€ 200	First Offer	
	First counteroffer	No counteroffer; asks for a better offer. Says beyond €120 would be difficult.
	Step two (after a day or two)	
	Telephone Conversation No conclusion	
	Step three (probably the next day)	
€150	Second offer	
	Response to the second offer	Not acceptable
	Final offer	€135
	Step four (A few days later)	
€140	Agreement reached at	€140
Ultimately, this is the end-result		

200	150	140	120
(A concession of 30%)			(A concession of about 17%)

What do you think about this situation? Let's break down this negotiation. Despite the seller's best attempts, the buyer doesn't want to talk about a long-term relationship.

The buyer negotiates with the singular focus of a price reduction. The buyer also keeps telling the seller about limited time and multiple offers that he may have, thus creating a high degree of uncertainty on the seller's part. The buyer focuses exclusively on the price and doesn't let any other variable influence the negotiation. These are all tactics employed in competitive negotiations.

1. **Defending positions:** A competitive negotiation involves positional bargaining. In other words, in a competitive negotiation, you take a position and defend it while the other party. Likewise, the other party defends their own position, as illustrated in the previous example, wherein both the supplier and the buyer tried to keep the final price as close to their original stance as possible. The focus of the negotiation, therefore, becomes conceding the smallest amount of ground possible.

2. **Power-gaining arguments:** A competitive negotiation involves many power arguments. It's easy to imagine that the supermarket procurement office making some of the following points:

    a. They have many other suppliers waiting to sell.

    b. They don't have much time.

    c. If they don't get the quotation soon, the negotiations would stop.

    Generally speaking, the challenge in competitive negotiations is to move the least from one's original position. In order to concede as little as possible, negotiators employ two types of power-gaining arguments.

    I. *Power-enhancing arguments: arguments* that help a negotiator strengthen their position and establish the validity and acceptability of that position. These arguments are mostly about the positive sides of negotiator's claim—why the product deserves a certain asking price, why the buyer deserves the requested discount, etc.

    II. *Power-countering arguments:* arguments that help a negotiator strengthen their position by reducing the power of the counterpart. These arguments focus on the other party's weaknesses and seek to undermine their position.

3. **Lack of information:** A competitive negotiation often involves high levels of uncertainty. Negotiators prefer to create tension by manipulating information in their favor, also known as information asymmetry. Negotiators keep certain pieces of information hidden in order to gain the upper hand over their counterpart. One of the reasons why it's effective to create such a gap is that it helps the negotiator maintain control over the situation. To that end, competitive negotiations can involve a lot of evasive responses to critical questions because the negotiator doesn't want the other side to figure out their limits. However, it's particularly important to watch out for lies and misinformation as well. In such negotiations, we often come across negotiators who stake claims and come up with arguments that might not be completely true.

4. **Short-term focus:** A competitive negotiation quite often focuses on short-term goals. In competitive negotiation situations, concentrating on the long run doesn't usually help if it happens at all. When the focus of a negotiator is on defending a particular position, it becomes difficult to see its long-term impact.

Now compare the negotiation above with the following example:

One day, Mr. John Smith, an experienced sales director in the food and beverage sector in southern Europe, received a call from a potential Japanese buyer. The buyer asked for a specific variety of almonds. John asked if they were only looking for that specific type of almond or if they had anything else in mind as well. The potential buyer, a young procurement officer named Taka who represented a multinational company, replied with an emphatic "no". John gave him the market price of that variety of almonds. The buyer said that many other competitors had quoted similar prices, and that he was only interested if John could offer a better price; at the end of the call, Taka said he would call again some other time. John didn't expect to hear back from him, but to his surprise, he received the call two days later. The first thing John noticed was that it was already evening. He asked Taka, "Isn't it late over there?" Taka replied that it was indeed close to midnight in his time zone. John joked that if he ever stayed that late, his wife made him sleep in the garage. Taka laughed and said that he was still single and didn't have to deal with that sort of problem. They shared a good laugh, and Taka sounded more comfortable than before. In the conversation, John got to know that Taka was Japanese-American, and had only recently joined the multinational company after graduating. Taka soon steered the conversation towards his objective and asked whether or not John would offer him a better price on the variety of almonds he needed. "Taka, I want to help you," said John. "You are almost my son's age. But there really isn't much I can do. Tell me something—why does your company need this specific kind of almonds?" "I thought you would already know," Taka replied. "We have a huge annual meeting with more than two thousand representatives from all over the world. I oversee operations and am also coordinating the in-house kitchen. We want to offer the best service to our representatives, and I am buying only the best ingredients."

John had a little chuckle. He said, "Taka, have you worked in a kitchen or a restaurant before?" Taka said he hadn't, and John asked for more information on this particular dish. Finally, he explained to Taka that the kind of almond he was asking for wasn't the solution to his problem. He told him buying a costly variant doesn't mean you are purchasing the right one. "You don't buy gasoline, even though it's more expensive, if the engine runs on diesel, right?" Taka understood the point.

John had sensed that Taka was a young executive who had just arrived in a new country (despite being of Japanese descent, he was an American citizen). He must have wanted to prove himself in front of his superiors. John suggested other varieties of almonds that were less costly and more appropriate for the kind of cuisine Taka had planned. He asked Taka to take his time, consult a few experts, and come back. Taka agreed. The next morning, Taka called again and placed a massive order for the variety that John had suggested; they also discussed future requirements for other dry fruits and nuts. In the end, John and Taka became friends and conducted frequent business transactions.

How is this negotiation different from the one we analyzed earlier? Here are some essential points to consider:

1. **Discovery of mutual needs:** The negotiation we've just observed begins on a rather competitive note. Taka asks for a lower price, a request with which John is unwilling to comply. However, once John identifies Taka's true need, the two of them can accommodate each other's objectives. John doesn't have to offer an unreasonable discount, and Taka doesn't pay an exorbitant price. Both parties walk away happy. In a collaborative negotiation, the discovery of mutual needs plays an important role. Only through the discovery of mutual needs can both sides expand the zone of possible agreement.

2. **Reduced uncertainty:** There are fewer uncertainties in collaborative negotiations than in competitive ones. Had Taka not shared his needs, John would never have been able to help him find the best solution. However, Taka was open about sharing his needs, and that helped John seek a better alternative. If both had been too stubborn to budge from their positions, they would have either failed to close the deal or fallen prey to an agreement bias in one direction or the other.

3. **Equilibrium of power:** In collaborative negotiations, we don't see power arguments. Negotiators try to avoid showing how much more power they have than the other side or, on the flip side, why they don't have much power. As we saw in the discussion on competitive negotiations, using power-based arguments quite often attracts retaliation. The negotiation becomes all about who gives in first.

4. **Shadow of the future:** In collaborative negotiation, the shadow of the future is enlarged. The negotiator is interested in establishing a long-term relationship of trust, so there's a higher level of exchange of ideas and information.

2. FRAMEWORK FOR ANALYZING THE SITUATION

Richard Pascale and Juan Roure developed a situation based negotiation model which addresses situation analysis through the factors we have discussed so far.

A summarized study of the two previous examples reveals four essential elements that help us understand the direction of a negotiation. We've already seen how a negotiator needs to know if a particular negotiation is competitive negotiation or collaborative.

1. **Need:** Needs are contrary and are generally expressed through specific positions. In collaborative negotiations, needs are expressed through interests and are typically shared between parties. We have also seen that a negotiator can turn a competitive negotiation into a collaborative one by exploring a common element of necessity.

2. **Power:** A negotiator's assessment of the negotiation depends a lot on their perception of power. Power in a negotiation refers to the negotiator's ability to influence the outcome. As we have seen, the fundamental source of power in a negotiation is BATNA (Best Alternative to Negotiated Agreements). Power in a competitive situation is unbalanced, and the negotiator generally attempts to tilt that power in their favor. However, in a collaborative situation, power is balanced.

3. **Information:** In a competitive negotiation, information is spread asymmetrically, creating higher levels of uncertainty. On the other hand, in a collaborative negotiation, information is distributed more symmetrically, reducing uncertainty on either side.

4. **Relationship:** A one-off negotiation situation creates a competitive situation while a long-term or recurring negotiation relationship creates a long-term perspective, facilitating a more collaborative dynamic.

Pascale and Roure's Negotiation Model

	Situation	
Competitive ←		→ Collaborative
Win-Lose Proposition		Win-Win Proposition
Contrary	Need	Common
Unequal	Power	Equal
High uncertainty	Information	Low uncertainty
One-off	Relationship	Long-term

3. SUMMARY

Preparation is the first essential step in the negotiation process. During the preparation stage, the negotiator should analyze four factors; need, power, relationship, and information. The negotiator needs to know what needs both sides are trying to satisfy as well as the relative power of both sides. It's important to understand both sides' alternatives in order to assess relative strength more accurately. It's also important to understand the current relationship between both sides and how to maximize its evolution during and after the negotiation. Finally, it's essential to assess who has an edge in terms of relative information. Who knows what about the other side? What are the most critical aspects of what we don't know about the other side, and how can we collect that information?

> **Food for Thought**
>
> Go back to negotiations you have thought about in the Food for Thought section in the previous chapters. Try to understand what these negotiation situations were like and how that influenced the negotiation's outcome.

NEGOTIATION PROCESS: FIRST STEPS

CHAPTER 4

So, what exactly does the term *negotiation process* mean? During our courses and seminars, we often converse with executives about some of the main challenges they face during a negotiation. These are some of their frequent comments:

"I don't know whether I should make the first offer or not."

"I don't know how to respond to a very high or a very low first offer."

"It's difficult to deal with someone who doesn't budge. Sometimes the other side shows so much obduracy that we don't know what to do."

"When someone asks me to adjust the price I've already quoted, I find it difficult to do. After offering a very fair price, how can they expect me to give a discount?"

"I don't know how to deal with people who don't share any information."

"I don't know how to deal with someone I can't trust."

Can you relate to any of these issues? As you can see, most of these concerns are linked to the process of negotiation. There are two critical questions most negotiators fail to answer. First, should the negotiator make the first offer? Second, how should the negotiator gauge the potential value that can be created from the negotiation?

1. EXPECTATIONS AND PROCESS

Clarity of objective has a powerful impact on the negotiation approach and, consequently, on the negotiation process. Look at the difference between the following situations. David is the regional sales manager for an international pharmaceutical organization, and he has to negotiate a two-year supply order of a specific medicine with a local private hospital. His immediate boss has asked him to close the deal at any price above $120 per batch (the current market price is $146.30). The hospital has set rules for the period and payment terms, and his boss has said that given those terms, that's the best they can do.

On the other hand, there is an MBA student, Dina, who is negotiating her first salary after finishing her MBA. While she wants to accept this job because it's her dream to work for the organization in question, she doesn't know what a fair salary would be. She knows a salary above 40,0000€ per annum would be suitable, as it would cover her rent and loan installments, but she doesn't know what she should ask. Before finding out what happened in each case, ask yourself how you would negotiate them. How would the negotiation process differ? Now let's see how they play out.

Assuming he can go as low as $120, David starts with the highest offer at $140. The client says that they were paying $125 to the previous supplier and were expecting a better price. They proposed $115. David said the best he could do was $120, at which point the client agreed, allowing them to close the deal.

Dina, on the other hand, doesn't ask for a specific amount and eventually accepts a $39,650 salary, as it's close to what she thought was a good salary. David makes the first offer, and Dina doesn't. They both adopted different strategies but attained the same outcome.

2. APPROACHES FOR DETERMINING THE NEGOTIATION PROCESS

In general, negotiators use two main approaches in the negotiation process, known as the marking approach and the waiting approach.

1. **Marking approach:** The marking approach implies that the negotiator takes the initiative and sets the tone to mark the zone of a possible agreement by making the first offer. In the examples above, David makes the first offer of $140. The moment he makes that offer, he knows he has a margin of $20 for the negotiation. He shouldn't let the deal go anywhere below $120.

2. **Waiting approach:** The waiting approach takes a different route—the negotiator waits for the other side to mark the zone of possible agreement. Dina wanted a salary of $40,000. She had received the offer of $39,650. The moment she received the offer, she knew it would require some hard work to get an additional $350. What are the pros and cons of both these strategies? Let's have a look.

	Marking Approach	Waiting Approach
Advantages	1. When one marks the price, one knows more or less the direction in which the negotiation will go. 2. One gains a better sense of control over time. 4. One forces the other side to react, thus finding out the other side's expectations. 5. Marking the price also has a catalyzing effect, allowing one to receive a counteroffer in return.	1. The waiting approach helps when there is absolutely no idea of the potential for value creation. 2. Often, negotiators who have incomplete information in a negotiation use the other side's first offer as an essential source of information. 3. If the negotiator has several options, this approach helps them relax and keep all their options open.
Disadvantages	1. The significant disadvantage here is that one would never know the real potential of value creation. 2. It is difficult to recover from an excessively ambitious first offer.	2. If the other side's offer is entirely unreasonable, it is difficult to recover the negotiation. 3. It is also essential to understand the risk of agreeing to what the other side wants by default if the offer is 'reasonable.'

Let's take another look at our two examples. What mistakes are being made? Both the negotiators, David and Dina, are happy with their deals. David thinks he achieved a good deal by making an excellent first offer, and Dina believes she did well by not making any first offer at all, as it would have reduced her chances of succeeding. When asked to reflect on their performance, this is what they had to say.

David: "I did a good job by starting at $140. If I had started a bit higher, they would have probably not negotiated further because they were already buying at $125. This allowed me to resist any pressure for a big discount and eventually manage to get the price my boss had already set."

Dina: "I did a good job by not telling them my expected salary. If I had asked for $40,000, they would have offered something much lower or just stopped the interview. I would've ended up with a low salary or no job at all. By not revealing my expectations, I managed to get both the job and a salary close to what I had hoped for from the beginning."

On the surface, both strategies seemed to work. But is this the best way to analyze results? Both negotiators missed something fundamental. They both omitted a critical parameter to evaluate their expectations. For David, $120 was a fair price because that was what his boss mentioned. Likewise, Dina's best friend had told her that $40,000 would be a fair salary. However, neither David nor Dina knew whether the result is optimum because they had no information about the other side's expectations. For example, what was the expectation of David's client? They were already getting the material at $125. Why were they looking for a new supplier? Why could they not negotiate a better price with the previous supplier? How urgent was their need to get a new supplier?

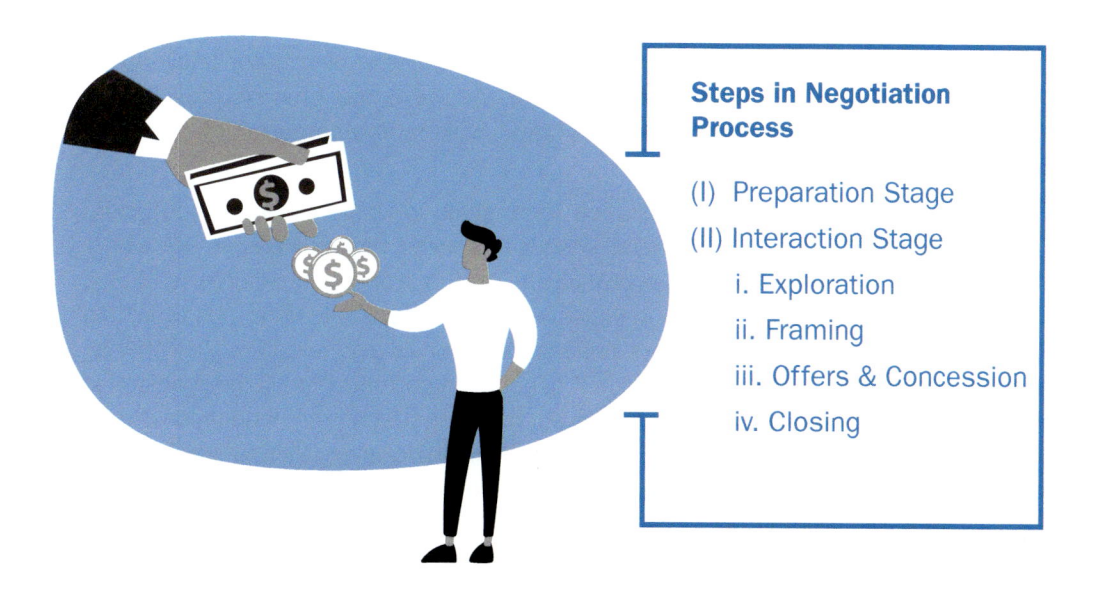

Steps in Negotiation Process

(I) Preparation Stage
(II) Interaction Stage
    i. Exploration
    ii. Framing
    iii. Offers & Concession
    iv. Closing

In Dina's case, was $39,650 the best offer from the company? What if they thought the counterpart would try to negotiate, and that's why they deliberately offered a lower salary? These little details will never be known to us. That's why it is vital to get information from the other side before making an offer. In the next section, we will see how to design the process of negotiation in a way that provides insight into potential expectations in order to maximize our results.

The negotiation process has three main stages—the pre-negotiation (or the preparation stage), the interaction stage, and the post-interaction stage. Moreover, each of these three stages of negotiation has its own sub-stages as well.

3. STAGE I: PREPARATION

A negotiation doesn't start when the two sides meet. Negotiation starts during the preparation, well before the meeting even begins. In the previous sections, we've seen how important it is to prepare and understand both sides' expectations. Preparation has a decisive impact on the negotiation process and, therefore, on its resolution. The effectiveness of the remaining phases is determined mainly by how we have prepared for them.

In his book *Checklist Manifesto*, author and surgeon Sanjeev Gawande talks about two types of mistakes professionals make: errors of ignorance (insufficient knowledge) and errors of ineptitude (not knowing how to use knowledge). Negotiators can avoid both these mistakes through thorough preparation. As we saw in the previous section, negotiators have many blind spots. A negotiator doesn't know what the other side wants, nor the potential of creating value that the negotiation situation offers.

For this reason, it is crucial not only to know enough but also to know what we don't know. An excellent and rigorous preparation helps a negotiator know about issues and elements they are not aware of. At the same time, it provides an opportunity to think of every negotiation step and identify an appropriate strategy for each one of them.

The principal element of preparation is a study of expectations. Two factors determine expectations in a negotiation—needs and power. Rigorous preparation allows negotiators to be more aware of their own needs and those of their counterparts. During the negotiation, they can move beyond desires and positions and find ways to satisfy mutual needs. Another advantage of understanding one's own needs is that it helps the negotiator know how to measure their negotiation performance. Good preparation also involves understanding the relative power one may have in the negotiation. Power is determined by various sources, as seen before. However, alternatives are the fundamental source of power. It is essential to know what alternatives one may have and what alternatives the other side may have in the negotiation.

4. STAGE – II INTERACTION STAGE

In the next stage, the negotiator and their counterpart begin interacting, whether by telephone, email, or other audiovisual (or synchronous) media (Google Hangouts, Skype, etc.). Generally, the principles we will discuss below are equally applicable to all of them. However, there are some specific issues that one has to be concerned about within the case of some particular media, which we'll make note of separately.

4.1. Exploration

Exploration should be the first step in the interaction phase of the negotiation. You may argue that during preparation, if you get enough infomation, you can start the negotiation with an offer. However, it would be an erroneous strategy as we don't know what we don't know. The negotiator needs to explore any available information about the other side. To come about this information, we need two things to work in our favor. First, we should be asking the right questions, and second, we should be getting the proper responses to our questions. To get the correct answers to our questions, it's essential to earn the other side's trust. During the exploration phase, negotiators need to use two primary strategies: active listening and trust generation. Let's break down each of these concepts.

Active Listening

During the 1970s, active listening, or empathic listening, emerged as a popular technique during crisis negotiations, particularly in the case of hostage situations. Active listening gained popularity because of its two significant benefits—the establishment of empathy and the collection of information.

Listening is not a passive, unilateral process. It is often an active and bilateral process. Imagine you're bored and looking for some stimulation or entertainment on an early summer afternoon. You start surfing channels on the TV, and you pause on a music channel when some visual element or other grabs your attention. You stop because of the visual, but you find the music pleasant as well. It's a genre you haven't heard before. The soft, melodic tune and the husky voice of the singer leave a strong impression on you. As soon as the song is over, you switch the TV off. You open YouTube, search for the musical numbers of that same singer, and spend the rest of the day listening to more of their songs. By the evening, you've also read the singer's Wikipedia page, where you learn about all their musical influences. Six months later, you attend their live concert in your city, and it ends up being one of the most memorable experiences of your life. Memorable because at the concert you finally meet someone who can understand you, you fall in love, and spend the rest of your life together blissfully. This entire process, however, isn't as serendipitous as it sounds. It involved a series of decisions and choices. First, you were looking for something interesting on television to stimulate your mind or to entertain you. The visual that made you stop was something you found attractive because it somehow appealed to your senses. You invested your time in that song because, in part, it was something that you were looking for (at least visually). Later, you were curious about that new singer and music genre, but you invested your time and effort in exploring more of their songs. You developed an interest in the singer's career trajectory and invested more time and effort in exploring it. In other words, four factors made this entire chain of events possible—your pre-existing interests, your willingness to explore, resources (time and money), and build-up through action. Think of how some of your strongest friendships were formed. They all started with a simple conversation between two individuals who were curious about each other. This is the essence of active listening.

Now go back to that same summer afternoon. Once again, you're bored and looking for some stimulation. You take the TV remote in your hand, hesitate, and then put it back down. Instead of turning on the TV, you dig through some of your music CDs. Once your favorite music is playing, you doze off and take a nap. None of the aforementioned events ever happen. This time, you acted strictly based on your pre-existing interests. You went for something tested and proven and listened to a song that you had heard many times before. That is the essence of directive listening.

Sometimes, negotiators slip into the habit of directive listening when they should be engaging in active listening. Let's go back to the example of David we mentioned at the beginning of this chapter. David started his negotiation by asking, "So, what is the price that you want to pay?" This question leads to a very limited answer of just one

How to explore information effectively?

i. Be an active listener
ii. Generate trust
iii. Create an environment of trust through actions
iv. Win trust through evidence and knowledge
v. Check for reciprocity

number. Communication scholars often analyze communication according to key factors such as the receiver, the sender, the message, and the noise. There are two fundamental errors in starting a conversation this way; first, the receiver only obtains the information they ask for. Second, the receiver assumes that what they are asking for is the only thing that interests the sender. In directive listening, the receiver already determines what they want to hear. As a result, the relative amount of noise in communication is higher for the listener. Noise is the information that is of no interest. In other words, the receiver listens to the information conditionally, and their filtering of the information is biased.

Active listening strives to remove this bias from the information reception process. In other words, active listening depends on reduction in the noise and leads openness to more information. We can reduce the noise by eliminating pre-determined criteria. For example, when David asks, "What is the price you are willing to pay?" he only receives the information related to the price. But when he asks questions like, "How can I help you?" or "What are you looking for?" he is likely to get more information about his counterpart's needs. Therefore, the first step of active listening is to ask open questions. Closed questions, where the answer has to be very precise, lead you to directive listening. However, you may need some accurate information as well —for example, what price the seller wants to offer, how long the contract should last, etc.—. Nevertheless, we need to understand that, while directive listening helps us understand positions, it seldom reveals the real underlying needs. When your supplier tells you that they would charge a 10% more for the next shipment, what you don't know is the rationale or the interest underlying this bump in price.

Imagine you've asked open questions and that your counterpart provides you with a good amount of information. Then what? Sometimes, negotiators look at open questions as a mere superficial tool and fail to explore the potential of value creation that they offer. An effective strategy for putting the acquired information to good use is paraphrasing. There are three steps involved in paraphrasing: capturing key concepts, presenting a summary, and seeking confirmation.

When your counterpart shares information, you must capture critical concepts that the other side is offering through paraphrasing. Think of the following statement that an aggrieved party made while talking about the conflict with a neighbor. "We've been living here for such a long time, taking care of the neighborhood as well as the apartment building itself. Soon after *they* arrived, though, they started talking as if they were the building owners." The conflict was about the children of a young couple who had just moved in who, while playing on the balcony, threw toys onto the balcony of the neighbor downstairs. The neighbors living downstairs were an elderly couple, and this caused them a lot of distress. One day they asked their neighbors upstairs to discipline their kids, and the neighbors argued that they should not interfere with their parenting. When you read the paragraph given above, you can see no talk about kids or harassment. Instead, the elderly couple is feeling deeply disrespected. The mediator summarized this statement as, "I can see that your new neighbors have not been respectful and aren't adapting to the lifestyle and environment of the building. Does this mean there are other neighbors who agree with you?"

The moment the mediator spotted a critical and revealing piece of information, he built upon it. That's why paraphrasing is a must. Paraphrasing has two significant advantages. First, it shows you've been listening carefully. In some complex negotiations, listening on its own isn't enough—one also has to demonstrate that they've been listening. The second advantage of paraphrasing is internal to the person. Paraphrasing provides the time it takes to process information. In other words, when you summarize your counterpart's information, you are also repeating it to yourself, and this gives you another opportunity to make sense of it.

Trust Generation

As previously noted, it is crucial to establish trust during the exploration phase. It's important to use open questions and have patience in paraphrasing the information received to establish trust with the other side. Let's do another quick mental exercise. Think of a strong bond, relationship, or friendship outside your immediate family. Think about how you gained the trust of the other person. Your answer may very well be, 'I did something they wanted.'

That is the story of trust in most cases. A lot of factors influence the growth of trust. Social psychologists talk about two types of trust, cognitive and affective. Affective trust means confidence born out of emotional ties with the other person. On the other hand, cognitive trust is based on evidence and knowledge about the other person. In the context of negotiation, there are three essential elements to be taken into consideration. First, it is crucial to work with the counterpart in an environment that favors trust. Second, it is critical to win trust through evidence and knowledge. Third, it is also essential to gauge how much our counterpart trusts us.

Environment of Trust

Some individuals prefer a more relaxed and informal environment in which to meet others and establish trust, while others prefer to establish trust by a fact-based conversation and sharing information transparently. It is vital to bring the counterpart into a positive frame of mind, at least in the initial part of the negotiation. When an individual is in a negative frame of mind, trust becomes all the more difficult to build. That's why it's imperative to figure out which environment would best help win the counterpart's trust before the negotiation. You may have a chance to interact through emails or phone calls before meeting face to face, and you can use these opportunities to figure out how the counterpart establishes trust. If they lean more towards relationship and using an emotional approach in interpersonal communication, trust might be an even more critical factor. You may establish trust by showing genuine interest in the relationship and by trying to develop an emotional bond with the other side. On the other hand, if you notice the other side is more rational and task-focused in their interactions, you may focus more on factual information related to the negotiation and establish trust through transparent and informative exchanges.

Winning Trust through Evidence and Knowledge

That brings us to the second important factor in establishing trust—winning trust through evidence and knowledge. Psychologists have shown there are many factors related to an individual's personality and appearance that makes them seem trustworthy. However, even if you're the kind of person who is generally well-liked by others, you cannot assume you'll have the other person's trust in a negotiation. That's why it's essential to identify all the critical points in the negotiation before it begins. Once you have all the crucial information from your side, try to determine what you can share without jeopardizing your position. Then you'll be able to communicate without being afraid of revealing too much information. You can also be forthright about your own approach, which will help your counterpart trust you as well.

Reciprocity Check

During this phase of the negotiation, use something we call a 'reciprocity check.' A reciprocity check is a system of evaluation of information coming from the other side. In other words, when you share information, you should determine whether or not the other side is sharing information as well. Also, try to gauge if the information transmitted is establishing a collaborative relationship or a competitive advantage. If you see that the other side is sharing information with you and responds positively to your prompts, use the opportunity to establish a trust relationship. On the other hand, if you see that the other side is not interested in sharing information, be prepared for a more competitive approach and be prepared to defend your future positions.

5. SUMMARY

In this chapter, we've seen the importance of understanding the most appropriate negotiation approach. To cover the blind spots and gather better information in a negotiation, it is better to explore information about the other side before rushing to make an offer. Active listening is an important skill to be more effective at earning trust and gathering information. However, it is equally important to see whether the other side is reciprocating appropriately. In the event that we don't see enough signs of reciprocation, it means the other side is not interested in engaging in a collaborative negotiation.

> **Food for Thought**
>
> Think of your past negotiations and the processes you followed. How did you prepare? How did you gather information? What kind of questions did you ask? Try to analyze your own approach to questions and the collection of information.

CHAPTER 5

FRAMING

Rebeca is a young student about to start the final term of her MBA. Rebeca's mother is the president of their family business. A few months ago, Rebeca spent three weeks working in the family business, and by the time she finished, she had made up her mind that she would eventually join the family business. Rebeca's mother explained the company's strategic plans and told her about the new ambitious expansion she thought the company should undertake. Rebeca had always admired her mother's dedication and her ability to strike a balance between her family, her children, and her company. She never made any of them feel ignored. Just before her final term, Rebeca went home and had an honest conversation with her mother about her future career. She made it clear that she wanted to join the family firm and lead the expansion project. At first, Rebeca's mother expressed her joy that her daughter intended to join the family business. However, after a few minutes, she said that it would be better if Rebeca took up a job elsewhere—probably in a multinational company—received training, and joined the family business later. Rebeca disagreed. She asked why she should spend her time elsewhere if she knew she wanted to join the family company anyway. Her mother said that she thought it would be better for both Rebeca and the company. Rebeca got upset. She asked, "Weren't you happy with my work last month?" Her mother, with a surprised look, said, "Of course I was!" Rebeca waited, demanding an explanation through her silence. Her mother finally gave in. "Look. I'm your mother. I've also been the president of the company for the last fifteen years. I know what's best for both you and the company. You should get some external exposure and then come back." The conversation ended there. Rebeca felt upset.

Now compare this conversation with the following one. Albert is a management trainee in a multinational company, and at one point, he joined the company's rotational program. During the rotation, he spent a few weeks in Poland, where the company was setting up a new plant. Albert enjoyed working in a small team and participating in every aspect of the job. When his rotational program was over, he had to talk to his manager to decide his eventual position. Albert had already written an email and expressed his desire to work in the Poland plant. His rotational manager called him for a meeting. He said, "Albert, I have chosen the best place for you. But before that, I want you to tell me where you see yourself in the future." Albert said, "I see myself in the Poland plant. Probably leading the distribution channel or something similar." The manager said, "Be a bit more ambitious! Let's say you plan to be the country head or the CEO, in case the Polish plant is spun off as a separate entity. Wouldn't that be the best?" Albert laughed and said, "Of course!" He felt a little bit embarrassed.

The manager then said, "However, to achieve that, you should join the Berlin division." Albert was puzzled by this suggestion. The Berlin division was the company's most significant division, and his experience there had been very different from that in the Poland plant. It was the most bureaucratic of all the divisions. Before Albert could put his disinclination into words, the manager said, "I understand your discomfort, but let me explain. The Poland plant, as you have seen, is still in its initial stages. When you worked there, many strategic decisions were being taken. Obviously, you liked working there and people over there liked you as well. It will take about three years for the plant to get completely operational. The Berlin division would be a smarter move for you. Why is it the most efficient unit of the company despite being set up like a maze? Study the distribution network over there. Within a couple of years, when the Poland market gets more active, you can start getting more involved there, and maybe when the Poland plant is ready to operate, you can move there and start establishing the distributors' network. We know you will relish the Polish challenge. But remember, we want you to be well-prepared." Albert left the meeting happy, relaxed, and full of enthusiasm.

What difference did you see between these two exchanges? Both the events follow a similar pattern. A younger individual asks for a professional assignment, and their senior rejects the immediate acceptance, promising instead that the job will be theirs at some point in the future. However, in one case, the aspiring young person walks away upset, while in the other, they're enthusiastic. The difference between both cases can be attributed to how the information is presented. In the first case, Rebeca's mother tells her what she thinks is best for Rebeca. In the second case, Albert's boss first affirms what Albert wants and tells him why his suggestion is the best for those plans. Arguments given for presenting offers or claims in a negotiation is known as framing. How an offer is framed has a significant influence on the counterpart's reaction and perception.

In order to get a positive response from the counterpart, A negotiator needs to present their case in such a way that the offer becomes credible and acceptable.

When we negotiate, we want to achieve one or more objectives, and we have a set of underlying interests. We may also have a particular perspective on the situation of the negotiation. Our framing of the negotiation presents our view about the situation, puts forth our demands, and responds to the counterpart's claims.

Let's try to understand how we frame our negotiations. Framing in a negotiation has a cognitive aspect and an interactional aspect. The cognitive aspect of framing seeks to address the mindset of the other side. The interactional aspect of framing seeks to present our position advantageously. The effectiveness of framing depends, in turn, on the effective exploration of information. The availability of useful information leads to a better understanding of the other side's mindset. If you understand the other side's mentality well, it becomes easier to present your case by using their perspective convincingly.

A particular company wants to hire a consulting firm for advice regarding the potential business model for a new product. A team from the company and another from the consulting firm meet to discuss the project. The company's team is led by the Chief Marketing Officer (CMO), while a senior partner of the consulting firm leads the other team. The Chief Marketing Officer briefs the consulting firm about the latest product, its features, its potential benefits, etc. After presenting the new product, the Chief Marketing Officer said the following to the consulting firm:

"Our board is concerned that we have not been dominating the market like we used to do a decade ago. The market is quite competitive now. That's why we've considered this new product. My team has worked hard, and they think it will give us an entry into a specific niche, and hopefully, it will help us regain our market share for the segment. I have high hopes for its performance. Our board needs to approve the strategy plan as soon as possible. The product is excellent, but we need the best possible business model. From you, we need to know whether it's better to use our dealers' network or to sell directly to the customer. Should we have a spin-off dedicated to this product? Or is there a better alternative? The launch of the product depends on whether or not the board sees its benefits. We want to work with you because you have experience in these matters. From you, we need robust market research as well as advice."

Once they finished their briefing, they asked how long it would take the consulting firm to advise the company about the new business model and its cost.

As we said before, to frame our negotiation position advantageously, it is essential to understand the other side's framing. The consulting firm needs to share how long it will take them to finish the project and how much it will cost. Now put yourself in the shoes of the consultant. What information do you need to respond to these questions? You need to know the company's expectations of the assignment in order to give an accurate estimate of time. The estimation of time will determine the amount of resources the firm needs to commit to the project, which, in turn, will provide you with the price.

1. UNDERSTANDING THE COUNTERPART'S FRAMING

If possible, before moving on to the next paragraph, take a pen and paper and jot down the essence of the Chief Marketing Officer's statement from the previous section. Let's answer a few fundamental questions to decipher the CMO's message.

1. What does the Chief Marketing Officer want?

    He wants to know the best possible business model for the new product.

2. Why?

    Because the company wants to regain the market share in the product segment through the success of the new product.

3. Who is he representing?

    He is representing the company and the board.

4. What does the company want?

    The company needs to regain its lost market share.

5. And the board?

    The board needs confirmation that this indeed is the best solution. If we reread the sentences, we realize that he needs to prove to the board that the new product and the proposed business model are the best solutions for the given situation.

6. How does the chief marketing officer feel about the entire situation?

    He has mixed emotions. On one hand, he's hopeful and optimistic. On the other hand, he has some concerns regarding the board's approval.

7. What does he really want from you?

    He wants you to come up with a business model, after some robust research, that would convince the board. He doesn't want you simply to prove whether the product works or not. He also wants you to figure out if the board will be convinced.

In other words, it's a negotiation where the Chief Marketing Officer needs your help to come up with a business model that would help the company regain its market share through the launch of this new product. In other words, the Chief Marketing Officer needs three things: advice, research, and help.

This was an example of how you can analyze the cognitive frame inherent in the negotiation. In analyzing cognitive frames, a negotiator needs to examine the following elements:

- **Identity**

   We have multiple identities. An individual plays various roles, e.g., that of a parent, a professional, a boss, a subordinate, etc. It is essential to understand the negotiator's identity in order to understand their motivation, needs, and relationship within the negotiation context. For example, if we go back to the text of the Chief Marketing Officer's explanation of the assignment, what do we see? We're talking to...

   (1) The Chief Marketing Officer of the company.

   (2) Someone who owns the idea.

   (3) Someone who needs help to sell the idea to other stakeholders.

- **Agency**

   That brings us to the next element in cognitive framing that we need to understand. Who are we talking to? Are we talking to the principal? Or are we talking to the agent? One time, we interviewed a politician who had recently participated in a negotiation to form the national government in their country. One of the statements that the politician made was that whenever they negotiate with another political party, they always need to keep in mind the narrative—the narrative they are going to present to their constituency. They negotiate not just for themselves but also for the people who vote for them in elections. When we negotiate, the communication changes according to whether we deal with the principal or with the agent. Marketing executives who mainly deal with purchase managers of big corporations in a b2b transaction often present statements such as, "I'm fine with your quotation, but my boss will not approve. Please give me a better price." It is essential to keep in mind the principals represented by the agent in a negotiation. Principals help us identify the issues at stake in a negotiation. In the example used here, we can see that the Chief Marketing Officer will decide on giving the job to the consulting company, but he is still an agent of the board. As a result, it's vital to keep in mind both the principal and the agent's needs and interests when we respond.

- **Issues and interests**

   During a workshop with some family business owners, a participant once said, "As a mother, I want all my children to participate in my business and work together happily. As the president of the company, however, I want the best and the most prepared professionals in my employment." This statement clearly shows how interests and identities are intertwined and why it is essential to understand them. Remember, not all the negotiation issues are needs or interests, and not all needs are framed as issues. In the example cited above, the Chief Marketing Officer needs the board's approval to go ahead with the launch because his team believes that launching this product will help them achieve their objective of regaining the market share. However, the issue is that the board will be convinced only when robust research is presented. Therefore, the need is not just research. The need is to do research to find out if the product would succeed based on the criteria the board may use to evaluate the proposal.

- **Alternatives**
  When we correctly identify interests, we're also able to explore alternatives more efficiently. It is vital to focus on all the stakeholders' alternatives, especially when the other negotiator is an agent and not the principal. In the example we're following, the company may have another way of increasing the market share. The board may have a competing plan from some other executive or department. Likewise, the Chief Marketing Officer may have some other consulting company in mind to do this research.

- **Emotions**
  Emotions have a significant influence on our ability to negotiate. What's the emotion of the negotiator in this case? It's important to see how each issue may provoke different feelings or responses. It's also crucial to divide emotions into three classes: positive, negative, and neutral. If we go back to the example, we can see that the Chief Marketing Officer has a positive emotion attached to the product.

  On the other hand, getting approval from the board may put pressure on the same negotiator. It's crucial to highlight and enhance the positive emotions in the negotiation, as well as to recognize any negative emotions that show through. In some negotiations, the negotiator may not necessarily find themselves in a negative mood, but you may still pick up on negative responses to some part of the negotiation. For example, in recruitment negotiations, candidates often feel that the recruiter shows signs of aversion when they try to negotiate their salary. The recruiter may not display any outright anger, but the candidate still senses negativity. It's important to recognize negative responses and avoid—or at least reduce—them during the negotiation.

- **Relationship**
  We need to understand the existing relationship between the two negotiators in the context of the negotiation. Let's go back to the earlier example of a family business owner. When the president of the company said she wanted her daughter to get involved in the business because she knew her daughter loved the work, we saw the relationship between a parent and a child play a prominent role. However, when the same person also said she preferred her daughter trained elsewhere before joining the company, a professional relationship layer was added to the dynamic.

Negotiators generally use two types of relationship frames—power frames and trust frames. We need to pay attention to the language and observe the predominant message. In the case of the Chief Marketing Officer's brief, we can see that he uses more of a trust frame. He seeks out a relationship of trust in order to set up a successful negotiation with the board down the line. To figure out whether the frame being used is a power frame or a trust frame, one may use a 'footing' test by asking a simple question: 'Are we on the same footing or not?' *(Bonito & Sanders, 2002)*. Chances are that footing may change for the negotiator as the negotiation issues evolve. It's vital to keep the counterpart on the same footing to have a more collaborative negotiation. When we are not on the same footing, we make the negotiation more vulnerable to competitive tactics and potential deadlocks.

- **Relational Flow**
Given the issues, interests, alternatives, power, trust, and other factors discussed above, negotiation relationships don't remain static; rather, they change during the process of negotiation. We call these changes relational flow frames. You can understand relational flow by paying attention to the evolution of the negotiation conversation. Scholars in psychology have shown that affiliation and interdependence reveal how the relationship is moving (Donohue, 2001). There are potentially four types of relationship flows that emerge from affiliation and interdependence and their respective degrees. These four frames are moving toward (high affiliation, high interdependence), moving away (low affiliation, low interdependence), moving with (high affiliation, low interdependence), and moving against (low affiliation, high interdependence).

	Interdependence - High	Interdependence - Low
Affiliation – High	Moving toward	Moving with
Affiliation - Low	Moving against	Moving away

Relational flow is the interaction frame mentioned earlier. So far, we have discussed the Chief Marketing Officer's example who wants to hire a consulting firm to suggest a business model. Now think about the consulting firm. Imagine that you represent the consulting firm. What is your position? Let's try to construct a scenario here.

2. CONSTRUCTION OF FRAMING

You're working with a new client. This job could be a way to get into the sector. However, you know that the consulting firm is inundated with a lot of work, and you may not get enough people to work on this assignment. As a result, it may be difficult to do the appropriate amount of research within the client's requested timeframe. Regardless, you don't want to just let it go. In other words, you are in a high-interdependence but low-affiliation zone. To move forward, you need to increase the affiliation. How can you do that? One solution could be to suggest a research program divided into shorter periods, starting out with a smaller focus group and then expanding to a larger scale. By doing this, you can ensure a quick, low-cost opening for the project, which could eventually give you enough time to garner resources internally. At the same time, it should help your client start assessing the viability of the product.

In other words, by staying focused on affiliation and interdependence, we move the negotiation toward an agreement, for which we need to improve both the affiliation and interdependence. Affiliation can be enhanced by showing the other side how close we are in terms of objectives and how our goals are similar. On the other hand, interdependence can be improved by demonstrating why we're better than the alternatives. It is essential to show we're moving closer to each other in our framing of negotiation.

If we go back to our example, we can frame the negotiation in the following manner:

"We are good at doing good research. We have a lot of experience in doing this kind of work. We may have to put in an extra effort to deliver it fast, and we will need additional resources."

Compare that framing to this second statement.

"We understand the importance of this product. It looks like a great idea. However, you're right; without robust research, we can't reach a conclusion, and we need to help the board make the right decision. We have experience in doing so. We will design the best possible research program, keeping in mind the board's past criteria, to help you in your mission of recovering the market share." What difference do you see between both statements? Conceptually, they are similar. Both statements inform the potential client that they would do the job. The framing is different, however. In the first statement, the consultant says, "I will do it because I can." In the second one, the consultant says, "I will do it because you want it." The latter is likely to get a better response.

To make the statement that you'll do something because your counterpart needs it, you have to meet two essential conditions. First, you need to know what the other side needs, and second, you need to align what you propose to do with what they need. Proper framing helps you accomplish this. To frame your position appropriately, pay attention to the other side's framing and make sure you avoid contradictions as much as possible. Some contradictions, though, are inherent to the negotiation situation, and you cannot prevent them. For example, if you are a buyer, then your identity as a buyer will never be the same as that of the seller.

Nevertheless, you can always create a superior issue-frame and a partner identity in the problem-solving process. As shown in the example above, the consultant can position themselves as 'experts who will deliver the service' or as 'partners who will help the Chief Marketing Officer convince the board through rigorous research.' You can see what each framing device reveals about the other side and how you should incorporate it into your proposal.

Frame	How does the counterpart use it?	How should you use it in your negotiation?
Identity	Who are you negotiating with? How does your counterpart define themselves?	Try to create a common identity. Try to avoid an openly conflictive identity.
Agency	Is the negotiator the principal? Or they are agents representing the interests of other principals?	Address the needs of both. Show that you appreciate the agent and the principal, and that both are equally important to you.
Issues	What are the significant issues you are addressing?	Highlight in your framing that you have understood the issues and that you will address them in your proposal.
Alternatives	What will happen to the negotiator you are dealing with if there is no agreement? What will happen to the principal if this negotiation does not reach an agreement?	Show why you are preferable to any alternatives the other side has.

Effect	What emotion does the other side feel?	Show you appreciate their emotion. If the emotional state is negative, try to avoid aggravating it.
Relationship	Are you on the same footing? Is the other side using more of a power frame or a trust frame?	If the other side uses the power frame, try to take their focus toward trust. If the other side is using a trust frame, avoid any unnecessary use of power frames.
Relational flow	What does the other side want from you? Why do they want it from you specifically? How are they trying to get it?	Show in your proposal how you're on the same page and how you both need each other. Move closer by increasing affiliation and interdependence.

3. SUMMARY

Strive to understand how the other side uses framing in a negotiation, as well as what needs they might have. Understanding their needs isn't enough on its own—you should be matching your own framing of the negotiation accordingly.

> **Food for Thought**
>
> Think of your regular negotiations. How do you frame them? Can you try and adopt a different approach? Think of negotiators you admire. How do they frame their negotiations?

CHAPTER 6

OFFERS AND CONCESSIONS

Making an offer is arguably one of the most critical events in the negotiation process. Every negotiator needs to prepare to make and receive the first offer since it has significant ramifications for the outcome. We have already talked about the marking approach and the waiting approach. The marking approach involves making the offer and allowing the counterpart to respond, while the waiting approach means allowing the other side to make the first offer and then responding ourselves. We need to address the question of which approach is better, marking or waiting? Let's consider the advantages and disadvantages of making the first offer.

1. ADVANTAGES OF MAKING THE FIRST OFFER

1. Focus: Robbie started his meeting at 11:00 a.m. He expected the negotiation to finish by the noon. However, his counterpart, Mr. Solorzano, didn't share the same sense of urgency. Robbie's company wanted to hire Solorzano's construction company to take up renovation work of four of their factories. Solorzano's company had done some work for them in the past, and before seeking tenders, the company asked Solorzano for an estimate. The company was also under pressure to increase capacity in order to meet the sudden rise in international demand. Robbie was the manager in charge of the renovation project. He knew the project had to be expedited, and he also needed to get a reduced quote. After a chain of several emails and meetings, Solorzano's company gave an estimate, which Robbie knew was on the high side. Robbie suggested they meet and discuss the estimate in person. Robbie expected Solorzano to come prepared with a new quotation. However, when the meeting started, Solorzano started talking about how his grandson won a drawing competition over the weekend. Robbie reminded him politely about the task at hand. Solorzano then launched into an explanation of the last big project they had taken up and how he couldn't go watch the World Cup because of the lousy schedule, which of course led him to talk about how much he loved soccer and how he had managed to see at least one game in each big stadium of the world. Finally, Robbie said, "Thanks for your

time today. Let me get to the point. Unless you lower your estimates by 20%, we can't accept your offer."

Robbie felt that Solorzano was beating around the bush to tire Robbie out and make him lose control of the negotiation. Making the first offer gives the negotiator a sense of control, and the same happened for Robbie. His first offer helped him bring the focus back to the negotiation. Negotiators with a very competitive mindset often try to wear down their counterpart with irrelevant conversation. With such negotiators, making the first offer helps bring the focus back to the task at hand.

2. Sense of Certainty: Most negotiations carry inherent uncertainty. Imagine you're working on an important project, and you have severe budget limitations. You're negotiating with an important raw material supplier for the project. You're concerned it would be tough for you to meet the deadline for your project if you don't meet the budget. In the negotiation, your primary objective is to meet the budget deadline. You start negotiations with the supplier. You've made your calculations, and you figure a maximum price of €250 per unit of material. Your research shows that prices range from €225-260. You're uncertain what offer you may receive, and you don't want to get stuck in a long negotiation. What do you do? Early on in the negotiation, you make the first offer, probably around €225. You're confident the rest of the negotiation will be centered around a reasonable margin of this offer. One reason for such a sense of certainty is something known as the anchor effect.

3. Anchor effect: In our negotiation class, we once had a fascinating conversation. The students had engaged in a negotiation exercise about sale of a company. We asked one seller about his negotiation. The seller said he thought he would sell the company for about 500 million US$. However, the buyer started with a first offer of 150 million US$. The seller made a counteroffer of just

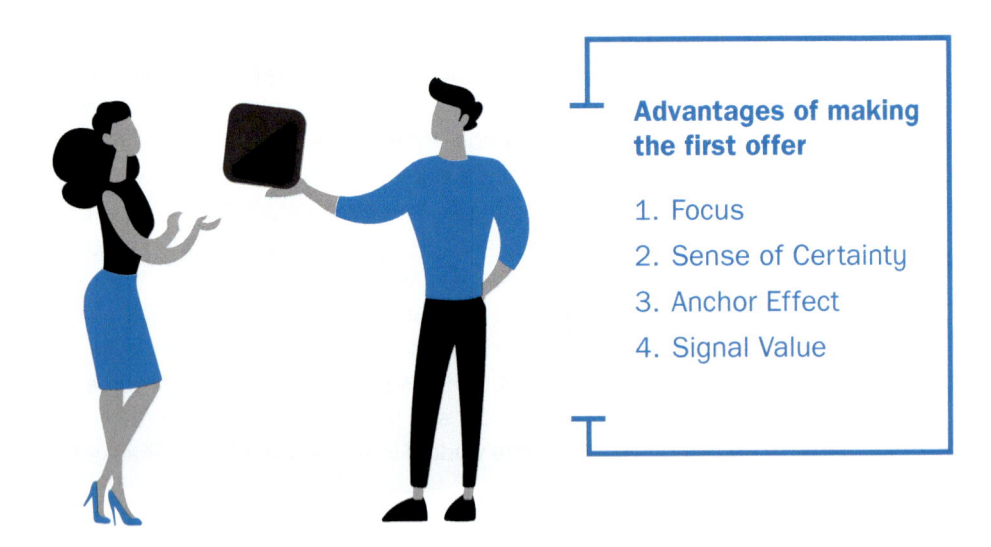

Advantages of making the first offer

1. Focus
2. Sense of Certainty
3. Anchor Effect
4. Signal Value

200 million US$. When we asked why he made such a low counteroffer if he thought his company's value was 500 Million US$. The seller said he didn't want to make an offer too far from the first figure to avoid a deadlock. The seller made such an assumption because he didn't know the counterpart's expectations. Negotiators frequently rely too heavily on the initial information (or the initial offer) in the absence of relevant information. This is also known as the anchor effect.

Here's another example. In a different negotiation exercise, buyers and sellers were negotiating the potential sale of a used motorbike. When asked about the expected price, one buyer said he had made an offer of €10,000, while the other buyer offered €4,500. The first seller had mentioned that a similar bike sold as a classic for about €20,000. This steep price anchored the buyer, and he ended up making a higher first offer accordingly. The anchor effect plays a vital role when the negotiator is not well prepared. We often see in salary negotiations that newly graduated students do not know how much their salary should be if they have not done enough research. As a result, they end up accepting a salary offered by their employer with minimal adjustments.

4. Signal value: Another significant advantage of making the first offer is the signaling effect. The first offer signals how much value the negotiator attaches to the product or service, as well as their willingness to negotiate. Raquel, a documentary filmmaker, wanted to make a documentary in a foreign country. She reached out to different production houses for collaboration. These production houses sent their estimates for their services. However, one of the production houses sent three separate offers. The first one was only about hiring the equipment. The second one showed how much it would cost if she hired the equipment as well as an additional cost in case she needed professionals to handle it. The third one was a partnership proposal. The company showed how they could help in the post-production work and eventual distribution of the documentary. When Raquel received this offer, she immediately sensed the company's interest. The offer was not just a signal for collaboration—it was also a signal that they had understood her idea and were willing to help her make the documentary. Hence, the first offer is not just an economic value of the deal. It's also an indication of your willingness, needs, and often your understanding of the deal.

On the other hand, making the first offer also presents certain disadvantages.

2.   DISADVANTAGES OF MAKING THE FIRST OFFER

1. Excessive Ambition

Can ambition be a disadvantage? If it is in excess, yes. Richard had a car his father left for him after driving it for about ten years. For Richard, it was his first car. After using it for about seven years, from eighteen until twenty-five years of age, he decided to sell it off and buy a new car. A couple of days later, he was visiting his professor at the university. Even though he had left the university two years ago, he would discuss his future and the challenges at work with his former professors from time to time. His professor introduced him to a young assistant who had recently moved from another country and had just joined the university. During the conversation, Richard discovered the young professor wanted to buy a car.

Given that the university was a bit far from the city center and that public transportation options were not convenient, the young professor thought he should buy a new vehicle. On the other hand, since he was just starting to work, he didn't want to spend too much money. Richard saw an opportunity and offered the young professor his car. Upon being asked for the price, Richard hesitated and said he would ask his mechanic and let him know. Richard didn't want to make an offer without preparation. After getting the opinions of a couple of mechanics and car salespeople, he concluded he couldn't ask for more than €1,200-1,500. The next day, the young professor called Richard, and they agreed to meet and have a look at the car. Before the young professor's visit, Richard thought he might sell the car at a high price. He felt that there were two factors in his favor. First, the young professor wanted the car and hadn't had time to look for an alternative. Second, even if someone was willing to sell a used car, Richard had an advantage. He the young professor through a common acquaintance, the senior professor, which made Richard more trustworthy.

Richard wanted to sell his car at a fair price. However, his research showed that more than €1,500 might be a stretch. Richard also inquired about new cars, and he knew that at least €10,000 would be a normal budget for a new car. He thought that since the young professor was single and probably had more purchasing power, he could aim higher.

Disadvantages of making the first offer

1. Excessive Ambition
2. Excessive Reasonableness

The next day, the young professor came over. After doing a quick inspection of the car, he said, "I like it. I think it should be fine for me at this point. I'll take it. For how much are you selling it?" After thinking for a moment, Richard put out a figure of €4,000. He couldn't resist the temptation of a bit more money. The young professor very politely replied, "I am so sorry. Our friend (the senior professor) told me that used cars generally sell for about €2,000. Only last evening, I spent most of my savings on rent and furniture, and kept about €2,500 aside. I didn't know this car was so costly. Thanks for your offer." And then he left. Richard didn't know how to invite him back. Telling him that he was okay with almost half of what he had asked for earlier would be tough because he didn't want to lose face.

If we consider our previous points regarding the anchor effect, an ambitious first offer should have, in theory, laid down a sufficient anchor, and Richard should have earned a lot of money. However, one of the most significant risks in negotiations is that if one makes a very ambitious first offer, there is a risk of losing credibility and interest from the other side.

2. Excessive Reasonableness

Can being reasonable ever be a disadvantage? Once again, if it is in excess, yes. Rizwan is a sales Director for a client service agency. His company generally provides customer support services to banks and financial service companies. Being an early entrant, the company had grabbed some big banks in India and Bangladesh. Gradually, they started losing their clients to new players who are more adept at providing multi-channel customer support services. Rizwan's company didn't make the right investments at the right time. Rizwan knew the company needed some quick cash flow to invest in becoming a more efficient multi-channel customer support company. One day, Rizwan received a call from an upcoming fintech startup. The startup was a neobank that needed an experienced customer service operator. Rizwan was impressed with their growth, and he realized they could be the high-volume client his company was looking for. On average, the service rate was between 11 and 13 US$ per agent per hour. Rizwan estimated a workload of about 40,000 agent-hours a year and thought that this could easily become a million-dollar client over the next three years. He didn't want to lose the contract. He could have offered anywhere between 11 and 13 US$. However, he offered a contract for two years with a 10 US$ rate, expecting to close a contract for two years. The company came back with a very aggressive counteroffer of 7 US$ per hour and a nine-month commitment. Eventually, they closed the deal for 9 US$ per agent per hour and an eighteen-month commitment. For Rizwan, it became really difficult to convince his superiors of the reason why he had sent them such a low quote. Rizwan had made a first offer that was not ambitious enough. He never imagined that the fintech startup would come back with a very aggressive counteroffer. In hindsight, he realized sending them a low quote was a mistake, and that he should have either asked them to make an offer first or made a more ambitious offer himself that would have left some room for negotiation.

So, what is the conclusion? Should we make the first offer or not? The answer is...you decide. If you are comfortable making the first offer, make the first offer, and if you are not, avoid it. Either way, always be prepared. Think of an athlete. Every athlete has a particular playing style. For example, in soccer, a player may prefer to play a more offensive game. Nevertheless, the same player (and the entire team) also prepares to play defensively as well in case the match demands it. Therefore, always be ready to make the first offer by balancing ambition and reasonableness. In the following paragraphs, we will see how to prepare to make the first offer.

3. STRATEGIES FOR MAKING THE FIRST OFFER

Preparation for a response to an offer is as essential as preparation for making an offer. Frequently, negotiators are caught unprepared when they receive excessively complicated or ambitious offers and lose control of the negotiation process. Let's start with some strategies for making the first offer.

3.1. Set your ambition

The first offer establishes the limit for the creation of value. The best indicator for the limit of ambition is the alternative of the other side. What would the other person do if they do not close the deal? This is a question a negotiator should always try to answer while preparing for the negotiation and getting information from the other side.

A negotiator should always get sufficient information about two critical issues while preparing for making an offer—first, the alternative of the other side, and second, their reservation price. The reservation price is a walk-away price that is either set by the negotiator or given to the negotiator. If we don't know the other side's reservation price, it's essential to at least have a good estimate.

Here is an example to reinforce the difference between an alternative and a reservation price. Stuart is an executive in an infrastructure company and has recently joined the company's corporate finance division. In one of his first assignments, his senior manager asked him to prepare a project report and negotiate a bank loan. The manager said that they already had an offer for a 3.5% interest loan from a competing bank. However, the manager also said that Stuart should try to get a 3% interest loan. Anything above 3% would not make it worth switching banks and would put existing relations in jeopardy. Imagine you are the banker who negotiates with Stuart. You know the competitor bank has offered a 3.5% interest loan for the project. To beat the competitor, you offer a 3.2% interest loan. Will it work? Even though it's a better offer than the alternative Stuart has, he may not accept it. Stuart will reject the bid because his reservation price is 3%. In a negotiation, always think about the counterpart's alternative and the reservation price.

3.2. Be credible

As we discussed earlier, the first offer has substantial signaling value. When you make the first offer, you not only show what you are willing to pay or charge, but also how willing you are to close the agreement. We have seen many negotiators who invest a lot of time in building up their argument a certain way and then ask for a first price which isn't at all coherent with the framing they used. Being vague or evasive proves detrimental to the negotiator's credibility. To make the first offer credible, it is crucial to support it with a positive negotiation context.

3.3. Strong anchors

We need to set our ambition reasonably. However, that doesn't mean there is no anchor effect at all. Studies have shown that stronger anchors bring more robust results. Consider the following example. A friend of ours once approached a lawyer to understand the intricacies of international law regarding a new export order he had received. He asked the lawyer how much he charged. The lawyer said, "Look, a task like this would take me about four hours of work, including reading and preparing the agreement you need to send to the client. I charge €200 per hour. However, this is the first time we are working together, and you have been referred to me by a friend of mine, so I'll only charge €575 in all." Our friend immediately accepted the offer. Later on, we asked him why he didn't ask for any further discount. His argument was the following.

> "How could I have asked for anything more? First of all, the lawyer told me how much time he would spend and how much he charged for his services. Secondly, he told me he was going to give me a discount. Finally, the amount he asked for was so specific; I didn't know what to do. Should I have suggested €550 instead of €575? Also, when you ask for a fee in this manner, it is difficult to argue against it. After all, it sounds perfectly reasonable"

Strong anchors achieve two objectives. First, they help make an offer reasonable. We decide if an offer is fair through comparison. In the example, the lawyer already established that he would provide a service worth €800 but that he was making an exception and giving a discount of about €225. On the other hand, the price he had given was €575, which was neither €550 nor €600. Some studies have shown that while interpreting numbers, we pay attention to the most significant digit. In this case (575) even though the number is exactly halfway between 600 and 550, the receiver perceives it to be closer to 550 than 600 because 5 is the most significant digit. This is also why many marketers tend to use what is called 'charm pricing.' It refers to offering prices like €2.98 or €4.99, which to a customer feel lower than what they are.

Therefore, whether you wish to make the first offer or not, always be prepared. Whenever you make the first offer, make sure you are reasonably ambitious, credible, and armed with references and arguments that can show the other side why your offer is too good to refuse.

4. CONCESSIONS

When you prepare for an offer, you also need to prepare for concessions. Making concessions is as vital as making an offer in a negotiation. Let's look at an example. Reginald was in the process of selling his factory. He set the price of the factory at €540,000. Reginald was in a hurry to sell the factory. He had a couple of estate agents who brought him new potential clients who wanted to either buy the land or buy the building and use it for a motion picture studio. However, Reginald preferred to see the factory go to someone who would keep its current purpose. He talked to the estate agent who had brought in some clients, and the agent told him that a certain buyer wanted to maintain the factory's current function. The buyer sent him a written offer of €450,000. Reginald was confused. He already thought that the price he was asking for was quite reasonable. The price that the buyer had offered was not very close. The negotiation stalled.

His friend Peter, who had always given him advice in crucial moments in life and business, told him that it might not be difficult for the buyer to come closer to matching the set price. The next day, Reginald sent a message to the potential buyer through the agent and told him he wouldn't change the offer. However, he said that he would love to meet the potential buyer to talk about any specific questions he may have had. The meeting took place a few days later. The buyer told him that he had seen three sites, and he preferred Reginald's factory for its proximity to his home.

However, the other two factories were available for a lower price. Reginald said he could lower the price to €520,000, which would be his final offer. The buyer said that it was not a significant decrease.

Finally, before leaving the meeting, the buyer said that the best he could offer was €467,000. This was based not on his assessment of Reginald's property's value, but on resources he could gather. Reginald asked for some more time to think. The next day, Reginald sent another message to the buyer and said the best he could do was €500,000. The buyer responded with an interesting counterproposal. The buyer said that he was ready to deposit €500,000 in an escrow account to continue the negotiation. If no deal was reached within the next month, he would reclaim the money. He insisted, however, that he would not be able to spend more than €467,000 for this property.

On one hand, this gave Reginald some confidence, but at the same time, he did not know how to respond in terms of price. If he accepted the buyer's offer, he was effectively admitting that the price was still negotiable. On the other hand, rejecting the proposal might mean closing the conversation. Reginald decided to wait and look for some more potential buyers. He received an offer of €485,000 from a residential property developer. However, the developer needed Reginald to undertake some renovation of the property, and Reginald was not interested in any further investment. In the meantime, Reginald went to meet his brother-in-law in the hospital, who was recovering from a cardiac trouble. His brother-in-law was talking about some of the problems that arise due to a lack of cash liquidity at old age. He said it is always better to keep money in stocks or deposits instead of stressfully locking it up in real estate properties. After hearing this, throughout his journey back home, Reginald kept thinking about his factory. When he reached home, he called his agent and said he wanted to make a counteroffer for €475,000. The agent asked him if he was sure. Reginald said that he was making an offer very close to the one made by the interested party to close the deal as soon as possible. However, the other side did not budge from €467,000. Finally, Reginald made another call a few days later and said he was ready to accept the offer.

Let's try to understand the pattern of offers in this case.

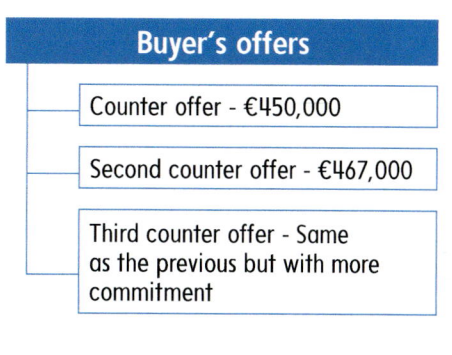

Seller's offers	Buyer's offers
First offer - €540,000	Counter offer - €450,000
Second offer - €525,000	Second counter offer - €467,000
Third offer - €500,000	Third counter offer - Same as the previous but with more commitment
Fourth offer - €475,000	
Fifth offer - €467,000	

Did Reginald do the right thing? Should he have waited? If we look at the pattern of offers, we see two things. First, the seller made many more offers than the buyer. Second, every time the seller made an offer, he didn't demand a counteroffer. Also, we see a steady trend of concessions from the seller. Even in the absence of any reciprocal concession from the buyer, the seller continues with concessions. So far, we have talked about the importance of making a good first offer. However, making a fair first offer is often not enough. The negotiator should also be careful with concessions. A bad concession may have as bad an effect as a bad offer. Let's try to understand the problem with a bad concession.

4.1. Impatience

Negotiators sometimes get impatient and make unreasonable concessions to close the negotiation quickly. Here's another example. A chemical manufacturer needs to buy a particular chemical product to be used as a raw material. The chemical mix needs to be produced according to certain specifications, and hence no direct reference of the price is available in the market. The seller gives a quote of €28 per kilogram of the material. The buyer doesn't want to pay more than 20€ and reaches out to a new supplier. The new supplier does not give an immediate response because they need more time to figure out the process and the cost involved. The buyer gets a bit restless and sends a quote to the original potential seller, making an offer of €22 per kilogram, which is still a bit more than what the buyer wants to spend. When asked why, the buyer said he wanted to make an acceptable offer, so he made an offer that was a bit higher than what he had in mind. For a couple of days, the buyer does not receive any response from either of the sellers. The buyer sends a message to the first potential supplier again. The supplier says that €22 is difficult. The buyer offers €26, and they close the deal. The second supplier contacts the next day and gives a quote of €21.50. When a negotiator gets impatient and feels that no alternatives are left, they frequently make bad concessions.

4.2. Irrationality

The second problem with concessions is irrationality. Think of the example above and put yourself in the position of the seller. You receive an offer for €22 per kilogram. When you reject it, you get an offer for €26 per kilogram. What do you think? What message do you receive? Why this increase of almost twenty percent? If the buyer can pay €26, why was he offering €22 in the first place? On what basis is he now offering an additional €4 per kilogram? In the heat of negotiations, we often fail to consider these questions. However, when we think about the situation from the outside, we are baffled by some negotiators' irrationality. Irrational concessions not only affect the value one creates in a negotiation, but they also create a lack of trust. A negotiator who receives such unreasonable concessions starts doubting the other side's intention and trustworthiness simply because an irrational concession makes the previous offer look like a lie.

4.3. Types of Concessions

There are three types of concessions—exchange concessions, sacrificial concessions, and quasi concessions. Let's take a look at each one of them separately.

1. **Exchange concessions**

These are the safest types of concessions because you create value in return. For example, an executive negotiating her salary may give a concession in her fixed salary because she might receive better stock options or a better bonus. Exchange concessions are easier to justify by means of a logical motivation.

2. **Sacrificial concession**

The negotiator who makes a sacrificial concession doesn't generate any direct value in return. In other words, you leave your position and try to accommodate the demands of the other side. This act requires effort; therefore, while making a sacrificial concession it is essential for negotiators to show how much of an effort they're making.

3. **Quasi concessions**

Quasi concessions may not necessarily be concessions in the exact meaning of the term but may still be presented as such. For example, in online shopping clubs, we often read lines like, "An excellent tie for €42 down from €90." The seller is offering a concession, but it isn't a real concession. The negotiation does not start at €90; rather, it starts at €42. Negotiators use such quasi concessions to establish credibility and also to avoid any further pressure for an actual concession. It's imperative, therefore, to be careful while making a counteroffer.

5. STRATEGIES FOR CONCESSIONS

How can we make sure that we don't end up committing the mistakes mentioned above? Here are some helpful strategies.

5.1. Concession order

Negotiators must prepare a concession order before the negotiation. A concession order is a list of priorities in reverse order. Of all the issues we work on, which issues can we concede most easily? The other implication is that as long as there are multiple needs at stake, it's easier to make concessions. Preparation and reflection on the needs at stake are vital before the negotiation. Also, it is essential to understand the needs of the other side. It is important to offer as concession, something that is more valuable to the other side than for us.

5.2. Justification

In order to make sure the concession doesn't provoke suspicion or affect trustworthiness negatively, it's essential to have a justification ready. In other words, when you modify your offer, you need to explain why and how you can afford that change. A philanthropist once told us that whenever somebody approaches him for a donation, if he is convinced by the importance of the need and seriousness of the institution, he offers twenty percent (20%) of the requested amount. Then, if he wants to make an additional donation, he asks for a few days. This gives him some time to rethink and do further research. However, it also convinces the other side that the philanthropist is making an effort and needs time to manage funds for his donation. Whenever you make a concession, you need to show the other side that you're making an effort. Generally, that effort is demonstrated through the explanation and justification of the concession. Remember, we aren'tt asking you to fake an effort. We are simply asking you make sure the other side sees the effort you make.

5.3. No Free Meals

It is important to remember that no concessions should be given away for free. When we give a concession without claiming any value in return, we commit two serious mistakes. First, we reduce the potential of value creation. Second—and more severely—we send a signal that we are willing to give concessions and that the original offer wasn't genuine. This may well work in a context where such behavior is a norm (a typical bazaar in a city like Cairo, Delhi, or Jakarta). Still, this approach may prove to be detrimental to the negotiator's interests in a high-level corporate negotiation.

5.4. Hitch-hiking

The next logical question is what to do when we don't have a rational justification and don't want to give away a free concession. The answer is to wait. When you run out of arguments for a concession, the best strategy is to let the other side give you an idea you can use in the justification. When you lack rationale, you can still hitch-hike on the reasons given by the counterpart. Give the other side an opportunity to come up with a good excuse. When the other side is not able to provide you with a proper justification, you may also orient them by asking suggestive questions like, "Why should we give you a discount?" or "By paying the extra amount, we are going to create an imbalance in our budget; how can we balance it again in the long run?" This strategy solves an important ethical dilemma. You don't have to lie or make anything up. You can effectively use the reasoning provided by the other side to justify your own concessions.

6. MULTI-ISSUE OFFERS

So far, we have discussed offers and concessions in terms of their single-issue variety. Making offers is especially complicated when the negotiation involves multiple issues. Look at this example:

A consulting firm and an electronics company are going to negotiate a contract for research and recommendation on the internationalization strategy for a new product. The product has been tested in the domestic market and has done reasonably well, and now the company wants to explore the options for making it a success internationally. On behalf of the company, the Vice President of the International Business Department led the negotiation along with the General Manager of the same department and a young Assistant Manager. On behalf of the consulting firm, a senior associate led the negotiation, supported by a junior associate and a newly recruited researcher. While the company's Executive Director of Marketing had already decided to recruit this firm, he had asked the Vice President to take care of various details pertaining to the deal. They had to determine the total fee for the assignment, the timing of the payment, the number of deliverable meetings, and the time span for the assignment. The company wanted to pay less, pay later (after receiving the final report), finish the project within three months, and have at least two to three meetings to discuss the interim results of the research. On the other hand, the consulting company did not want to give any discount and wanted to have a considerable share of the total fee paid upfront because that kind of a project might require liquidity in terms of travel costs and other expenses. Even though such incidental factors would be covered by the client eventually, past experience with the same company had shown that getting reimbursement for expenses was not an easy task. The consulting company thought they would need anywhere from six to nine months to finish the project. However, the consulting company also wanted more than one meeting for the deliverables to make sure that they were on the right track.

The negotiation kicked off in a friendly manner, and they started discussing the payment mode. The company said that, due to the brief nature of the assignment, they would like to make the payment at the end of the tenure. The senior associate of the consulting firm saw this as an aggressive tactic. Ultimately, to avoid tension, the consulting firm agreed to a 25% payment up front and the rest at the end of the term. However, they also decided not to reduce at all the consulting fees. They had, in fact, initially quoted a slightly higher price, thinking they might have to provide some discount. The discussion on these two issues took some time, and both sides were tired, so they took a lunch break. After the break, when the two sides met again, they picked up where they had left and began to discuss the time frame. The consulting firm said they didn't want to compromise the rigor and quality of the project. This was a research project, and it required special attention. They didn't want to finish any sooner than within six months. However, the Vice President of the company was adamant about completing the project in three months. At this point, the General Manager of the company made some comments about the competence of the consulting company compared it to some of its competitors. The comment irked the junior associate, and he, in return, reminded the company of its recent failures in the international market. This exchange resulted in a complete collapse of the negotiation. The senior representatives from both sides decided to stop and meet again after a few days.

When both teams regrouped at their respective offices, they had intense discussions about what had happened. The Vice President of the company was not happy with the way the negotiation had progressed, and he asked the General Manager to stay out of the second meeting. He also stressed that it was important for them to get the consulting firm to start working as soon as possible. The objective was to have the blueprint for internationalization ready before the next shareholders' meeting in six months' time. On the other hand, the discussion at the consulting firm's office played out slightly differently. The junior associate who had lost his temper apologized and offered to stay away from the next negotiation. His colleagues, however, supported him. Yet, they agreed that it was important to close the deal, and they decided to be as cordial as possible in the next meeting. After a few days, when they got together, they agreed to do the project in five months. This happened through a brief and cordial conversation. Then the Vice President asked, "How many meetings for the deliverables do you want? Just one or more?" The Senior associate replied, "Well, one is okay, I guess." On those terms, they closed the deal.

In the return journey, the researcher, who was in the meeting, asked the senior associate, "Why did you ask for just one meeting? We should have pushed for at least two meetings for the deliverables." The senior associate replied, "I didn't want one more point of disagreement. I just wanted to close the conversation." Meanwhile, in the company headquarters, the Vice President was updating the Executive Director. The Executive Director asked, "Did you not want at least two meetings for the deliverables?" The Vice President replied, "Yes, I did. But given the last meeting, I really wanted to avoid any conflict. Since they agreed to a shorter time frame, I thought they would prefer to have just one deliverable meeting."

Now we can see what happened. Despite having many issues at hand, the negotiators tried to close the deal one issue at a time. As a result, each issue created competitive tension. Not only that, but even on an issue where both of them wanted the same result, they were not able to achieve it. In the following section, we're going to take a look at some of the risks of negotiating variable-to-variable in a multi-issue situation.

6.1. Risk of Deadlock

As we saw in the previous example, if there are issues where the interests of different parties are completely at odds, the risk of a deadlock increases. Once we get stuck in a particular issue, it may be difficult to proceed in the negotiation. Often, if such a contentious issue emerges earlier in the negotiation, negotiators lose the opportunity to explore common ground and end up abandoning the negotiation altogether.

6.2. Overshadowing

When negotiators focus too much on one or two competitive issues, it overshadows other issues that may have collaborative potential. As seen in the example, even when both sides could have easily collaborated, they ended up competing on most of the issues and ultimately settled for a sub-optimal result.

6.3. Strategy

In the event of a multi-issue situation, offers should also be multi-issue. Flexibility is a luxury in a negotiation. In multi-issue negotiations, a multi-issue offer provides this much-needed luxury. Imagine the consulting firm from the example makes the first offer. "We will do the assignment for X amount, 75% of which must be paid upfront. The project will be delivered in nine months, and there will be three interim presentation meetings to discuss the progress of the project." This gives the company a chance to see that both parties want the same thing as far as the number of meetings for the deliverable is concerned. However, from the very beginning, the company assumes their positions are in opposition to those of the consulting firm. The proposed first offer might give the company an opportunity to present their positions in a package as well. More importantly, it leaves room for a discussion that isn't as likely to get stuck on a single issue.

Nevertheless, multi-issue offers are difficult to make. We often see even experienced negotiators getting stuck on a single issue and not being able to get out of the deadlock. Here are some of the reasons why multi-issue offers are particularly challenging.

7. FACTORS INHIBITING MULTI-ISSUE OFFERS

1. **Lack of trust**

    When we run negotiation simulations, we sometimes ask participants why they shy away from making multi-issue offers. The most common response that we have received so far is the absence of trust. When a negotiator doesn't trust the other side enough, they don't want to share information. When you make an offer, you reveal all your positions. At times, negotiators don't want to reveal these positions too soon.

2. **Lack of knowledge**

    Another important factor that inhibits multi-issue offers is the lack of knowledge. For example, negotiators may argue that they don't know the priorities, needs, and preferences of the other side, so they don't feel safe sharing information through multi-issue offers.

3. **Futility**

    The third argument that we hear is that, even after making a multi-issue offer, negotiators don't perceive any guarantee they won't be stuck defending their positions. This is a valid point. When one side makes a multi-issue offer, the counterpart may respond with a single-issue counteroffer, all but shooting down the entire point of the multi-issue offer.

4. **Over-concession**

    This issue is partly linked to the previous one. Some negotiators feel that when they make a multi-issue offer, they end up over-conceding, especially when the matters are unquantifiable. For example, in the negotiation mentioned above, how would a negotiator measure the value of finishing the project faster by a month? How would the negotiator measure this concession? Because of the fear of over-concession that arises from the lack of ability to measure the value, negotiators avoid mixing quantifiable issues with unquantifiable ones.

How can a negotiator overcome these issues?

It's crucial to consider the following principles when making a multi-issue offer.

8. PRINCIPLES OF MULTI-ISSUE OFFERS

8.1. Offer a negotiable package

While making a multi-issue offer, a negotiator may be tempted to propose a deal rather than an offer. What's the difference? Let's go back to the initial example we were talking about. If the consulting firm, while making the first offer, starts thinking, "We're going to ask for the entire payment before the project begins. However, let's at least give the other side something so that we don't appear too aggressive. They should get a discount on the price. Let's provide them with a discount of 15% of the original quote." The moment the multi-issue offer is made based on a consideration of what's good for the other side, competitive pressure starts building up so long as there's a lack of proper research. That's why, while making the offer, it's vital to keep in mind that the other side may negotiate, and one should leave an appropriate margin for negotiation.

8.2. Build trust

It's essential to gauge the level of trust with the counterpart. As mentioned in the previous chapters, negotiators need to adopt an incremental strategy to build trust, investing a bit of information and seeing if the other side responds positively by sharing some information of their own.

8.3. Discover priorities

To build a package that would attract the other side, it's fundamental to discover the other side's priorities. Trust and productive questions lead to an understanding of preferences, and this needs to happen before jumping to make an offer.

8.4. Create an evaluation system

One of the best ways to deal with concessions is to prepare an evaluation system of different issues. In the following example, we've developed a point system for the evaluation of variables. In creating a point system, two issues need to be taken into account. First, one needs to identify the relative importance of each issue. Second, there are many other options within each issue, and it is crucial to assign points to these options as well. Negotiators must work at two levels because, on the one hand, they should know what their own priority is, and, on the other hand, they should also understand to what extent value can be created on each issue.

For the Consulting company

Issues	For the Consultant Importance (%)	Points	For the client Importance (%)	Points
Getting all the payment at the beginning	50	10	25	0
Getting at least 75% at the beginning		8		2
Getting up to 50% at the beginning		6		4
Getting 40% at the beginning		4		8
Getting between 25 and 40% at the beginning		2		10
Getting less than 25%		0		10
9-month tenure for the project	25	10	50	0
8-month tenure		9		0
7-month tenure		8		0
6-month tenure		7		0
between 6 and 4 months		5		4
less than 4-month tenure		0		10
Number of meetings for deliverables				
Three meetings	25	10	25	10
Two meetings		5		5
One meeting		0		0
Optimal Deal				
All the payment made at the beginning		5		0
Less than four month's tenure		0		5
Three Meetings		2,5		2,5
Total		7,5		7,5
Actual Deal				
25% payment at the beginning		1		2,5
Five months of tenure		1,25		2
One meeting		0		0
Total		2,25		4,5

In the point system, we've assumed that for the consulting company, the most critical issue was to get the payment sooner rather than later, while for the client, the most pressing issue was to finish the project as quickly as possible. We've given 50% weight to the priority issue based on this information, while the other two issues have been assigned 25% each. Next, we've tried to allocate points, on a scale of ten, to individual options for each issue. For example, getting the entire payment at the beginning is worth 10 points for the consulting company, while getting anything less than 40% at the beginning is worth 0 points. On the other hand, reaching 25% or less of prepayment is worth 10 points for the client.

For the consulting firm, completing the project in about six months is worth 5 points, while anything more than six months is unacceptable for the client. With this point scheme, we can see that while the consulting company is more sensitive to the payment, the client is more sensitive to the project's tenure. We can also see that if the company agrees to pay beforehand, and if the consulting firm agrees to work faster, it will create more value for both sides. Both sides also wanted more interim meetings. Based on the point chart, both sides could easily have achieved a deal worth up to 15 points in total by scoring 7.5 points each. However, the actual deal is only 6.75 points total (2.25 points for the consulting firm and 4.5 points for the client.

8.5. Always close the package

As we saw earlier, the problem with multi-issue offers is that negotiators inevitably get stuck and don't seize the opportunity to create value. One of the essential rules of a multi-issue offer strategy is to always close the package. Even after you make a multi-issue offer, it is crucial to make sure the counterpart doesn't push you towards closing issues one by one.

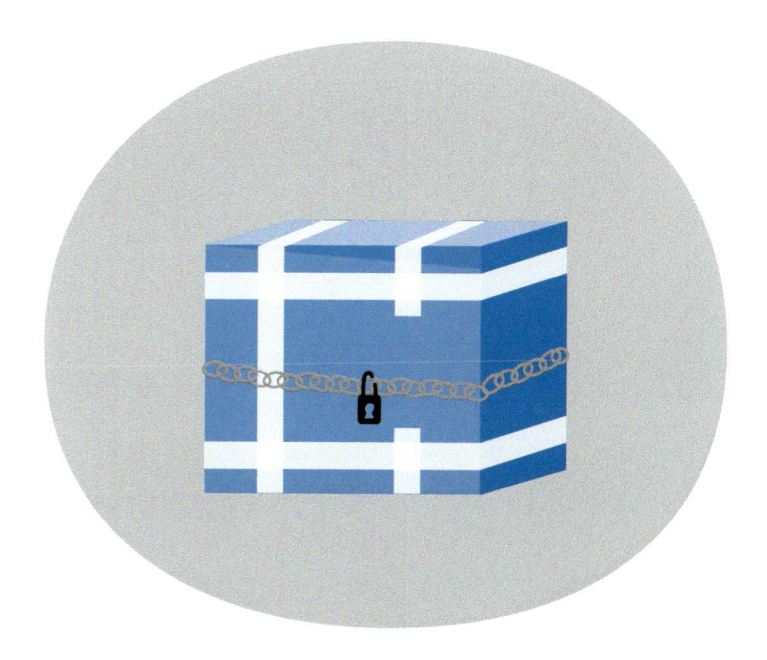

Offers and Concessions Preparation Guide

	Needs		
Our side		Their Side	
Common Needs			
Positions		Positions	
Strategy for identifying priorities and creating valuable exchanges.			
	Issue I		
	Issue 2 ...		
	Issue n		
Issues crucial for us, not for them			
Positions		Positions	
Strategy for determining position. Not giving up on them soon. Identifying and avoiding potential deadlocks.			
	Issue I		
	Issue 2 ...		
	Issue n		
Issues crucial for them, not for us			
Positions		Positions	
Strategy for identifying their positions. Identifying and avoiding potential deadlocks. Using them actively during concessions. Creating valuable exchanges with the issues above.			
	Issue I		
	Issue 2 ...		
	Issue n		

CHAPTER 7

CLOSING THE NEGOTIATION

The closing of a negotiation determines the successful execution of the deal. Consider the following example. A friend of ours once moved into a new apartment as a tenant. When they signed the contract, the owner said that the tenant would be responsible for any minor repairs, to which the tenant agreed. After some time, a leak appeared in the bathroom sink. The tenant called the owner because low-quality plumbing had caused the leak. The owner said, "As per the contract, you need to take care of these small repairs." Our friend didn't argue. He called a plumber and got the problem fixed. The plumber warned him, however, that more leaks were likely to show up elsewhere. A few days later, his suspicion was confirmed when a leak appeared in the kitchen sink. Our friend called the plumber straight away. When the plumber was leaving, our friend asked, "Last time you were here, how did you know this would happen again?" The plumber told him that the plumbing looked old and that the pipes were a bit rusty. In the end, our friend ended up spending a lot of money on these little repairs. He sent all the invoices to the landlord and asked for a refund. The owner showed the contract and said that all the invoices were for 'small repairs.' According to the contract, they were the tenant's responsibility. Our friend threatened to go to court, but the landlord refused to concede. Our friend realized the cost of a lawsuit would be more than was worth his time and effort. In total, he had asked for the plumber to visit eight times and had paid €487 (four hundred and eighty-seven euros). Had he known these numbers ahead of time, he would never have agreed to deal with that first leak as a 'minor repair.' Ultimately, he left the apartment for good. What was his mistake? His mistake was to leave a poorly-defined term in the contract—minor repairs. Often in negotiations, especially in conflict-resolution negotiations, negotiators do not spend enough time closing the negotiation. Here are the issues we need to pay attention to while closing the negotiation.

1. REACHING AN AGREEMENT

It is vital to make sure that the agreement is reached. It is important to refer to the preparation document before closing the agreement and make sure that every important issue and need have been adressed.

2. MAINTAINING CALM

Negotiations often derail because of a lousy closing. Negotiating is like building a house of cards—even at the last moment, a small lapse in attention may destroy all the hard work. Some negotiators use the tactics of throwing a fit of anger in the closing moments to extract a little more value; hence, it is imperative not to lose control over the negotiation process. In a very complex negotiation, take a break just before closing the negotiation to make sure you have an acceptable deal at hand. If the counterpart shows anger in the closing phase of the negotiation, don't make any quick concessions out of panic. It's important to recognize their emotions, but those emotions shouldn't pressure a negotiator to make quick concessions.

3. CHECKLIST FOR CLOSING A NEGOTIATION

Samir was a sales representative in a medium-sized food processing company which frequently supplied some of their products to a particular retailer. However, there was a quality problem in one of the shipments. While Samir and his colleagues denied the issue, the customer demanded a full refund. The situation escalated during a couple of heated telephone conversations. Finally, after the intervention of some seniors, both sides decided to have a conversation. The negotiation was mainly about two issues, resolving the conflict about the unpaid bills and getting more business for the future. In the end, both sides reached a few conclusions. 1. The customer will only pay half of the bill; 2. In the future, a third party would oversee quality control; and 3. The order for the next quarter would be raised by 30%. A month later, when Samir sent a new invoice, he added the inspection report by a consultant and also the invoice from the consultant. This triggered another confrontation. Even though the inspection amount was not huge, the client insisted that they should not be paying it. Samir said that the client should cover at least half of the inspection cost because their agreement said, 'an external party will be hired to certify the quality' and never specified that the cost will be paid by the supplier only. The purchase officer who was negotiating on behalf of the customer agreed that it was a moot point. He also said that they would not mind paying half the cost. However, the consultant hired by Samir's company was relatively unknown and was too costly. The purchase officer did not deny the quality inspection and said it was satisfactorily done, but it would be difficult for him to justify such a high cost with the finance department. Finally, they decided to have another negotiation to resolve these pending issues. However, this incident affected not only the relationship between the two companies but also the situation of these negotiators internally in their respective organizations.

Here is a checklist that a negotiator has to use to ensure that the negotiation has ended well and no loose ends have been left.

3.1. Needs

Make sure all the needs have been met. Use the preparation document elaborated in earlier chapters to ensure that all the objectives of the negotiations are taken care of.

3.2. Agreement

Write down the agreement in clear, well-defined terms.

3.3. Time

What is the time frame for the execution of the agreement? Make sure the date and time for implementation are clearly identified. Avoid terms like 'soon' or 'in a few days' or (the most dangerous) 'at an appropriate time.'

3.4. Allocation of Tasks

Identify who is responsible for what during task execution. This is especially important in the case of contingent agreements. As we have seen in the example above, it is important to identify who will execute which task.

3.5. Precision

Vague agreements easily lead to future conflicts. Make sure to eliminate any ambiguity from the agreement.

3.6. Measurability

One way an agreement can be made precise is by making sure every aspect of its execution is measurable. For example, when we include terms like 'we will talk beforehand,' that doesn't establish when and how the conversation will occur. Instead, incorporate a clause that says, 'every three months, starting from this particular date, meetings will take place...' Measurability is especially important in internal negotiations within an organization. We often see two departments agreeing on a collaboration using terms like, 'our team will work enthusiastically,' or 'a detailed report will be given.' Subjective terms like 'enthusiastically' or 'detailed' often invite misunderstanding. How much detail is necessary? How do they define enthusiasm? Substantiate these claims by clearly defining each point in measurable terms. For example, 'our team will spend 50% of our time on the project' or 'our report will include analysis on the following items (followed by a list of issues).

3.7. Dispute Resolution Mechanism

If applicable, this is an essential element to be included in the negotiation document. It is crucial to identify who will resolve differences or conflicts, especially when negotiators are in different regions and therefore subject to separate jurisdictions. It becomes imperative in cases of provision of services through virtual channels. For example, a Sweden-based firm hires an accountant based in Spain to keep their books. It is easy, given the nature and volume of work, to manage it virtually. However, they both need to identify which jurisdiction applies in the event of any conflict regarding delivery, payment, the definition of work, etc. How will they resolve conflicts, disputes, and disagreements? If they have to resort to mediation, where will they find mediators?

In short, the negotiation agreement should act as a control document for the execution of the deal. Every time any of the parties are confused about implementation, the contract should provide guidance. In fact, while writing the agreement, negotiators need to imagine that they are writing the constitution of a little republic—the republic of their relationship. Every time differences of opinion or conflicts arise, this agreement should provide a clear path ahead.

4. STAGE III POST-NEGOTIATION

A negotiation shouldn't be considered resolved until the post-negotiation task is complete. If a supplier navigates a tough negotiation and gets a great contract from their buyer, their job doesn't end there. Once the negotiation is complete, the supplier also has to complete the job as promised, and the same can be said for the buyer. A negotiator, therefore, always has to keep the post-negotiation scenario in mind. In complex, high-level negotiations, each negotiation has significant implications on many other current and future negotiations. Furthermore, each negotiation adds to the personal prestige of the negotiator. In current times where people are more connected than ever, impressions matter a lot.

Food for Thought

1. Think of your past negotiations and describe them. Try to understand the process within the context of the steps we have just elaborated. Take note of what you could have done differently.

2. Think of a negotiation that you are going to engage in soon. Write out your preparation using the framework devices we have developed so far. Also, describe the process you will engage in and share it with a colleague or a confidante for some feedback.

CHAPTER 8

SIX TENETS OF AMBIDEXTERITY

What does 'Negotiate Good, Negotiate Well' mean? It means a negotiator not only needs to negotiate a good outcome but also needs to focus on the process in order to negotiate well. In order to have a strong command over negotiation process, the negotiator needs to be very good at analyzing situations. So far, we have looked at a framework for situation assessment, preparation, and the negotiation process. There are moments when we have to compete and others when we need to collaborate. However, it is important for a negotiator to be ambidextrous, able to negotiate in both competitive and collaborative situations. In this chapter we will present the principle of ambidexterity and its basic tenets.

A sports agency represents a soccer player named Sweetstrike. At the age of 32, he is approaching the twilight of his career but is still a sharp and a deadly player in front of the goal. However, competition for roster spots at his current club is intense, and he is finding it increasingly difficult to compete with the club's younger strikers for a place on the first team. Rather than continue to warm the bench, Sweetstrike has asked his agent to seek a loan arrangement with another team. During the January transfer window, a struggling club in the same league needs to find a replacement for its lead striker, Mr. Goalmachine, who recently tore his Achilles tendon.

Unable to find a promising young prospect to fill in, the club's manager is desperate to sign Sweetstrike, who played for the club at the beginning of his career and wouldn't need much time to fit back in. Despite concerns that he may not be as prolific, the club is prepared to offer Sweetstrike almost the same salary that they have been paying Mr. Goalmachine. However, Mr. Goalmachine's current salary is significantly lower than what Sweetstrike gets paid at his current club.

For Sweetstrike's part, this mid-season switch offers the prospect of more first-team playing time and would improve his chances of revitalizing his career. What he most wants is to preserve his chances of playing for his national team in the World Cup in two years' time, which he sees as the perfect swan song to his career. Indeed, he wants the switch so badly that he has told his agent that he would even be willing to play for free, although he would never say no to more money. On the other hand, the coach of the struggling club has told the club that they should sign Sweetstrike, and that even though he may not have the same recent statistics as Mr. Goalmachine, he should be offered the same salary and incentives.

What do you think about this negotiation? Will it be difficult? You do not think so at all. It seems like a purely collaborative situation with an inevitable win-win conclusion. However, when we have asked participants in our training programs to assume roles of the agent of the player and the director of the club, negotiations often become tense and end up in a deadlock.

Why do negotiations with a lot of collaborative potential sometimes fail to create as much value for both the sides as they should? The answer is simple. Negotiators frequently misread the situation and choose the wrong approach. A negotiation ultimately stems from the approach taken by both the sides. What can we do to avoid this pitfall? The solution is to be ambidextrous.

Being ambidextrous in a negotiation means being able to handle both competitive and collaborative tensions with equal dexterity. Lax and Sabenius talked about the competitive-collaborative tension that exists in a negotiation, referring to it as *negotiator's dilemma*. In a way, it was an ode to the term *prisoner's dilemma,* which had been coined earlier by game theorists. Because of the inherent uncertainty about what the other side would do, the negotiator is always in a dilemma. For a negotiator to compete or to collaborate, that is the question.

Figure 8.1 breaks down the possible outcomes of choosing either option.

Figure 8.1. The negotiator's dilemma

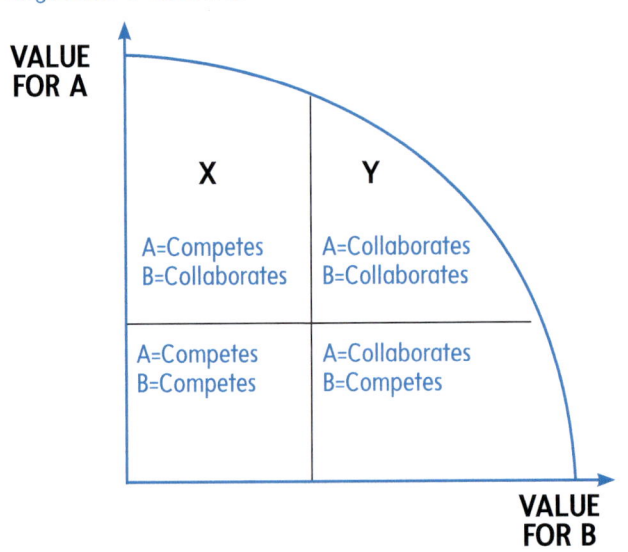

	X	Y
(upper)	A=Competes B=Collaborates	A=Collaborates B=Collaborates
(lower)	A=Competes B=Competes	A=Collaborates B=Competes

VALUE FOR A (vertical axis) / VALUE FOR B (horizontal axis)

If both the sides take on a competitive mindset, the result will be mediocre for both of them. On the other hand, if both the sides collaborate, they'll maximize their created value potential. That being said, if one side tries to collaborate while the other chooses to claim value by being competitive, the benefits will be largely one-sided.

Some people might say that, according to this chart, choosing a collaborative approach is not advisable. If you choose a collaborative approach, and the other side chooses to collaborate as well, value creation is high for both sides. If, however, the other side chooses to compete, your value may plummet. While this reasoning sounds logical, a very significant factor has been overlooked: reciprocity. Reciprocity pushes a negotiation toward a stalemate. Let's go back to the original example of a negotiation between Mr. Sweetstrike's agent and the representative of Struggling FC. Take a look at the following dialogue.

Agent: My client, Mr. Sweetstrike, is happy to know your club is interested in signing him. He once played for your club, thirteen years ago as a teenager. Now, as a veteran player, he would love to contribute to the club again. We are really looking forward to making this happen.

Representative: Of course. It's a shame such a good player isn't getting any chance to play in the first eleven.

Agent: Well, you know how it works. You may be the best, but if the coach has a different plan, you may not get the role you deserve. After all, football is a team sport. I think his playstyle and his effectiveness as a striker would be a good fit for your team's culture and approach.

Representative: I agree. Nevertheless, as you already know, we are not a top team in terms of resources, and Sweetstrike hasn't been having a great season so far. We really can't afford to pay a top-tier salary.

Let's stop here for a moment. Sweetstrike's agent is trying to highlight how the player and the team are a good fit for each other. The representative of the club, meanwhile, is pointing out the player's liabilities and how he may not command a very high market value. The agent is approaching the negotiation collaboratively, but the club representative is being competitive. The agent picks up on this fact and adapts his strategy as the conversation continues.

The agent: Yes, I understand you can't offer a very good salary, but you don't have a lot of other options, either. Your main striker, Goalmachine, got injured in the last game and may be out for the season. If you want to survive in the competition, you need us.

What has the agent done? He has reciprocated, responding to the representative with a competitive approach of his own. When two sides become competitive, negotiations become more vulnerable and are often likely to get stuck in a deadlock. To avoid this situation, the negotiator needs to demonstrate ambidexterity. The following section presents the basic tenets of ambidexterity.

1. FOCUS ON MULTIPLE NEEDS

Focusing on needs is the first tenet of ambidexterity. An impasse occurs when two negotiators get stuck on a single issue and refuse to budge from their respective positions. When focused on winning a position, negotiators may completely forget the multiple needs they need to address and satisfy throughout the negotiation. Staying focused on the need always brings the negotiator back to the negotiation table and helps create common ground with the other side. The failed negotiation between U.S. President Ronald Reagan and General Secretary of the Communist Party of the Soviet Union Mikhail Gorbachev at the Reykjavik Summit of October 11-12, 1986 is an interesting example of this phenomenon. While the talks may have collapsed at the last minute, the summit represented the first step toward the gradual normalization of relations between the United States and the Soviet Union.

After the meeting, Gorbachev said, "Reykjavik is not a failure—it is a breakthrough which allowed us, for the first time, to look over the horizon." A year later, the two countries signed the Intermediate-Range Nuclear Forces Treaty. Such an agreement would have been unthinkable had one or both of the participants been unwilling to sacrifice certain strategic interests for common gain. Even though the talks faltered, they at least established all the demands of both parties, as well as all the potential concessions that both sides could offer and, hence, left everyone in no doubt as to where probable solutions could be found.

This is the key to resolving deadlocks: understanding multiple issues and identifying areas of concession, which can help both parties move beyond the one stumbling block that caused the deadlock in the first place.

2. DO YOUR HOMEWORK

All too often, negotiators enter a negotiation lacking a clearly defined objective. In order to focus on multiple issues that can be addressed through the negotiation, it's crucial to prepare for the negotiation beforehand. This is not to say that you need to enter the negotiation with a fixed position in mind or your heart set on achieving one single objective—quite the opposite, in fact.

As we have already seen, negotiators should establish a negotiating position that has two key elements: a minimum or resistance point also known as a reservation price, and an objective or target point. These two poles serve to establish the parameters of the bargain, while at the same time giving you some room in which to maneuver.

The same applies to the counterpart. Think about their needs, positions and alternatives. As they say, knowledge is power. The more you know about the people sitting across the table from you, the greater your chances of making creative initial offers or counteroffers that will align their interests with your own. This will also avoid conflicts and provide the basis for the development of integrative solutions.

3. LISTEN CAREFULLY TO THE OTHER SIDE

When it comes to financial matters, negotiators make the mistake of focusing too much on their own position. They try to bargain based on assumptions that go untested due to the negotiator's inability or unwillingness to truly listen to what the other party is saying.

As we have seen already, listening is not the same as hearing. Listening is about understanding what is being said and grasping its implications for the negotiations at hand. It doesn't mean picking out only what you want to hear. Negotiators should be attentive to everything their counterpart says, regardless of how trivial it may seem.

By actively listening to the other party, a negotiator may stumble upon a bargaining chip that can unite both parties, raising the prospects of a more creative outcome.

4. USE OFFERS STRATEGICALLY

Making offers is one of the most important steps in the negotiation process. We've already seen that making an offer is more than a formality; when we make an offer, we are, to a certain degree, stating how much importance we're giving the deal. How, then, can offers be strategic tools for achieving ambidexterity in negotiations?

1. Multi-issue offers to avoid deadlocks: Successful negotiation is not just about listening to what the other party says; it's also about acting upon the new information you've gleaned by incorporating it into an attractive counteroffer. In fact, failure to do just that is one of the most common mistakes in negotiations. When the counterpart takes a stern position on a single issue, try bundling different objectives into one and offering a package deal.

2. Use Multiple Equivalent Simultaneous Offers: Scholars like Victoria Medvec and Adam Galinsky have eloquently highlighted the importance of MESO (Multiple Equivalent Simultaneous Offers) in complex negotiations. Imagine you're negotiating on behalf of a supermarket chain, trying to close on a food supply contract from a producer. Factors in this negotiation probably include prices, quantities, number of deliveries, and quality control. Picture the following figure as a summary of your positions.

Issue	Position (Desirable)	Position (walk-away)
Price	€20	€25
Quantity	10000 kgs	14000 kgs
Deliveries	50 per month	20 per month
Quality inspection costs	Carried out by a third party; cost covered by the supplier	Quality inspection carried out by you

During the negotiation, you're unsure about what your counterpart really wants—their needs and objectives. Ultimately, you present them with three offers which are all equally good for you.

Issues	Offer 1	Offer 2	Offer 3
Price	20	22,6	24
Quantity	13000	12500	12000
Deliveries per month	20	30	40
Quality inspection	Inspection carried out by you	Inspection by a third party and split costs	Inspection by a third party; cost covered by supplier

Your calculations seem to suggest all these options are equally beneficial for you. As you can see, when you offer a higher price, you slightly reduce the quantity and you also increase deliveries. When the total quantity is spread over many deliveries, your total inventory cost goes down, which results in clear savings.

The moment you make the offer in this form, you send the signal that you're willing to negotiate and that you have a certain amount of flexibility. At the same time, you force the other side to reveal their preferences. For example, if the supplier starts paying more attention to the third option, you know they're willing to increase deliveries and lower quantity but prefer to have a higher price. On the other hand, if the supplier shows greater interest in the first option, you know they're flexible regarding prices. However, as mentioned before, always close the entire package and avoid closing one issue at a time. Closing one issue at a time will take you right back to a competitive setting.

5. ALWAYS SEEK THE COMMON GROUND

As any manager of a large corporation can tell you, it's one thing to reach a satisfactory outcome in a negotiation between two individuals; it's quite another when the two sides of a negotiation are corporate behemoths. As a general rule, corporate negotiations take more time than most. They also tend to be more involved and may include larger groups of people. Decision-making tends to be slower, especially if authority is dispersed across an organization.

As a matter of fact, the closer corporate negotiations come to reaching a conclusion, the more tedious the process, as contract and legal departments must review any paperwork prior to signature. This is simply a fact of corporate life.

When two corporations are fiercely battling it out, the chances of reaching a win-win outcome are minimal. Naturally, when the potential gains or losses can run into the billions of dollars, there is far greater pressure to achieve a win-lose outcome. That's why, even in the most fierce and competitive situations, always look for common ground.

This was a lesson that Steve Jobs learned during Apple's struggles with its larger competitor, Microsoft. Explaining his decision to partner with his longtime rival, Jobs said, "Apple was in very serious trouble at that point, and what was clear was that if the game was a zero-sum game where for Apple to win, Microsoft had to lose, then Apple was going to lose."

Jobs realized that trying to drive a hard bargain with Microsoft would be of no benefit to his company. Instead, he reached out to Bill Gates in the hopes that the two could forge an agreement that would be beneficial for both companies. The Mac Development Team at Microsoft became one of Apple's best developer relationships, according to Jobs.

This is a perfect example of integrative negotiation in action: seeking to find common ground by listening to and understanding the interests of the other party. This is a far more effective way of achieving ambidexterity.

The Apple vs. Microsoft negotiations also underscore the usefulness of negotiating a group or bundle of interests together, as opposed to treating each issue separately, which we will discuss next.

6. DON'T IGNORE THE MUSIC

Edward T. Hall, one of the most prominent cross-cultural anthropologists of the 20th century, spoke of a "perpetual ballet" in his description of a Mexican marketplace, where many pairs of buyers and sellers from different cultures bargained over goods.

It's fitting that he would liken negotiation to a dance involving two skilled performers who need to understand each other, adjust to each other's steps and respond to the common music in order to create an elegant choreography.

Problems arise when the dance partners don't listen to this common music. They need heed that common ground in order to arrive at a sustainable deal that satisfies the needs and requirements of both parties.

How can you pay attention to this common music? By paying attention to the process. Before the negotiation, always prepare yourself for the process. Do your best to foresee how the negotiation will proceed. During the negotiation, pay attention to every verbal and nonverbal cue you receive from the other side. Musicians and dancers don't learn how to make a masterpiece; they learn to play their instrument or control their body to move with the music. The masterpiece comes to life as a result of minute attention and the hard work the artists put into every little aspect of their skill. The same is true for negotiations. Pay attention to every aspect of the process and achieve your masterpiece of a deal.

7. SUMMARY

Tenets of Ambidexterity

1. Focus on Multiple Needs
2. Do Your Homework
3. Listen Carefully to the Other Side
4. Use Offers Strategically
5. Always Seek Common Ground
6. Don't Ignore the Music

> **Food for Thought**
>
> Based on our discussion thus far, prepare a personal plan of action and approach for your future negotiations. Identify what negotiations you are going to engage in. Come up with a plan. Try to script the process you want to follow. Once you finish the negotiation, see how well you succeeded.

SECTION II

NEGOTIATION IN SPECIAL CONTEXTS

CHAPTER 9

NEGOTIATING IN A TEAM

A participant in a negotiation course once confessed that he hated to negotiate in the presence of his wife. When asked why, he said he found it difficult to close the negotiation when she was with him. For example, he once found himself negotiating the price of a used car. Both he and his wife had agreed that fifteen thousand euros was a fair price for the car. However, the seller didn't want to go below sixteen thousand, five hundred. "If I were negotiating alone, I would have agreed to his price, but I generally find it difficult to concede in the presence of a family member. I couldn't concede in that negotiation, and we ended up walking away without a car. Whenever I'm with my father, brother, or wife, I become a bit adamant. Maybe I don't want to look weak in front of them," said the participant. Negotiating in a team involves more complexities due to the unique, interpersonal nature of teamwork. Some of us are more comfortable negotiating as part of a team, while others are more comfortable negotiating solo.

1. IMPACT OF TEAM NEGOTIATIONS ON OUTCOMES

Let's try to understand the team as a negotiating unit by answering two questions. First of all, what happens when an individual negotiates as part of a team? Second, what happens when an individual negotiates opposite a team? A study led by Leigh Thompson from Northwestern University found that teams negotiate better in almost all situations. Not only that, but teams were also a better counterpart than a solo negotiator. When teams negotiate with individuals in competitive or distributive scenarios, they generally create more value. However, individuals are still better off negotiating with a team in the opposition than negotiating opposite another individual. In other words, in a competitive scenario, teams help not only in getting a better result than the counterpart, but they also help the counterpart get a better result. On the other hand, in a collaborative negotiation situation, teams actually help increase the joint gain. In a nutshell, teams achieve overall better results in negotiations.

There are two main reasons why teams create more joint profits—better information and better control. When teams negotiate, they have an advantage of a larger network, more information, and a more thorough analysis. With more participating members, teams can come up with better ideas because they have a broader perspective. Another reason why teams create more joint profits is their control over the negotiation process, which is often greater due to having a wider range of tactics at their disposal. Different team members can even play tactics like good cop and bad cop, which is difficult in a solo negotiation.

2. CHALLENGES IN A TEAM NEGOTIATION

Despite their numerous advantages, team negotiations also face several inherent challenges, which we'll break down in the following section along with some strategies for overcoming them.

2.1. Lack of Coordination

One of the biggest problems team negotiations face is a lack of coordination. Teams may lack coordination for a variety of reasons, but internal conflict is usually at the top of the list. It's essential to avoid internal conflict in a team by carefully studying sources of potential conflict even before the team formation. There are two main types of conflict that affect teamwork: interpersonal and task-related.

Negotiation teams need to function as a cohesive unit, but interpersonal conflicts are difficult to foresee and therefore difficult to avoid. Most of the interpersonal conflicts stem from strong emotions. The best way to avoid emotional hiccups in a team is a careful selection of its members. Furthermore, negotiation teams should spend time together before the negotiation process begins. Some organizations overlook the impact of teams on negotiation performance and don't give them enough warm-up time to develop a sense of camaraderie.

Task-related conflict, on the other hand, can be avoided in two ways. First, negotiations teams need a high degree of functional coherence. If the team is homogenous in terms of the functions and expertise of its members, they'll understand each other's perspectives a lot better. However, this may work only if the negotiation is limited in terms of functions. In many complex negotiation situations, a team needs experts from different fields. It's common to see representatives of finance, marketing, operations and human resources negotiating together in representation of their organization. In order to avoid task-related conflict in a multifunctional team, it's important to provide the team with some 'grooming time' in order for them to understand each other's objectives and priorities. It's also important to use this mutual understanding to create a common ground for negotiation. If team members negotiate for conflicting goals, not only will the unity of the team suffer, but their overall performance will fall short of its potential.

Type of Conflict	Reasons	Preventive Measures
Interpersonal	Lack of harmony, lack of mutual understanding, lack of trust	Careful selection of the team
Task-Related	Lack of understanding of each other's functions and priorities	'Grooming time' for the team

2.2. Poor Control of the Process

Team negotiations sometimes tend to get a bit off-track and take up too much time at the negotiation table. This is the second problem that surfaces from team negotiations. The following graphic compares how the sharing of information is distributed throughout the negotiation process between team negotiations and individual negotiations.

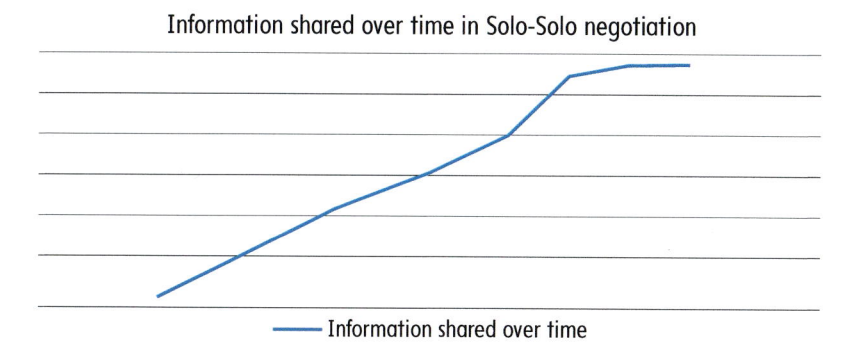

Information shared over time in Solo-Solo negotiation

——— Information shared over time

As the graph illustrates, it can be difficult to share information in team negotiations. These situations often feature sudden spikes in the amount of information shared. As a result, it's very important to keep track what information is being presented. During team negotiations, these spikes occur when the team spends a lot of time warming up; later on, team members start contributing a lot of information at once. Because of this pattern, it's often difficult to keep track of all the information that is being or has been shared. The best way to avoid information overload is to manage the process through role assignment.

Information shared over time in Team-Team negotiation

—— Information shared over time

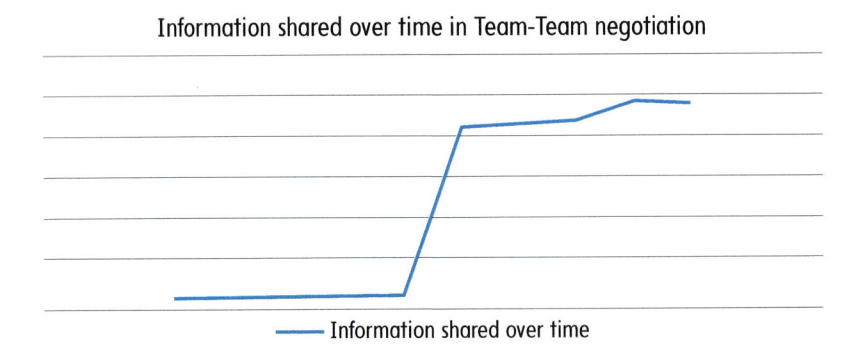

3. ROLE-ASSIGNMENT FOR MANAGEMENT OF INFORMATION

In order to maintain control of the negotiation process, it's important to assign roles for negotiation. Assigning roles helps the negotiating team achieve two objectives—information management and process management. In a way, the management of both information and process are interrelated. Poor management of the flow of information leads to a poor management of the negotiation process, which ultimately results in a bad deal. Ideally, roles should be assigned in two ways: functional assignment and processual assignment.

Functional assignment is essential in a multi-functional negotiating team. In a joint-venture negotiation where issues related to human capital, valuation of the company, and product portfolio need to be decided, it is advisable to have an expert of each area present at the negotiation table. This will ensure that each and every important aspect that needs to be shared or explored is taken care of.

Processual assignment means assigning every team member their role throughout each step of negotiation process. For example, assign someone to establish contact, someone to frame the negotiation, or someone to manage offers and concessions. There are two important advantages of processual assignment. First, no single member of the negotiating team has the pressure of taking the initiative at each and every step of the negotiation. Second, it aids team synchronization with the negotiation process. Each member of the negotiating team needs to know their role in the negotiation. Proper assignment of these roles in the negotiation process demands clarity on two fronts: what information each member needs to explore or collect and what each member's role is during each step of negotiation process.

4. COLLECTIVE PREPARATION

The previous paragraph explains how a negotiating team needs a great deal of synchronization. In order to address issues related to the assignment of roles, it's absolutely essential that teams prepare together. Preparation for a team negotiation should ideally be managed over two phases: individual preparation and team preparation. During the individual preparation phase, each member needs to understand their particular objective and needs from this negotiation. It's important to understand how the negotiation is most likely to affect personal objectives. Once individual preparation is completed, the team should get together and prepare for the negotiation as a unit. Prior work in individual preparation helps the team focus on issues that need greater clarification.

5. CAUCUS

Another vital part of a team negotiation is caucus. Caucus refers to the break a team takes in negotiation in order to assess the negotiation's progress and check its effectiveness. Caucuses are important. Many teams, however, don't take caucuses because view them as a sign of weakness. For this reason, it's essential to convey in advance that the team will use caucuses to evaluate information and the progress of the negotiation. Caucuses are also taken to deal with unforeseen situations. In complex negotiations, teams frequently find themselves in situations where they need to deal with information or issues they had not foreseen. During a caucus, it's invaluable to maintain strict discipline and not get distracted, as well as to summarize all the issues that have been discussed before getting back to the negotiation table. It's not just important to manage our caucuses; it's equally important to manage the counterpart's caucuses. Imagine you've been doing well in a negotiation and are feeling optimistic. Suddenly, the counterpart asks for a caucus. The biggest risk in this situation is to lose all the hard work you've done so far. Before granting the caucus to the counterpart, take consent over what has already been agreed upon and establish a time limit for the caucus. If the time limit is not properly set, there is a significant risk of losing focus.

6. CONFLICT DURING THE NEGOTIATION

Caucuses also help deal with any conflict that arises during the process of negotiation. At times, negotiators disagree on a certain issue during the negotiation, and these disagreements may lead to conflict. In these situations, the following steps should be taken. (I) Caucus: If possible, it's always better to avoid continuing the negotiation if the team is in conflict. Caucuses can be essential for resolving internal conflict, which affects not only the team's focus but also employee commitment toward the negotiation. (II) Conflict Redressal System: in order to avoid conflict, it's important to prepare together as a team and also set up a system to redress conflicts that may arise in a negotiating team.

7. LEADERSHIP

Last but not least, every negotiating team should have a leader. As we have established in previous chapters, negotiation is a skill, and in a team negotiation, it's important to make sure that each and every member's skill is put to the best possible use. However, it's possible that in a team negotiation, individual members might simply get overwhelmed by a few particular issues, and that's why it's important to have someone who is specifically in charge of keeping the big picture in focus all the time. It's also important to designate an approving authority in the heat of crucial decisions. That's the reason why each negotiating team should appoint a leader—a leader who can keep the team intact, who can take control whenever needed, and who can make final decisions about the negotiation.

8. PREPARATION GUIDES

Individual Preparation Guide

My Side		Other Side
	Needs	
	Alternatives	
	My BATNA	
	Organization's BATNA	

Processual Role Assignment

	Teammate 1	Teammate 2	Teammate 3	Teammate 4	Teammate 5
Establish contact					
Framing					
Generate options					
Making first offer					
Concessions					
Creating an agreement					
Closing					

Team Preparation Guide

Our Side		Other Side
	Needs	
	Alternatives	

9. ESSENTIAL INFORMATION SHEET

Write down all the important issues on one side, and on the other side, identify who will deal with which information and what questions need to be asked.

	Teammate 1	Teammate 2	Teammate 3	Teammate 4	Teammate 5
Issue 1					
Issue 2					
Issue 3					
Issue 4					

MULTIPARTY NEGOTIATION

CHAPTER 10

Two sisters are fighting over an orange. Their mother intervenes and finds out that one sister wanted to have the juice while the other needed the peels to make a pie. The mother gives the juice to one sister and the peels to the other, and both girls walk away happy. You've probably read this story in many negotiation books before. However, let's add a few more participants to the scenario—a third sister who wants the orange peels for cosmetic purposes, a grandmother who thinks the orange is overripe and should be thrown away, a toddler who mistakes the orange for a ball and wants to play with it, and an older brother who wants the orange just to mess with everyone else. This is a perfect example of multiparty negotiation. In these types of negotiation, it can often be challenging to identify who wants what, and even more so to pursue our own objectives. Let's take a look at some of the biggest challenges multiparty negotiations tend to present.

One of the reasons we need to understand multiparty negotiations well is that they're a lot more frequent than we realize. In our negotiation programs, we frequently ask participants what kind of negotiations they participate in the most—individual, team, or multiparty negotiations? They rarely mention multiparty negotiation as a frequent exercise. However, when we conduct the negotiation simulations, the same participants often confess they hadn't realized how often they engage in multiparty negotiation situations. Many internal negotiations, such as department meetings, family reunions to discuss property issues, business or interpersonal conflicts, community meetings to sort out issues related to the neighborhood, or even a meeting between friends to discuss where they should vacation together are all examples of multiparty negotiations.

1. IDENTIFYING OTHER'S INTERESTS

One of the biggest challenges in a multiparty negotiation is to ascertain the interests of everyone present at the negotiation table. Simultaneously, it's also essential to be able to convey our own interests to everyone else. Negotiators who frequently confront multiparty situations tend to complain about their voices getting drowned out.

At times, negotiators are not able to share their point of view properly. It's imperative to manage the process of the negotiation in such a way that everyone gets an opportunity to participate in the conversation. One of the ways in which one can identify interests in a multiparty negotiation is through thorough preparation. It's vital to determine what we know and what we assume we know. For example, look at the structure below, in which you identify what you know and what you think you know. Determining in what information we have in concrete terms will help us identify which questions we will have to ask when we negotiate. The other objective is to stop us from acting based on sheer prejudice. We often assume what others want in a negotiation based on our own biases, and these assumptions are frequently inaccurate. Here is a little schema of how the needs of others can be analyzed before the negotiation.

Needs	Party 1	Party 2	Party 3
What I know for sure they need			
What I assume they need			

As we identify needs in this fashion, we can develop the framework for the questions we'll want to ask when we enter the multiparty negotiation.

2. POWER AND ALLIANCE

Another important factor that influences expectations in a negotiation is power. In the case of a multiparty negotiation, power plays a very crucial role. In a dyadic negotiation (two parties), it is relatively easier to identify both sides' needs because due to there being fewer situations and alternatives to. In a multiparty negotiation scenario, on the other hand, it's much more difficult to assess everyone's alternatives against our own. Moreover, it's important to note the relationship between multiple parties in order to know what kind of alliances they might be forming.

Forming an alliance before and during a multiparty negotiation is one of the most important tasks of a negotiator. Two separate skills or practices come into play.
1. Creating a formidable alliance
2. Protecting yourself against a hostile alliance.

Consider the following strategies for forming an alliance.

3. AFFINITY MAP

Our mentor Juan Roure has developed a tool that he always talks about in his lessons, called "affinity map".

Generally, during the negotiation, you have to manage both practices. Once again, preparation is key. As the old saying goes, "sweat in peace to avoid blood in war." A negotiator needs to be ready for both situations. The tool we recommend for preparing to form alliances is called an affinity map—it's a visual representation of the proximity of interests of different parties involved in a negotiation. Affinity maps show what kind of alliances are likely to emerge.

Let's assume a company's top management is getting together to determine the new production budget. They'll have to decide whether or not the company should invest in expanding the plant facility. Here is a list of each participant's objectives.

1. The CEO wants to do what's best for the company in the long run.
2. The Chief Finance Officer wants to reduce overinvestment in the plant facility because of higher interest rates.
3. The Chief Marketing Officer believes higher production means more stock, which in turn means a potential increase in sales.
4. The Chief Operations Officer believes higher production means larger scale, more efficient production, and better management of the facility.
5. The Human Resource Director believes a larger plant facility would put more pressure on current working staff, increase overtime costs, and raise a need for immediate recruiting.

Based on the information above, what would each participant's relative position be? Obviously, the Chief Marketing Officer and the Chief Operations Officer would be in favor of the investment while the Chief Finance Officer and the Human Resource Director would be against it. The Chief Executive Officer would maintain a neutral position and wait for a more detailed analysis before taking one side or the other.

Based on this information, we can create the following affinity map.

Affinity Map

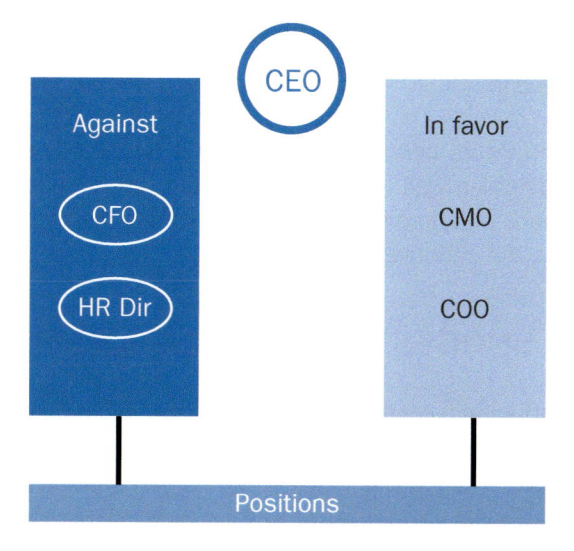

This diagram allows us to quickly identify potential alliances between different participants in the negotiation. This example may be an oversimplification, but it still illustrates the concept of an affinity map. Let's think about the eventual meeting of these five leaders. While the CEO takes stock of the situation, both the CFO and the HR Director try to convince the CEO about the disadvantage of the investment. In contrast, the CMO and the COO try to persuade the CEO to go ahead with the investment.

Using a tool like an affinity map, the CFO would realize that she has to create an alliance with the HR Director and collectively put forth strong arguments against the expansion. The CFO has to make sure that the HR director remains aligned with her position, as well as find ways to dissolve a potential alliance between the other members in opposition.

4. LISTENING TO OTHERS AND SHOWING YOU LISTEN

In order to understand what people really need in a multiparty scenario, it's crucial to listen to them. Listening well means making sure the negotiators present at the table get enough space and time to express their needs. The best way to ensure this happens is by taking the initiative with questions.

5. MAKING SUGGESTIONS ABOUT THE PROCESS

It is important to maintain control over the negotiation process, and presenting a recommendation about the negotiation process is a good way to do this. If the other negotiators haven't thought about the negotiation process, then there's a high probability they'll simply agree to your recommendation, placing control over the negotiation in your hands.

6. REACHING AGREEMENT AND MAKING ALLIANCES

Reaching an agreement in a multiparty negotiation is not only complex, but also vulnerable to several biases and difficulties. Let's think of an example.

Cunning Daddy and the Marquis of Condorcet

Picture a household of three members—a father, a mother, and a teenage daughter. Upon the arrival of winter, they decide to spend a weekend at a ski resort. They arrive at the resort on a Friday evening, and the father is the first to switch on the TV. To his dismay, he finds that there are only three channels available. One is playing a movie that he loves, another features a live tennis match, and the last one is showing news. The father wants to watch the movie, but the tennis match would be his second choice. The news doesn't grab his interest at all. The father knows the daughter would love to watch the tennis match, as she herself is an excellent player, and that the news would be her next choice. She doesn't like romantic comedies, so the movie wouldn't be for her. While the mother doesn't care for tennis, she might enjoy the movie, although but her first choice would definitely be to watch the news.

	Father	Mother	Daughter
First choice	Movie	News	Tennis
Second choice	Tennis	Movie	News
Third choice	News	Tennis	Movie

The father wants his first choice to be the ultimate decision, but he still wants the rest of his family to weigh in. What should he do? Well, this cunning man did something unethical. He told his wife and daughter, "Sweethearts, there's this film on TV, along with a tennis match. What should we watch?" The daughter said, "Hey! Tennis!!" The wife said, "No! I don't want to watch tennis at all. I prefer something else." At that point, the father said, "Well, I prefer the movie over tennis, too. So why don't we watch the movie?" And, sure enough, they ended up watching the movie.

If each family member knew about all the available choices from the beginning, there wouldn't be any selection because the father would want the movie, the mother would prefer the news, and the daughter would prefer tennis. This is also known as the Condorcet cycle, named after a nineteenth-century French philosopher, Marquis de Condorcet or Nicholas de Condorcet. In a Condorcet cycle, where choices are cyclical in nature (a>b>c>a), there is no clear winner. To make use of such a situation, at times, some negotiators present the situation, limiting the available choices in such a way that others might not be in a position to make the right decision. One should always be very clear about not being a victim of such a trick (like our clever father's trick) in a multiparty negotiation.

Two more vital elements in a multiparty negotiation are setting agenda and presentation of choices. Given that multiple parties are present at the negotiation table, it's extremely important to have a say in the setting of the agenda and the presentation of alternatives. In other words, for a more effective multiparty negotiation, greater control over the process is required. Another reason why the presentation of options is essential is because of the limited perspective that a negotiator develops when there are multiple options on the table. In a study conducted by Leigh Thompson, participants of a multiparty negotiation were asked, upon finishing the negotiation, how many potential solutions they thought were possible. The negotiation was about five different issues, and each issue had four to five clearly identified alternatives. On average, people estimated that there were about four alternative solutions possible[1]. In reality, the exercise offered about fifty potential solutions. We call this a problem of bounded negotiability. Bounded negotiability means our ability to see limited issues as 'negotiable.' Bounded negotiability is largely influenced by our preparation and how issues are presented in a negotiation. That's why it's important to understand all the issues beforehand and consider the big picture before the negotiation begins.

Quite often, we advise our participants and students to use the VIA framework for analyzing the needs of different parties present at the table. In the VIA framework, participants are encouraged to classify needs at hand as Vital (V), Important (I), and Additional (A). This system helps a negotiator manage time properly and allows them to focus on key issues.

Let's look at an example of a multiparty negotiation an executive once shared with us. An important negotiation is taking place in a pharmaceutical company, in which it will be decided how much of the total budget should be allocated to a new cosmetic product. The issues to be resolved are budget allocation, allocation of human capital, purchase of new equipment, and the lead time for launching the product in the market. Which issue is likely to generate the most debate in this case? Generally, when we ask this question, the answer we receive is budget allocation. However, the executive who was sharing the story with us tried to draw a VIA-chart for all the issues and all the parties present. In this meeting, the following negotiators were present: the CEO, the Chief Finance Officer, the Chief Operations Officer, the Chief R&D Officer, the Chief Marketing Officer, and Chief Human Resource Manager. In this scenario, allocation of human capital is a vital decision for the CEO, COO, and CHR. At the same time, budget allocation is a crucial decision for the CEO and the CFO, along with the Chief of R&D Officer. Here is a list ranking each issue for each individual.

---

1   Thompson, L. (2014) *The Mind and Heart of the Negotiator.* Pearson.

The VIA chart of issues and parties

Issue	CEO	CFO	COO	CRO	CHO	CMO
Allocation of funds	Vital	vital	Important	Vital	important	Important
Purchase of a new equipment	Vital	vital	Vital	Vital	additional	Additional
Allocation of additional staff members	Vital	additional	Important	Vital	Vital	Additional
The setting of lead time for the launch of the product	Vital	important	Important	Vital	additional	Vital

What do we see in this chart? The decision of whether to buy new equipment for the research project or not was a vital issue for the majority of negotiators present, while budget allocation was a decision that was vital for only three of the negotiators. Eventually, as the executive predicted, it was the decision regarding equipment that took up the most time. One reason why it created a little bit of conflict was because almost everyone had assumed that it might not be a critical issue for the rest of the negotiators. Hence, they all took up the issue slightly later in the conversation, and eventually, it created a significant amount of chaos and conflict in the team. Along with the affinity map, a VIA matrix for the negotiating parties helps identify potential allies very soon.

7. ESTABLISHING THE CORE

The owner of a family enterprise once shared an exciting story with us. There was a family business operating across Central America, and the enterprise was run by the eldest brother in the family. The eldest brother (let's call him Ramon), who was on the verge of being a septuagenarian, wanted to delegate more responsibilities to his two younger brothers and their six sons (each brother had two sons). Ramon was the president and the CEO of the company, while his two brothers were vice presidents. His two sons and four nephews were all involved in the business and were looking after different operations. However, Ramon wanted to restructure the company into autonomous business units and allow each son and nephew to take on a larger leadership role within those business units. At the same time, he wanted his two brothers to gradually take his place and respectively assume the roles of president and the CEO.

For a few months, Ramon talked to everyone individually, without revealing his plans, to test what everyone really wanted, both personally and professionally. Finally, he chalked out a plan. In one of the quarterly meetings for the performance review, Ramon called a meeting with his brothers, sons, and nephews and unveiled his plan of restructuring the business. Everyone welcomed the idea of change in the organization and showed willingness to take on more responsibility. However, as

Ramon told everyone what he thought everyone should be doing, their enthusiasm started waning. In fact, the meeting ended without any conclusion, and Ramon had to stop talking about restructuring because he feared tensions or even a rift in the family. Ramon couldn't figure out why his ideas had been received so poorly despite his best intentions for the company and his family.

After a few months, everyone got together again at an employee's daughter's wedding. Ramon figured it was safe to mention his restructuring ideas because, even if someone got angry, nobody would create a scene at a wedding. This time though, Ramon couldn't talk to everyone together. He was seated with his wife, his two brothers, and their wives. Ramon started talking about his plan to his brothers, and their wives also got involved in the conversation. In fact, Ramon's wife was very dear to both the brothers and his brothers treated her like a second mother. By the end of the lunch, Ramon had convinced his brothers and had also secured a commitment from them and their wives in convincing their kids in every possible manner. Slowly over the next two months, Ramon convinced his sons about restructuring and finally acquired everyone's commitment. He had made some adjustments to his plans as well. "I wanted to make everyone happy at the same time, but I was wrong," said Ramon. "I learned a fundamental lesson of leadership when I was about to leave the leadership position. No matter how well you wish for others, eventually, you have to build consensus slowly. You can't win them all at once!"

Generally, it's difficult to form the entire coalition because of a lack of trust among group members. It's vital for the negotiator to win a few crucial members first (the ones closest in the affinity map) and establish a core. Having a core makes it easier to gain the trust of new members, and it also makes it easier to expand the coalition without much disruption.

8. CIRCULAR LOGROLLING

Another advantage of establishing a core is circular logrolling. Circular logrolling means having trade-offs through other members. Think of a three-party situation where A and B have already established an alliance, and they want C to enter the coalition as well. However, for that to happen, A needs C to give up on a particular issue (x) where A and C have contradictory positions. In other words, A needs C to give up his position in favor of A. On the other hand, there is another issue (y) on which B can give up in favor of C. In this case, A can convince C to give up on (x) in return for (y), which will be given up by B. Such a circular logrolling or a circular trade-off is possible when a negotiator has already established a primary alliance and is trying to expand it.

Transfer of value on x from C to A

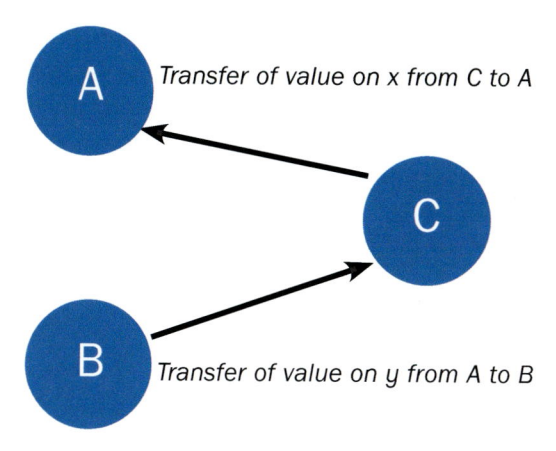

Transfer of value on y from A to B

An example of circular logrolling

Preparation Sheets

Name

Organization

Possible interests

Current position

Possible Relationships

Past experience with us

9. UNDERSTANDING OTHERS

In order to establish a formidable coalition, it's important to understand who is at the table, and a quick analysis of these counterparts using a uniform structure can help. Here is an example of a flashcard that can be used for a quick analysis of a negotiator at the table.

One of the objectives of doing such an analysis is to identify de-facto allies. De-facto alliances emerge beyond the negotiation table; they may influence the negotiation in an indirect manner. An executive in one of our programs told us an interesting story. The executive was going to do a negotiation where the bank and government of a country were going to be present. On the day of the negotiation, the executive negotiator was surprised when he realized the government representative was an old classmate of his with whom he had spent even some vacations during their university years. Due to work, the negotiator had left the country and had lost touch with many of his old friends. However, seeing an old friend reminded him of all the great times they had together, and it created a different dynamic in the negotiation. Quite often, such de-facto alliances escape our analysis, and they might turn out to be counterproductive even when we try our best to build an alliance.

10. FIGHTING A HOSTILE ALLIANCE

Another vital duty of the negotiator is to fight hostile alliances. It is imperative to make sure hostile alliances don't form during the negotiation; if they do, however, the negotiator should be ready to stand their ground. There are two main ways to push back against a hostile alliance.

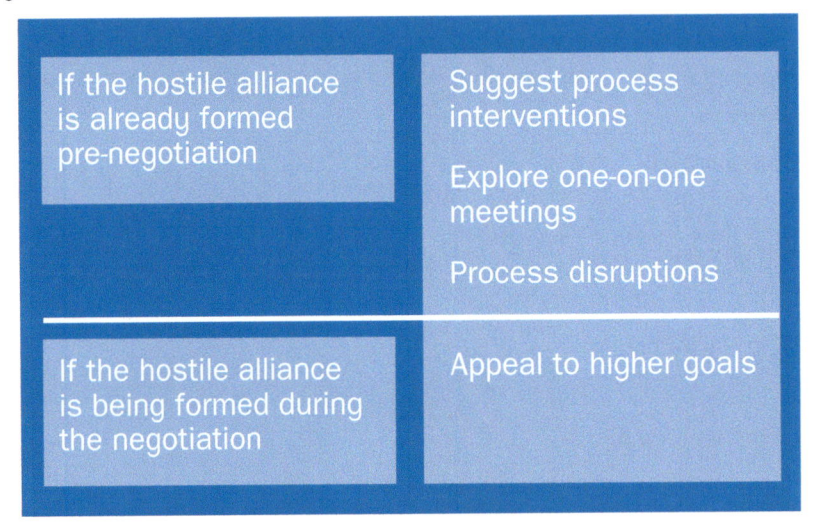

If the hostile alliance is already formed pre-negotiation	Suggest process interventions
	Explore one-on-one meetings
	Process disruptions
If the hostile alliance is being formed during the negotiation	Appeal to higher goals

If a hostile alliance forms, the negotiator needs to find a way to negate its impact. One way to go about this is to set the agenda of the negotiation in such a manner that the hostile alliance becomes less relevant so that the negotiator's opportunities don't suffer. Another alternative is break up the hostile alliance before the negotiation even begins. This can be done by organizing personal meetings with some or all parts of the hostile alliance. Generally, one-on-one meetings offer insight into different alliance partners and give the negotiator more flexibility in fighting the alliance. If the opposing alliance is built during the negotiation process, then it's important to disrupt the process. The negotiation process can be disrupted by raising secondary issues or drawing attention to issues that can take away the focus of other negotiators. Another method is to appeal goals that go beyond what is being discussed. In other words, appealing to a higher morality or a higher level of perspective can also help break a hostile alliance.

If consider the entire discussion on building and fighting alliances, one common factor that emerges is control over the negotiation process. In a multiparty and multi-issue negotiation situation, it's invaluable to control the negotiation process. One of the most secure ways of controlling the negotiation process is preparing and designing the negotiation process before the negotiation itself. This grants us a better opportunity to control the negotiation process.

At the end of the day, negotiation is a skill, and it's therefore better to prepare for the execution rather than the result. In any sport, a professional athlete doesn't prepare for the result, but focuses on the game itself.

NEGOTIATING IN DIRE STRAITS

CHAPTER 11

What do you do when you have to negotiate in dire straits? How do you get out? Can negotiating skills come in handy? In this chapter, we want to address these issues and understand how negotiation skills can help you when you in these situations. This chapter is based on a real story, and no characters are fictitious or imaginary. A young Brit from the English midlands suffered a kidnapping ordeal; this story tells how he survived through sheer negotiating acumen. This chapter is written in a dual voice. Since neither Kandarp nor Guido have ever been kidnapped or held hostage (and we hope it stays that way), we decided to include the first-person account of someone who lived this experience, turning this chapter into something of a reality television show. However, instead of commercial breaks, we'll be taking academic breaks. We will see what happens to our protagonist, and at different stages, we will have our academic narrator analyze our protagonist's negotiation skills. The objective of this exercise is to focus on the negotiation process and not to draw any conclusion on governance, politics, or the ethnicities of the individuals involved in the incident. Now, over to the protagonist!

1. THE KIDNAPPING

It was a sunny afternoon on Tuesday, 20th April 1993, and I was planning to go to the library to study for my upcoming A-Level exams. However, at 12:45 p.m. on the way to the library in the center of Leicester city, UK, I was kidnapped (abducted in my car). I was idling at a traffic light, surrounded by heavy traffic, when out of nowhere, a man with an imposing figure was knocking on my passenger window. He asked me to unlock the door and let him in. I said no, and suddenly another man reached in my window (which was half-open) and unlocked the rear door of the car. Within two seconds, three big men climbed into the back seat of the car and quickly opened the front passenger door. The last gang member got into the passenger seat. The man sitting behind me locked the car doors, and I was simply told to drive down a side street. In a panic and state of confusion, I did what I was told...Within a mile I ended up in a rough estate and was told to park the car. Now, within two minutes of these men (all about seventeen to nineteen years old) jumping into the car, I was in parking lot in a rough area that I did not know with four fairly large men in the car. Let's call them A, B, C and D. Person A was the biggest and the scariest, and he was clearly the gang leader. The kidnappers pulled out a knife and said that Person D would hurt me with it if I refused to comply (person D had a large scar on his shoulder, so I knew they weren't afraid of a fight). They wanted money, and I said I would give them anything they wanted so long as they let me go. They asked me to empty my pockets found a few bank cards in my wallet. I wrote the respective PIN codes on the back of each card. They also ransacked the car (it was a standard four-door Volkswagen Golf). In the glove box, they found my house keys and my driver's license, which had our home address—a remote farmhouse approximately thirty minutes outside Leicester. They also found a credit card statement for my father; they immediately recognized his company's name and realized that our address belonged to an affluent part of Leicestershire. Now they wanted more from each account, if not everything. They said they knew my address and would find me if I tried to escape. They reiterated that they would let me go once they had the money from the accounts. Two of the men (Person B and Person C) then walked off to a cash machine to get the money whilst I sat in the car with A & D.

1.1. Academic Break I - Where there is no negotiation, create one

I know you're already hooked. Is this a negotiation situation? When does the negotiation happen? Negotiation happens whenever an exchange takes place with the possibility of a give and take. The first lesson is, of course, *don't carry your father's credit card statement around, especially he is a respected entrepreneur*, or *don't give your credit card statement to your young children if you are a respected entrepreneur*. Other than that, however, we witness a simple exchange. The protagonist gives up his cards so that the kidnappers get the money they're after and let him go. In a situation like this, it's important to create a negotiation, to be demand something by offering something. Let's see if our protagonist is able to do that.

1.2. Whatever can Go Wrong

When the two guys came back from the cash machine, they said the cards didn't work (in the confusion, I had given them incorrect codes). They thought that I was lying and trying to keep the money from them (I honestly wasn't). It was at this point that A and B stepped out of the car and stood at the front near my side. I overhead them saying that they should just take what they could and kill me. My senses cleared—I realized they were serious about the threat and that I had to do something. I considered running but realized this was their area and that they were bound to know people here. I was a stranger to this part of town, and running would not bode well for me. I then realized I had to shake off any emotions and negotiate my way out of the situation. When A and B got back into the car, I began the negotiation by offering to do whatever it took to get them the money, even close the accounts if I had to. I didn't mention saving my own life, as I figured their main focus was the money and that actually harming me was a byproduct of what they were after. They took some time to discuss my offer outside the car and concluded, based on my tone and expression, that I was being honest with them, and that I truly wanted to reach an amicable agreement. They all got back into the car and agreed.

I had to constantly adjust my position as I was still exploring the relationship and discovering new pieces of information. However, our respective options changed the moment we left the car park, because Person A took another look at my driver's license (with my home address) and asked who was at home. It was at this point that I realized that their intentions were changing for the worse; they intended to take this situation to a far more severe and dangerous level. My father was alone at home and our house was in a remote location. My mind suddenly sharpened and knew that I had to step up the negotiation tactics and offer more alternatives to prevent any harm coming to my father. If they rejected the next option, it would be better for me to escape and pray that I got away rather than risk them reaching my house. I focused on giving them options, hoping I could avoid putting my family in danger.

1.3. Academic Break II - Determine Alternatives and Agreements

Let's understand what happened now that things have taken a turn for the worse for our protagonist. Now he has to fight for his life, so negotiating becomes all the more important. In negotiations, the concept of BATNA (Best Alternative to Negotiated Agreement) is essential. In every negotiation, the negotiator needs to ask the question, 'What is the best alternative if this negotiation doesn't succeed?' The BATNA establishes a reference. However, in extreme situations, the negotiator should also consider the WATNA (Worst Alternative to Negotiated Agreement). Quite often, thinking of the worst alternative creates a strong incentive for dialogue or negotiation. In his book *Power of a Positive No*, acclaimed mediator William Ury describes his negotiation experience in Venezuela in the year 2003. He states that in one of the meetings between two quarreling factions (pro and anti-establishment), he started the mediation by asking members of both groups to think of a person they loved or cared for. Then he asked each one to imagine the worst thing that could happen to this individual if they did not resolve their current conflict. In our story, the worst alternative to the negotiation (and the most likely one) is death. This immediately enhances the value of a negotiation. However, to only consider one's own worst alternative would be a mistake. In any negotiation, one must also focus on the value one could create for the other side. One tool for such analysis is the Zone of Possible Agreements, also known as the ZOPA. The ZOPA delineates all possible agreements that can happen. Let's analyze the zone of possible agreements (ZOPA) for both the sides of the kidnapping ordeal, comparing the initial situation to how things have evolved with the latest turn of events.

1.4. Zone of Possible Agreements

The Zone of Possible Agreements (Outcomes) for the Kidnappers - Beginning

The Worst Possible Outcome	The Best Possible Outcome
No Money	Lots of Money

The Zone of Possible Agreements (Outcomes) for the Kidnappers - NOW

The Worst Possible Outcome	The Best Possible Outcome
No Money (Kill the captive)	Lots of Money from the captive and the family

The Zone of Possible Agreements (Outcomes) for the Captive - Beginning

The Worst Possible Outcome	The Best Possible Outcome
Death	Survival

The Zone of Possible Agreements (Outcomes) for the captive - NOW

The Worst Possible Outcome	The Best Possible Outcome
Death, family harmed	Survival and safe family

The best possible outcome for the captive is to stay alive; for the kidnappers, it's to get money. We don't really see any conflict here. However, if the captive focuses on not losing his money, he enters a direct conflict. Before entering a conflict, a negotiator needs to gauge the relative power they have over the other side. Needless to say, in our story, the person with the gun holds all the power. However, if we concentrate on the need (getting money) we avoid the unnecessary temptation to use that power. Keeping this in mind, what can our protagonist do next? Here's a recap of the facts so far:

1. He has been kidnapped by a group of four criminals.
2. Their first attempt to retrieve money failed.
3. Now they are entertaining the idea of killing him.

It's actually not in the kidnapper's best interest to kill our protagonist. However, they can't be expected to behave like rational human beings (especially in the middle of an irrational kidnapping). The best option for our captive is to engage in conversation. The most important objective is to draw the other side into a verbal exchange. In extreme situations, what really matters is to bring the other side to the negotiation table.

2. WHAT CAN I DO?

I started weighing my options, but I could only think of two binary outcomes—life or death. I suppose the outcomes were binary for my kidnappers as well—money or no money. Only the degree of these outcomes could fluxuate. I might remain alive but suffer pain, while they might end up with a little money or a lot of money.

At that point, I focused on gaining their trust. I asked myself, "What are our best-case scenarios?" For me, the answer was simple. My best-case scenario was to stay alive and keep my family safe. For them, there was no limit. Is there any limit to greed? I don't think so. This realization scared me. Nevertheless, understanding the difference between my needs and theirs, my main drive became to build a relationship with them.

2.1. Who is the leader?

From the moment they agreed to let me try to get them money, I decided to establish some form of relationship based on trust. When we left the car park, I simply drove and listened to their conversations and absorbed all the information I could in case I needed it later. Person A told me to drive to the bank. As a complicit captive, I followed his instructions. He was the clear leader of the gang (and, ironically, the smallest in stature), which made him the chief negotiator and, therefore, the one whose trust I needed to earn first. I had to focus on Person A in order to fill in the gaps in our mapped expectations.

2.2. Academic Break III - Avoid a play of positions

Be it a business negotiation or a negotiation in dire straits, trust is essential. How can a negotiator gain trust in a situation like this? Generally speaking, conflict stems from opposite positions. For example, in a typical bargaining situation where the objective of the buyer is to pay as little as possible, and the objective of the seller is to get as much as possible, there is no trust; as a result, the negotiation is dominated by counterarguments focusing on positions. In order to generate trust, a negotiator needs to find a shared space. What could this shared space be? There are several possible options—establishing a common problem to solve together, highlighting similarities, or focusing on the future and avoiding conflictive positions, to name a few.

In team negotiations, establishing trust is even more difficult, mainly because of the number of participants involved. In these cases, it is important to identify and win the trust of the decision maker. The protagonist of our story identifies a leader and tries to establish a connection with them. Let's see what happens next.

3. EXPLORING OPTIONS

My first option was to suggest closing the bank accounts and giving the kidnappers as much money as I could. This option would buy me time. However, when my home entered the equation (around 2:30pm), I knew something more had to be offered to divert them from my house. I remembered A and D had been talking in the car about going to a party that A was hosting at 6:00 p.m. that evening (I figured they would need time to get ready and calculated that the latest they could be with me would be around 5:00 p.m.), so when they enquired more about where the house was (they recognized the area but didn't know the exact location), I told them that it was at least an hour-long drive each way without traffic (in reality it was about thirty minutes) and that we had men working in our home. I gave them time to think and myself time to assess my escape options. They were still armed; however, I preferred to risk my life than let those delinquents near my family. Luckily, A and B ran through some of their time calculations out loud. As I listened, I came up with a few more ways to divert their attention from my home—both now and in the future, since they had my house keys. I was actively pursuing two objectives: my own safety and the safety of my home and family.

I knew time was a key factor. The kidnappers couldn't risk spending too much time with me and getting caught. At the same time, they wouldn't let me walk away without getting money. I started mentioning the names of some banks and their branches. This gave them something to think about as they decided where to go first. They were thinking as to where to go first.

They decided not to go to my house, so their focus fell back on me, for which I was thankful. However, through this discussion, I was fostering trust—they were speaking more openly among themselves and revealing more information. There were two possible reasons for this—they were either relaxing due to an increasing atmosphere of trust, or they were going to kill me. For the sake of my own sanity, I decided to assume the first option was the case.

3.1. Academic Break IV – Analyze relative power and overcome imbalance of power

Growing up in India, Kandarp (one of the co-authors of this book) read a story in his Gujarati textbook. One time, a peace-loving gentleman with a very lanky frame was forced to join traditional Indian wrestling. Upon seeing his first massive opponent, he thought the end was nigh for him. When his opponent attacked, the thin gentleman dropped prone to the ground. His opponent backed off, confused, and attacked again. Again, the gentleman dropped to the ground. This happened several times before the wrestler got angry and said, "Why do you keep lying down?" The gentleman responded, "Isn't that what you want? To push me down on the floor and win? I'm letting you win, and I'm keeping my bones intact."

In every negotiation, there are three primary sources of power: alternatives, situation, and time. Alternatives are the most important source. A negotiator without solid alternatives has virtually no influence over the outcome. Situational sources of power are also common. For example, the kidnappers in our story obviously have more situational power because they have weapons and incentives to use them. Lastly, time is another important factor. In our story, both the kidnappers and the victim have equal power in terms of time, since both sides want to resolve the situation as quickly as possible, albeit for different reasons.

Here is an analysis of power for both sides.

	Power	
Alternatives 1. Kill the captive and risk getting caught 2. Don't kill the captive but risk captive revealing identity to the police	Alternatives	Alternative 1. Death 2. Family members get hurt
	Situation	
Kidnappers have more power because they have weapons		
	Time	
They both have the same time pressure. Kidnappers don't want the captive for too long as it increases the risk of committing mistakes. On the other hand, every second is torture for the captive.		

Something similar shows up in negotiation research. Use of power at an inappropriate place doesn't help. In situations of imbalanced power, the negotiator with less power should not only avoid use of power-centered arguments, but also disincentive the use of the power against them. How is this possible, though? They key tools are trust and creativity. Creativity in a negotiation entails creating common ground where the counterpart sees their objective being met and where the negotiator meets their objective—or at least avoids worst-case outcomes. Here we can see that creation of a new variable and how it avoids further conflict. The protagonist's offer to take the kidnappers to the banks and close the accounts generates some common ground. It's important to generate these kinds of options in any negotiation. There are two clear advantages of such a strategy. First, it helps create common ground and avoid conflict. Second, even it doesn't create common ground, it provides better insight into the mindset of the counterpart in order to understand what they really want.

4. GROWING TRUST

As time went by, the kidnappers's trust and respect for me grew. We visited three banks. Each time, I was escorted inside with Person D, who was huge, and in each bank I tried to close the accounts. Something interesting happened the first time D and I were left alone in the bank—he apologized and said he hadn't realized what they were doing. He had thought his companions had unlocked the door of my car because they knew me . I didn't know whether to trust him or not, since he was the man with the knife, the scar, and an obvious affinity for fighting. I told him it didn't matter and that I wanted to do whatever I could to get them their money. Ironically, the banks realized what was going on and refused to close the accounts, but they were too afraid for my safety to raise the alarm.

After visiting the three banks, I gained more trust in Person D, and he began to trust me more as well. Luckily, he relayed the message to the gang in the car that I was complying and genuinely trying to close the accounts. The situation was changing, and I could tell they were becoming more relaxed. Their attention started to shift; they realized I was just a normal person, a human being, who was on his way to the library. When I came back to the car from the third bank, their faces were more relaxed. The leader's ever-present scowl had disappeared, as had the intense glint in his eye. Our conversation turned to more personal issues, and he started opening up to me. I was genuinely interested in knowing these people a bit more. Why were they doing all this? What was the purpose? He started talking about his life and how he enjoyed being a DJ and why he and his gang did such criminal acts. In fact, the conversation turned into an interview of sorts, during which he revealed a lot about himself and the gang. He also revealed one of the main reasons for their criminal activity was boredom and lack of recognition in life. I told him I could imagine how frustrating lack of recognition must be in such a competitive and diverse society, and how being from a tough neighborhood often deprives people of good options in life. They started looking at me as someone who understood them.

Of course, the conversation did nothing to change the fact that they were criminals who had kidnapped me and would not mind killing me if they felt the need. Moreover, an incident occured that was quite revealing—we were waiting at a traffic light and I asked the kidnappers what kind of people they usually targeted. At precisely that moment, a young lady in a new convertible BMW pulled up next to us. Person A looked at her in the car and said, "Well, *she* deserves it." I realized these immature men (if you can call them that) lacked any sense of morality. I had to focus on reaching an agreement and getting out.

4.1. Academic Break V - Trust and Empathy

Once a common ground is established, it is very important to reinforce trust. The best way to reinforce trust is through actions. It's also important not to take trust for granted and to be diligent with its implementation. That's what our protagonist is doing here. He is reinforcing trust through his actions. In the process, he is getting to know the other side of his particular negotiation better. Most importantly, he is establishing a relationship of empathy and changing the way the other side perceives him. In case of an extreme negotiation, it is important that the counterpart stops seeing us as an adversary and starts seeing us as a partner.

5. CREATING AN AGREEMENT

I focused on the relationship and figured we would reach an informal agreement sooner or later. I knew we'd reached a turning point in the relationship when Person A said, "You know, you're kind of cool—it's a shame we met this way; we could have hung out." I replied that I thought so too, and we could still hang out if he wanted to, even though

I never wanted to see any of them ever again. At that point, the kidnappers declared the whole ordeal a shame and asked me to drive them each home.

The ironic part of this true story is that, despite the despicable nature of my predicament, I built trust with the kidnappers to the point where, around 5:00 p.m., I actually drove A and B home and dropped C and D off where they first got into my car.

Thankfully, I never heard from them again, but I was interviewed by the Leicestershire Police for a few hours, and the car was analyzed for fingerprints and DNA traces the next day. I was told to stay out of the city for at least three or four months and to take my car with me, since it was a rather recognizable color. My family were extremely shocked about what had happened, especially since they assumed I'd been quietly studying in the library the whole time.

6. EPILOGUE - PROCESS OF NEGOTIATION

When a certain English playwright penned the expression 'All's well that ends well' in the mid-16th century, little did he know he was coining what would eventually become one of the most popular idioms in the English language. However, in the context of negotiation, the saying isn't always true. A negotiation may have ended in an agreement, but that agreement may not be stable or feasible in the long run. The interesting thing about this negotiation story is that, by staying focused on the negotiation without losing control over his emotions, a young man found his way out of a very difficult situation.

Here are some of the factors that made this negotiation in dire straits conclude positively:

1. Focusing on the objective: In a situation where the loss of life is a realistic potential outcome, it's important not to lose focus on the objectives. Tense negotiation situations often create a great degree of emotional stress, which causes distractions. Here, as we can see, despite feeling threatened, our protagonist did not lose focus on his objective.

2. Trust and empathy: Another crucial factor in this entire exercise is the growth of trust and empathy. Trust stems from credibility—a credible negotiator does what they say they'll do. Trust also comes from consistency. Actions that are consistent with words (and the other way around) help generate trust between negotiation participants. Furthermore, in order to be trustworthy, it is important to empathize and communicate. When the protagonist of the story shares empathizes with the kidnapper's background, he shows he is trying to see the situation from the other side's perspective. That conversation of empathy played a key role in the entire process.

3. Process is paramount: Negotiation is a skill, and skills continually need to be practiced and polished. Professional athletes don't play for the score; they play to win, and they win by performing better than their opponent. Similarly, in a

negotiation, it is important to stay focused and to negotiate better than the counterpart. Managing the process well is paramount for this to happen. The negotiation steps our protagonist followed are exemplary. Here's a summary of the negotiation in dire straits:

a) Identify the objectives, both your own and those of your counterpart.

b) Analyze power. Study power from three sources.

   I. Alternatives

   II. Situation

   III. Time

   In a situation where the counterpart has lot more power, it is important for the negotiator to keep negotiating and avoid any power games.

c) Generate creative options

   The best way to avoid power games is by generating creative options. In order to generate creative options, one needs the following.

   1. Identification of interests of the other side
   2. Control over emotions
   3. Identification of self-interests (and how they can be aligned with the interests of the other side)

d) Establish a common ground

   Once we know what options the other side prefers, we can find common ground. The focus should be on not allowing the negotiation to move beyond that common ground.

e) Keep reinforcing trust

   The best way to make sure that common ground is maintained is by reinforcing trust throughout the negotiation. It is important not to take initial trust for granted. This can also happen through constant recognition of the objective we are working on.

f) Close an agreement

   Last but not least, it is important to close the conversation and reach an agreement by showing the other side what we have to offer.

In the end, negotiating in dire straits is a challenge that can be overcome through focus on goals and proper processes. Sun Tzu writes in *The Art of War*, "Do not repeat the tactics which have gained you one victory, but let your methods be regulated by the infinite variety of circumstances." A good negotiator should be prepared for each circumstance be able to mold his negotiation style to achieve victory.

CHAPTER 12

NEGOTIATING ACROSS CULTURES

Executives in our negotiation programs frequently ask, "How should I negotiate with people from a different culture?" Most negotiations in today's corporate world take place in a global context. While this has brought us all closer, it's also added to the anxiety business executives experience when they deal with unfamiliar cultures. Most executives with whom we interact point out culture as a significant factor in their negotiations.

Why does culture play such a significant role in negotiations? A negotiation is primarily an interaction between two or more participants with the goal of satisfying a particular need. Negotiating is a relationship between an individual's negotiation style and their interpretation of the situation. Culture influences both these elements.

1. NEGOTIATION SITUATIONS AND STYLE

Culture influences the way we behave and how we assess the behavior of other people. Culture, therefore, has a substantial impact on negotiations. Each culture has a cognitive component and a normative component. A culture's cognitive component deals with the different values the culture espouses. These values affect our understanding and judgment of what is acceptable and what is not, what is right and what is wrong, and so on. On the other hand, the normative component outlines standard rules of behavior—how to sit, how to greet people, how to eat, what to say, what not to say, etc. Rules and norms are outlined by cultures. Let's take a more detailed look at why and how culture influences negotiations and negotiators.

2. KEYS TO UNDERSTANDING CULTURE

If someone asked you how you knew a person was form a different culture, what would your response be? Whenever I ask our participants this question, their answers invariably point to behavior as a key reflector or identifier of culture. We detect differences in culture by looking at how individuals talk, meet, greet, and respond to different social situations. However, human behavior is driven by several factors, such as values, beliefs, norms, and mindsets. Behavior is just the tip of the iceberg[1].

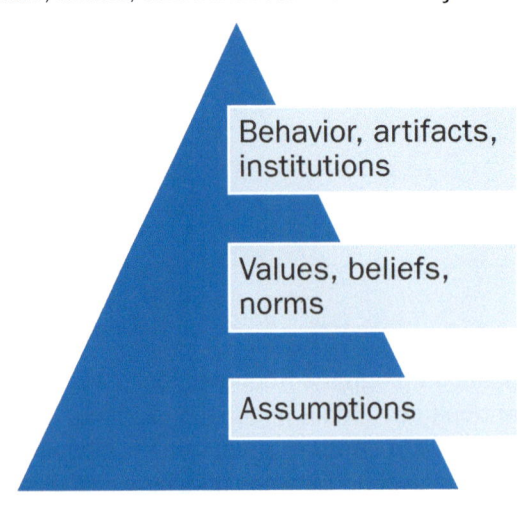

- Behavior, artifacts, institutions
- Values, beliefs, norms
- Assumptions

Cultures influence negotiation strategies in two ways. On the one hand, values, beliefs, and norms influence how the negotiator prioritizes their interests; on the other hand, they also dictate how the negotiator asks for what they're seeking. When negotiators exchange information, a range of behaviors is possible. However, these behaviors are deeply influenced by culture. For example, confrontation is a typical negotiation behavior, but while in some cultures direct verbal confrontation is a normal part of negotiation behavior, in others, verbal confrontation is not an option. Similarly, cultures influence the negotiator's interests and priorities. For instance, individualist cultures might inspire the negotiator to seek self-interest, while more collectivist cultures could inspire the negotiator to seek objectives that would satisfy the interests of their whole community. The influence culture has on institutions and systems is also important. A country's institutions often influence the values that drive the predominant culture of that nation. In order to gain a better understanding of these factors, we're going to break down the influence of culture on behavior, institutions, and negotiation.

The following section studies a few different cultural prototypes and their impact:

3. INDIVIDUALISM VS COLLECTIVISM

In individualistic cultures, the pursuit of happiness and personal welfare are paramount. People in individualistic cultures prioritize their personal goals even when these goals conflict with family, organizations or the nation itself. Collectivist cultures, on the other hand, prioritize harmony in interpersonal relationships individual

---

[1] Source: French, W.L. and Bell, C.H. (1923) Organization Development Behavioral Science in Interventions for Organization Improvement (p.18)

gains. In a collectivist culture, members tend to be sensitive to the effect of their actions on the collective group. This creates a certain degree of interdependency between members of the group.

4. HOW DO INDIVIDUALISTIC AND COLLECTIVIST CULTURES AFFECT NEGOTIATIONS?

1. Trust and relationships: the first major implication is on how individuals trust each other during a negotiation. For example, in an individualistic culture, one assumes that the other side is acting in self-interest. As a result, trust is based more on how a negotiator perceives the other's behavior, actions, and speech. Sharing information is crucial to establish trust between two negotiators, and a negotiator may have to face many questions throughout the negotiation process. Meanwhile, in collectivist cultures, trust is not just based on individual behavior, but also on the position of the other side within the collective group. As a result, trust is not merely a product of questions and answers. In fact, negotiatiors in collectivist cultures often don't depend on many questions and answers because trust has already been established on the basis of the common collective.

2. Collaboration: Culture prototypes also impact cooperation between negotiators. In collectivist cultures, negotiators are more likely to be cooperative than in individualistic cultures. Several studies have shown that negotiators from eastern cultures tend to be more cooperative than negotiators from western cultures.

3. Team efficiency: in collectivist cultures, individuals are usually more accustomed to working in a collective setting. Even when working alone, they are more likely to keep the benefit of the larger group in mind. Likewise, in collectivist cultures, teams are more likely to negotiate with a common objective. In individualistic cultures, if the individual gain and the joint gain have not been properly aligned, team members may underperform in the task. Hence, it is very important that negotiation teams prepare rigorously in individualistic cultures.

4. Conflict resolution: When negotiation conflict arises in individualistic cultures, the negotiator is more likely to ascribe it to the individual. As a result, the negotiator may develop suspicion toward their counterpart and seek formal mediation. On the other hand, in a collectivist culture, negotiators tend to ascribe behaviors to the situation. In an individualistic culture, conflicts are resolved through common procedures, mediation, and rules and regulations. In a collectivist culture, conflicts are resolved through informal means or through the intervention of authority. When making a deal during an international negotiation, it's crucial for the negotiators to not only determine how the deal will be executed, but also focus on how potential disputes can be resolved. Setting up a conflict resolution plan ahead of time is essential for a successful international negotiation.

5. EGALITARIAN AND HIERARCHICAL CULTURES

Hierarchical cultures feature more prominent power gaps than egalitarian cultures. As a result, in an egalitarian culture, negotiators expect to be treated as equals, while in a hierarchical culture, negotiators are more sensitive to power gaps, which often play an important role in the negotiation. Generally speaking, cultures with high collectivism also have high power distances.

5.1. How do hierarchical and egalitarian cultures affect negotiations?

1. Source of power: In an egalitarian culture, negotiation power is more situational, since it tends to stem from information and alternatives. Negotiators search for more detailed information in order to gain an advantage. On the other hand, in a hierarchical culture, negotiators may base power on status or even threats if the former doesn't provide enough leverage.

2. Identity of the negotiator: The identities of both sides of a negotiation makes a big difference in a hierarchical culture. While the context of the negotiation determines the equality of the negotiators in an egalitarian culture, negotiations in hierarchical cultures demand that both sides be of equal status and authority beyond the context of the negotiation. As a result, the selection of your representative in a negotiation becomes even more important.

6. LOW-CONTEXT VS HIGH-CONTEXT CULTURES

Low-context cultures are those where communication is more direct. A negotiator doesn't need a comprehensive understanding of context to understand what is being communicated. On the other hand, in a high-context culture, communication depends on an understanding of context. Communications are more indirect in such cultures. In a low-context culture, messages are explicit, direct, action-oriented, and strive for solutions. In high-context cultures, messages are subtle and contextual.

6.1. Impact on Negotiation

1. Negotiation pattern: In low-context cultures, where communication is more direct, negotiators often ask more questions and make offers based on sufficient rationale; offers, in turn, are supposed to be rationally derived. Once the offers have been made, negotiators don't usually engage in very many subsequent rounds of offers and concessions. In a high-context culture, however, negotiators may jump to making offers rather quickly. Offers become tools for gaining information as well as being the foundation of a deal. High-context cultures may also feature many more rounds of concessions and counteroffers.

2. Collaborative potential: In order to collaborate in a negotiation, it is important to have sufficient information about the interests and priorities of both sides. In high-context cultures, where sharing information is more difficult, collaborative deals are more challenging to reach. Even if collaborative deals are reached, they may not live up to the full potential of their value creation.

7. CULTURAL PROTOTYPES AND IMPACT ON NEGOTIATION

Cultural prototype	Impact on negotiation
Collectivist vs. individualist cultures	In a collectivist culture, negotiators are likely to negotiate for common objectives. Likewise, it's more common to negotiate in teams rather than alone. There may also be an aversion to direct confrontation. In an individualist culture, negotiators are likely to focus on individual goals and gains. Direct confrontation during the negotiation process becomes far more likely.
Low-context vs. high-context cultures	Low-context cultures prefer the direct exchange of messages and sharing of information. High-context cultures share information indirectly and meaning is embedded in many messages. As a result, in low-context cultures, sharing information is simpler and more direct. In contrast, sharing information is complicated in high-context cultures, and both negotiations and decision-making tend to take longer.
Hierarchical vs. egalitarian cultures	In hierarchical cultures, power gaps are greater. As a result, negotiation is possible only when power gaps have been reduced, which means negotiations are more likely to be held in teams. In egalitarian cultures, negotiations are simpler and tend to end sooner since individual decision-making takes precedence. In hierarchical cultures, there is a tendency to refer to higher authorities and, as a result, negotiations tend to take longer.

8. FALSE AFFILIATIONS

Robson is a marketing executive in a Brazilian company. He hails from a family of German descent since his paternal grandparents migrated from Germany; he also learned German while growing up. Robson worked for a company that produced submersible pumps. The company used to import parts from a Mexican plant and then assemble pumps in their plant in Porto Alegre before selling them all over Brazil. One time, they received a great offer for a joint venture with a German manufacturer who wanted to expand their network across Latin America. They invited the senior management for a presentation. The CEO of Robson's company selected him for the initial conversation. He told Robson, "You speak German. You look German. You're our best chance to close the deal as soon as possible." Robson put together a team of two assistants and traveled to Rosenheim, Germany. He felt he had arrived home, and he was excited to see the country from which his grandparents had migrated. He was planning to visit the town of Grunwald, where they had been born. Meetings with the chief marketing officer and the chief distribution officer started after a couple of days. At first, Robson loved the fact that he could speak German fluently, but after a while, he began to lament that fact. Eventually, he called his CEO to evaluate the meetings that had taken place so far. This is what he said:

> *I don't think I'm the best person for this job, not because I'm not prepared or qualified, but because I'm of German descent. The people here are treating me like a fellow German. I speak German, but that doesn't make me German. I don't get their jokes. I don't understand their references to German football. I don't know their unwritten rules. They were warm in the beginning, but now I feel a bit awkward. In fact, one of the marketing managers actually asked me if I was comfortable with German or if I wanted to switch to English.*

We often judge an individual based on their religion, ethnicity, or profession. For example, two individuals of different nationalities may form a strong bond if they discover that they support the same football team or they share the same religious belief. Affiliation bias frequently plays a significant role in an international negotiation.

8.1. Cultural Adaptation

Another important issue in cross-cultural negotiation is adaptation. Studies conducted by Jeanne Brett and her colleagues showed that value creation is significantly affected when negotiators meet from different cultures. Value creation decreases when the two sides have contrasting cultural makeup. One of the major reasons for this decrease in value creation is the lack of cultural adaptation. Imagine one side belongs to a low-context culture and is driven by dignity norm with direct communication and open sharing of information, while the other side belongs to a high-context culture and is driven by face norm where communication is indirect and information sharing is piecemeal and limited. Both sides would expect the other to adapt to their style of negotiation. When the other side doesn't conform to these expectations, it has a direct impact on the trust equation between sides. When trust breaks, negotiations invariably turn competitive. When too much information has been withheld, negotiators tend to defend their positions more vehemently and refrain from sharing their interests.

This raises the question—who should adapt to whom? Ideally, the decision should be based on the level of cultural familiarity between the two sides. In a situation where only one side is aware of the cultural nuances at hand, they should be the one to adapt. However, that isn't always possible. It's essential to assess the level of acquaintance with both cultural perspectives before the negotiation.

9. EAST VS. WEST AND BEYOND

Traditionally, the world used to be seen in the light of East vs. West. The Western hemisphere had a uniform concept of the East and vice versa. However, in the 20th century, this model was replaced by a more East-Middle-West cultural view. Cultural psychologists divide the world into three prototypes, each of which has a strong effect on negotiations. These culture types can be classified as dignity culture (Western culture), face culture (East Asian culture) and honor culture (Middle Eastern, Southeast Asian, and Latin American cultures). In her seminal work *Negotiating Globally* (2001; third edition, 2014), Jeanne M. Brett says the following about these cultural models:

> "In terms of six sets of characteristics: self-worth, power and status, sensitivity and response to insults, confrontation style, trust and mindset. […] Self-worth refers to a person's sense of his or her own value in society. Power refers to a person's ability to influence an outcome. Status refers to a person's position in a social hierarchy. Sensitivity and response to insults refers to the way a person is affected by and responds to another's offensive behavior. Confrontation style refers to how a person responds when faced with defiance, opposition, or hostility. Trust is the willingness to make oneself vulnerable to another person. Mindset refers to the way people reason and process information."

What are dignity, face, and honor cultures? Let's look at each concept in turn.

10. DIGNITY CULTURE

Dignity culture is the cultural prototype of the Western hemisphere. Dignity culture societies are more egalitarian, and hence the worth of an individual is self-determined. Since self-worth is independent of social status and does not depend on social opinion, it is also possible that negotiations will focus more on individual welfare. In such cultures, retaliation is less common because of the lower dependence on others for self-worth. At the same time, greater importance is attached to trust and reciprocity. In addition, due to the influence of Greek philosophy and especially Aristotelian logic, a highly analytical approach can be seen in negotiations.

11. FACE CULTURE

Face culture is the prototype of East Asian societies. The main feature of these societies is collectivism. Self-worth is socially conferred and depends on a person's relative position in a stable social hierarchy. The atomistic unit of society in a face culture is the family. Hierarchies and social relationships are especially important. As a result, there is less confrontation in negotiations, while interactions are more indirect and impersonal. Interpersonal trust is important in face culture, but this trust does not merely emanate from interpersonal interaction—rather, it also depends to a great degree on institutional approval. Some scholars even argue that forms of institutional surveillance (e.g., surveillance by the family, community, church, etc.) serve as reliable external guarantors of individual behavior. Another interesting characteristic that has a huge influence on negotiations is the holistic mindset of individuals in face culture. When negotiators analyze a situation, they focus both on the problem and on the context in which it is embedded. Many executives tell us that almost every negotiation in a face culture becomes a multi-issue negotiation.

12. HONOR CULTURE

Honor culture societies are probably the most diverse, which is why it is more difficult to identify the precise prototype of honor culture. Self-worth has been seen as a combination of an individual's assessment of his or her value in society and socially conferred value. In other words, it is important to have social approval of individually determined self-worth. In honor cultures, societies tend to be hierarchical, but these hierarchies are not always stable and so they need to be established. For negotiation, this is a particularly important issue. In a negotiation in honor cultures, there is an increased possibility of a confrontational approach. According to Brett:

> "In honor cultures, trusting means putting your self-worth in the hands of others. If you trust and your trust is reciprocated, then you gain honor because your self-worth is ratified. But there is the huge risk associated with trusting. If

your trust is not reciprocated, there is both a social loss of social face and also a personal loss of self-worth."

Therefore, negotiations in honor cultures sometimes rely more on the argumentative brilliance of negotiators than merely on their trustworthiness.

12.1. Mindset and Trust

Let's try to understand what makes these cultures different. One of the main elements that influences differences in behavior is mindset. Studies have shown that Western mindset is characterized by use of formal logic and avoidance of contradiction. On the other hand, Oriental culture is characterized by more holistic systems. Holistic thinking is characterized by keeping in mind the larger picture, while the analytical mindset is characterized by more formal and rational decision making. Holistic cultures are often characterized by high-context communication style as well. In a holistic mindset, one not only has to keep in mind the decision at hand but must also consider its larger impact on the entire social context surrounding the person.

12.2. Trust and culture

One of the reasons why intercultural negotiations sometimes fail is lack of trust. Different cultures trust individuals differently because the self-esteem or value of the individual differs across cultures. Researchers have identified two types of trusts: cognitive trust and affective trust. Cognitive trust is based on tasks and rational decisions. Affective trust, on the other hand, is based on emotions. In other words, when you trust someone because you are convinced by the evidence that the person will do what they claim to do, you trust them cognitively. Meanwhile, when you trust someone because you feel a strong emotional connection with them, you trust them affectively. In cultures where there is greater emphasis on maintaining harmony and social cohesion, cognitive and affective trust overlap a lot. In cultures where the mindset is more analytical and individual worth is self-determined, cognitive trust and affective trust do not overlap as much. In other words, in the US, a negotiator must gain trust through argumentation and evidence to show that what they claim, they will do. On the other hand, in a country like China or Japan, evidence alone will not be sufficient; establishing a relationship with the other side is also important.

For these reasons, in honor and face cultures we see that negotiations have a lot of important informal contacts interwoven within the negotiation process, whereas in dignity cultures, informal contacts, while maybe important for information sharing, may not help as much in gaining trust.

12.3. Social Motivation

Why do some negotiators negotiate competitively while others work cooperatively? Morton Deutsch (1949), who was one of the first scholars to construct the dichotomy of competition and cooperation, saw social motivation as an important factor when choosing between competition or cooperation. In the context of negotiation, social motivation refers to the concern the negotiator has for the outcome of the negotiation for themselves as well as the outcome for the other side. In cultures where personal success or gain is paramount, one would see less prosocial motivation. In other words, where winning over the other side is important, negotiators would tend to be more competitive. On the other hand, in cultures where maintaining harmony and saving face are important, one would see more prosocial motivation and hence more collaborative approach in a negotiation. One may argue that in almost all cultures there are individuals who wish to win over the other side as well as people who wish to help the other side.

13. FINAL ADVICE: DO NOT OVERLOOK THE INDIVIDUAL

Having gained an understanding of these three cultural paradigms, we must also understand that culture is not a static and stable construct. So many countries in the world today have education systems that are highly influenced by European systems. Many young men and women relocate to different parts of the world to pursue higher education, develop their careers, or simply to benefit from new experiences. As a result, there has been a great degree of cultural exchange and globalization. The framework that has been shown in this segment aims to help us understand one another better. Scholars of cross-cultural research have been working hard to separate cultural stereotypes from cultural knowledge. Therefore, we strongly advise all negotiators not only to make an effort to understand the cultural nuances of their counterparts but never to undermine the importance of the individual with whom they are dealing. Negotiations are strongly influenced by individual needs and insecurities. Culture influences the way these needs are expressed and prioritized, but this doesn't mean the basic needs of negotiators are absent. After all, across the world, a smile is always sweet, and tears are always salty.

Characteristics of Dignity, Face and Honor Cultures

Characteristic	Dignity	Face	Honor
Geographical location	Western Europe, North America, Australia and New Zealand	East Asia	Middle East, North Africa, Iberian Peninsula, Latin America, Southeast Asia
Self-worth	Self-determined Variable	Socially conferred Stable	Socially claimed Dynamic
Power and status	Egalitarian Dynamic	Hierarchical Stable	Hierarchical Dynamic
Sensitivity and response to insults	Low sensitivity	Medium sensitivity	High sensitivity
Confrontation style	Direct Rational Unemotional	Indirect Controlled and measured Use of superiors to resolve conflicts	Direct and indirect Expressive
Trust	Interpersonal High level of ingroup and outgroup trust	Institutional High ingroup and low outgroup trust	Interpersonal and institutional Low outgroup trust
Mindset	Analytic	Holistic	Analytic and holistic

Source: Adapted from Exhibit 2.2 in Jeanne M. Brett: *Negotiating Globally,* 3rd ed. Jossey-Bass, San Francisco, 2014.

14. RECOMMENDATIONS FOR NEGOTIATING WITH A DIFFERENT CULTURE

1. Understand the other culture beforehand. If possible, seek input from an external cultural advisor to help understand the other culture.

2. Anticipate strategies and tactics of the other culture. Try to understand how the other culture would...

    a) share information.

    b) respond to questions.

c) make offers and concessions.

   d) establish a relationship of trust.

3. Find out how to show respect to the other side within the parameters of their culture.

4. Understand how communication functions in the other culture. Is it direct or indirect?

5. Understand the needs of the other side.

6. Understand their alternatives. Compare them with your alternatives.

7. Master the art of dealing with multi-issue offers.

NEGOTIATING YOUR JOB OFFER

CHAPTER 13

1. AN APPROACH TO DRIVING NEGOTIATIONS

Experience and research teach us there tends to be a lot of room for improvement when it comes to approaching negotiations that take place during the hiring process. Numerous studies have demonstrated that successfully negotiating for a first job has significant consequences later on in the candidate's career—for example, in economic terms or in terms of promotion rate. Research has shown that candidates who try to negotiate their first job offer can potentially add an additional million dollars in value to their overall career during the next twenty five years.[1] Likewise, companies would get what they need more effectively if they considered the relevant factors in this type of negotiation and took advantage of the different phases the processes go through. Although each situation is different, the idea is to create a win-win situation, so everyone's needs are met, without necessarily implying a loss for the other party. Therein lies the art of negotiation, since people tend to walk away with less than they could have received.

No one doubts that a job is much more than its salary. However, people's actions don't always reflect this common knowledge. The reason is that what is obvious is not, in fact, the first thing that catches our attention. More than money is at stake for the potential employee and employer. The former brings to the table a significant portion of his or her life; the latter offers up part of the company's ability to compete and survive—in short, whether the company is able to fulfill the purpose for which it exists. For the candidate, the necessary condition is to be wanted and to convince the company he or she is the best choice. The rest will come later.

If one of the parties (or both) make a mistake in the selection and, down the line, in putting that selection into effect, there isn't much that can be done. The first principle is to not waste time —yours or other people's. If the offer does not meet the candidate's basic demands or the candidate does not have the key characteristics of the profile the company is looking for, it is better to be realistic and to avoid settling for half measures.

---

[1] Thompson, L. (2014) *The Mind and Heart of the Negotiator.* Pearson.

On the other hand, once the decision has been made to move on with the process, a negotiation phase begins that may (or may not) be a source for mutual creation of value and opportunities with any subsequent results. We have to accept the fact that negotiations involve a certain amount of risk. Negotiating a job offer is mainly a chance for the parties to get to know one another while laying the groundwork for a relationship that will continue over time, even for many years in some cases. Experience and research show that around 90% of companies expect candidates to be prepared to negotiate, whereas in reality only 25% of them actually do so and only about 15% of employees who are already hired renegotiate their employment conditions after some time has passed. That means there is a high probability that employees who remain loyal to their companies will end up below the market average in terms of salary.

The personal image transmitted by a candidate who negotiates is better than that of one who does not, so long as this behavior is not a deterrent for the employer. The best negotiations stem from a common understanding of what is important to both parties and an effort to overcome their ostensible differences and work toward the harmonization of interests and capabilities. This involves embracing not only the role of negotiator, but also the role of a fellow explorer traveling through unknown territory. It is worth investing in a revamp of the classic job-offer negotiation. In that sense, it is enough for the parties to put a bit of effort into replacing haggling with intelligent exploration.

It's a good idea to avoid the bias that leads negotiators to draw conclusions about the other party's future behavior based on their own fears or uncertainties.

First impressions leave a near-permanent mark, since the candidate uses them to glean information about how he or she will be treated during a regular workday at the company. Negative experiences (inconsiderate or high-handed treatment, pressure regarding salary terms, slowness in providing information, etc.), can and should be avoided without harming the company's position in the negotiations.

Being an effective negotiator boils down to knowing how and when to negotiate. In some situations, negotiating may not be the best option—for example, when the alternative to continuing negotiations is unfavorable, or when it is much better than the best offer the other party might propose;[2] when negotiating sends a message that would be misinterpreted or misunderstood by the other party; when the harm caused to the relationship by negotiating is worse than the supposed advantages and endangers future negotiations; when the other party doesn't expect negotiations to continue, etc.

Sometimes, it's simply better to accept the financial offer without any further negotiation. The idea is that, after a certain time, a more favorable atmosphere will be created in which to discuss adjustments and improvements, and which will be supported by actions that confirm the candidate's value, leading to more receptiveness on the part of the employer. Knowing when to wait is an effective negotiating tool.

---

2   When there is no zone of possible agreement (ZOPA), the best alternative to a negotiated agreement (BATNA) should be put into play.

2. THE QUESTION OF SALARY DURING NEGOTIATIONS

Employers will often ask candidates about their current or previous salary for a number of reasons: finding out what kind of salary they should offer the candidate if they are selected, seeing the discrepancies between what they are offering and what other candidates are earning, etc. The truth is that people on higher salaries tend to be perceived as having higher levels of performance and, inversely, people who have lower salaries are usually assumed to be worse at their jobs. However, that's not the case in many situations. If, for example, two professionals begin working at the same time at the same company, and one of them negotiates a salary deal while the other does not, the difference between their salaries will persist due to inertia.

If an employee wants something beyond what their employer offers, they need to think about the most effective way to let the employer know. What people earn tends to depend on what they contribute, their professional value, and how well they negotiate based on that value.

When should the salary be discussed? From the candidate's point of view later is usually better than sooner. Theoretically, the more time a candidate invests in a company, the more committed they'll feel. The best bet is to wait for an offer, since it is preferable for the employer to be the one to set the first number, given that this serves as the foundation for future discussion. Likewise, it gives the candidate an idea of what the company is willing to pay and thus limits the risk of going above or below that mark if the candidate proposes an initial figure.

Experience has shown that when MBA students are having their first job interviews and are faced with the question about their salary expectations, they tend to make two fundamental mistakes—they either lie or try to avoid the question. A job interview is a conversation, and any conversation needs to be fluid if the participants are to achieve their goals. Bypassing a question cuts off the flow and, in turn, the desired effects of the conversation. Understanding the question is better than trying to avoid it. To gauge the scope of the question, there are two important things to be aware of: 1) How will the possible answers affect my position in the negotiation? and 2) Why is the interviewer interested in this information? Thinking about these two aspects on the spur of the moment can be hard. That is why it is useful to prepare your responses to these questions ahead of time. In the **Exhibit** below (see p. 146), a preparation guide for salary negotiations is provided.

In some cases, instead of providing a rough salary range, the company representatives —especially those from the Human Resource Department— may ask candidates what they hope to earn or what they are currently earning. If that happens, it may make sense to respond with one of the following statements. *Money isn't the most important factor in my decision; I'd like to know more about the job's requirements and the company's priorities so I can think about what contributions I can make; I'll accept any reasonable offer; what would you normally pay someone in a similar position?* Ultimately, the goal is to gather more information in order to come up with an appropriate number.

If the company insists that the candidates give a precise answer, they must be able to provide a number supported by objective arguments, such as what the market offers, on average, for a similar profile; what is paid at the company as far as they are aware; and what they feel they are worth based on what they can contribute to the company and on their level of experience. It's a good idea to leave the matter open for discussion along with other aspects of the job, such as what the position entails, the level of responsibility, possibilities for advancement, the flexibility of work schedules and vacation time, training, etc.

Beth, one of our MBA students, once had an interesting experience. Her potential employer asked about her expectations, and she didn't give a precise number. In turn, the company made an offer that was extremely low, not just compared to her expectations but also by normal salary standards for fresh MBA students from our institution. She was upset and considered writing an angry email to the company. However, we took a different approach. We asked her to explain to the organization that the salary was too low and support her arguments with statistical information. She wrote a polite email in which she showed the average salary of MBA students from premier institutions as well as average salaries offered to students with her profile. The company answered favorably, explaining that they were creating a new position and had never hired an MBA from a premier institution, and promised to revise their offer. Eventually, Beth received an offer that was almost sixty percent higher than her original offer, and the company received a bright and happy employee.

3. HOW SHOULD YOU APPROACH A JOB INTERVIEW?

3.1. Help Them Help You

When we observe Beth's experience, we realize that what really helped her was her initiative to benefit the organization. Following, in part, the ideas of Deepak Malhotra,[3] the main goal of a job interview is for the company to want to meet with the candidate again—either due to a good first impression, a pleasant initial surprise, or the recognition of a good fit. The better the impression left by the candidate, the stronger his or her negotiating position will be. It's enough for the candidate to avoid anything that the other party might not like, such as having an untimely, unjustified, or excessive interest in the economic component, being petty about small details, or needless impatience.

Arrogance is lethal, although it is possible to temper it and change it into healthy ambition through justification, based on objective references, of why you deserve what you are going to end up asking for further on in the process. The reasons behind any request for more must be based deservedness, which will not make them disagreeable. If this foundation is lacking, it can be prudent to wait before presenting any kind of demands.

3.2. Understanding the Other Parties: Sharing Their Criteria and Constraints

Let's go back to Beth's example for a moment. Notice how her potential employer took pains to understand what Beth wanted to express. Negotiating is an activity between people who don't always behave as they should or as we would expect. The employer in this case tried to understand the candidate's point of view, which led them both into a positive dialogue exchange. On the other hand, candidates may find themselves in a different situation altogether if, instead of negotiating with the person who will be their boss, they do so with a representative of the Human Resources Department, since they won't necessarily use the same criteria (the sense of urgency may be different for the boss than for the head of human resources), nor do they attach the same priority to the criteria they do share (for the boss, the question of remuneration tends to be less of a limiting factor than for human resources).

All negotiators have two types of interest: those of the company or the department they represent, and personal interests. Candidates must keep this distinction in mind when dealing with different interlocutors in order to maintain realistic expectations, expand negotiation options, and handle any obstacles that may arise.

---

3   Malhotra, D. 15 Rules for Negotiating a Job Offer. *Harvard Business Review 2014;* 92(4):pp. 117-120.

Once the firm decides to hire the candidate, it's possible that the company won't be able to offer what the candidate asks for. The candidate has to find out, before beginning the process or during the first conversations, what the real limitations of the interlocutors are regarding the matters that interest them (fixed and variable compensation, nature of the position, reporting level, promotion options, flexible working hours, training, relocation, insurance, allowances, etc.). The more these factors are known, the better a position the candidate will be in to deal with them to the satisfaction of both parties.

It can be useful to draw up a list of both parties' needs (whether these have been made explicit or not; in the latter case, the list would be based on approximations and plausible hypotheses that need verification through conversations and research) and to sort these in order of priority (using the same tools mentioned earlier) with the ultimate objective of maximizing reconciliation.

The VIA (vital, important, and additional) framework enables the aforementioned organization of needs and packages to be prepared for the purpose of carrying out exchanges through value creation for both parties. The parties rarely have two vital needs in confrontation, but if and when they do, obstacles will surely emerge.

4. THE TREES ARE NOT THE WHOLE FOREST

Negotiating a job offer goes far beyond money, since life is not about material things alone. For this reason, it's necessary not to lose sight of the fact that it is a multi-factorial negotiation with consequences for the future—not only does the negotiation deal with more than one *what,* but the *how* and the *when* can be essential sources of value creation for both parties as well.

Considering all the pieces of the puzzle regarding what both parties can get from the negotiation enables a flexible attitude and prevents blindness—that is, being trapped by one or several matters that cause a conflict of interests. It's also advisable to deal with them all at once in search of package deals that will add up to a positive result for both the employer and the candidate and avoid one-sided outcomes.

Continually haggling for a more will annoy the other party and discourage future generosity, limiting the employer's desire to negotiate and create value with the employee. Workplace relationship 'break-ups' are all too frequently caused by unbalanced negotiations that heavily favor one party over the other.

5. ANCHORING IN THE NEGOTIATION

Furthermore, it should be noted that whoever speaks first, if they do it well, anchors the process in their favor. Academic research into the impact of anchoring has confirmed time and again that it plays a decisive role in negotiations. A negotiator who makes a more ambitious first offer almost always ends up receiving more. Nevertheless, declaring yourself first entails two risks: first, the counterpart may lose interest in the negotiation simply because the base or lower limit seems unachievable to them, and secondly, an ambitious first offer may not seem credible. In salary negotiations, it is always necessary to be prudent when answering questions about salary expectations. One strategy for tackling this question is to answer in ranges. Research in experimental psychology has shown that negotiating in ranges leads to a stronger anchor. For example, instead of answering, "My salary expectation is €40,000 a year," it is preferable to opt for, "Applicants of my profile in the market, from what I've observed, make between €40,000 and €42,000 a year." Negotiating in ranges presents a series of advantages, such as the establishment of a double anchor[4] that will favor our expectations. Another advantage is open dialogue. Talking in ranges and justifying the range not only protects interviewees from the risks of unjustifiable offers, but also invites the other party to explore the reasons for this range; this provides interviewees with an opportunity to explain their expectations more efficiently.

6. IT'S NOT PERSONAL—IT'S NEGOTIATION

There is a series of direct questions that increase the competitive temperature in a negotiating process. *What is your current salary? Have you had other offers? Where are you looking? How long have you been looking? Are you changing companies because of the money? Could you start right away?*

The same thing happens with pressure or ultimatums. *Take it or leave it; we can't go beyond this limit; you have to answer within twenty-four hours or you're out; etc.* In these contexts, it is essential to react calmly and professionally. Fundamentally, they are providing information that should be decoded correctly and, to do this, it is necessary to understand the constraints, concerns, and needs of the speakers. Why are they doing this? What do they really want?

Generally, these constraints indicate that the company is interested in how the candidate is going to react. They also demonstrate how the employer processes the uncertainty typical of the negotiating process and that they want to clarify any gray areas or gain negotiating power in order to enjoy a more comfortable position. There is rarely an underlying personal issue or desire to annoy. The negotiation, rather, is taking place in all its splendor; the best thing to do is focus on the details, keep calm, and enjoy the challenge.

When faced with a threat or ultimatum, the most sensible reaction is to attach no great significance to it and not insist on any confirmation. This way, whoever issued the statement will be less disposed to act on it and may even withdraw it. Helping the interlocutor can provide a foundation for value creation, conflict resolution, and the

---

4 Ames, D.; Mason, M. Tandem Anchoring: Informational and Politeness Effects of Range Offers in Social Exchange. *Journal of Personality and Social Psychology* 2015; 108(2):254-274.

overcoming of obstacles. The key lies, once again, in investigating what is behind the threat, because it will come up again if it's real.

In short, negotiating effectively requires managing expectations wisely even in situations of uncertainty by way of an inquisitive approach that focuses on the underlying interests of both parties.

Exhibit
Workplace Negotiation: Preparation Guide

First job	
An open process	Campus recruitment
Try to find out how many candidates are in the process.	How many students are part of the process?
It is more difficult to discover what the company is offering in general.	It is easier to find out what is being offered.

General (Applicable for all the salary negotiations) Analysis of negotiation	
My side	**The other party**
Where do I want to live and work?	What profile are they looking for?
In what position?	Why do they need a professional for this position?
What kind of job do I prefer?	How does this position help create value in the company?
Will I like my colleagues and the management style?	What skills should a good candidate have?
Will I fit in with the company culture?	What experience and training should the right candidate have?
What will my career be like?	

Power	
What alternatives do I have?	What alternatives does the company have?
How long can I wait?	How long can they wait?

Expectations			
Need			
What monthly salary do I need?			
Fixed salary	Variable	Stock options	Other factors
			Promotion
			Level
			Various: insurance, pension plans, notice of dismissal or additional compensation, flexible hours, teleworking, vacations.

NEGOTIATING IN A VIRTUAL WORLD

CHAPTER 14

The procurement manager of a pharmaceutical company, a young MBA who has only held the position for a year, is called on by the Director of Research and Development to source a new material within a week. The company has its existing suppliers, and the price negotiations nearly always follow a predictable course. However, this time, the situation is different. There's a lot of pressure to find a supplier, and the only feasible option is located in another country. The negotiation is conducted via email, and the price demanded by the supplier is notably high. The procurement manager sticks to the normal policy and asks for a discount but receives subsequent counteroffers to no avail. The limited time frame means this is the only supplier that can serve their needs. Fortunately, an interesting opportunity arises: the following week, there is a convention attended by both the Director of Research and Development and the potential supplier. At the end of the event, the director, after face-to-face negotiation, returns having come to an agreement in under twenty-four hours, at the preferred price, and with a long-term contract. After the successful conclusion of the negotiation, the procurement manager asks what went wrong with the negotiation by email.

The COVID-19 pandemic rattled the world in the year 2020 and forced countless people to learn new ways of living and working. One important change was a shift toward online work. Many executives and directors were likewise forced to negotiate via online channels. Negotiations can be drastically different in nature when conducted online. In the post-COVID world, companies and other organizations are conducting more and more negotiations online. In this segment, we are going to analyze online communication based on two important parameters: space and time. We are going to explain the influence of online negotiations and then see how the process of negotiation changes in an online negotiation.

1. HOW DO SPACE AND TIME INFLUENCE NEGOTIATIONS?

The classic *in situ* negotiation process implies that two (or more) negotiators are present at a single venue at the same time. This setting provides an opportunity to interpret non-verbal signals such as body language, gestures, and facial expressions. With the latest technological tools, which are driving an unstoppable wave of digitalization, space and time as elements of communication have been transformed. Media that facilitate transmission and reception of the message at the same time are called synchronous media, while media that do not allow this facility are referred to as asynchronous media (see Table 14.1).

Table 14.1. Space-time model of social interaction

	Same place	Different place
Same time	Face-to-face	*Email* (simultaneous response) Telephone call Instant messaging Video conference
Different time	Negotiation rounds Shared files	*Email* (asynchronous response) Instant messaging Shared files

Source: Compiled by the authors.

Face-to-face negotiation and emails are on two extremes of the spectrum. In a face-to-face situation, the negotiator gets the message from their counterpart at the same time and in the same place, while the same can't be said for email communication. Bearing in mind the binomial of the space and time dimensions in which the communication between the parties takes place, four situations are identified:

- **Same time, same place:** A traditional negotiation takes place in a shared space and in a simultaneous manner. The parties involved rely on direct and immediate communication and a wide variety of signals that allow quick interpretation of information, identification of interests, and the addressing of any offers put forward. Whenever we ask our program participants if and why they prefer face-to-face negotiations, we generally get two answers—better information and better trust. Face-to-face negotiation allows for immediate clarification and explanation in the event of misunderstandings or questions, as well as lower levels of uncertainty. Some negotiators express themselves much better in speech than in writing. Given the opportunity for immediate feedback on the communication, the negotiator also has an opportunity to modify their communication to avoid misunderstandings altogether. Moreover, negotiators who rely on an emotional connection with the other side can develop a trust-based relationship with greater ease. As a participant once said in our class, "In person, I can show how genuine and trustworthy I truly am."
- **Different time, different place:** This situation is diametrically opposed to the previous one. Negotiators neither share the same physical space nor are the messages exchanged at the same time. These situations include negotiations that take place through email. It needs to be noted that emails are becoming borderline synchronous tools as well. The proliferation of the smartphone has made it the

most commonly used device for accessing the Internet all over the world. As early as in 2016, more than 49% of all emails worldwide were read on mobile devices and tablets (IBM Marketing Cloud, 2016)[2]. If face-to-face negotiation gives an impression of establishing better relationships, emails provide a sense of more accurate analysis to negotiators. Asynchronization can be turned into an advantage when used with logical and deductive rigor to construct proposals, identify back-up points, elaborate reference-based arguments, and present the facts and data that support them. Time and the sequencing level of exchanged information allow us to understand the messages of the other party more precisely.

- **Same time, different place:** This is the mode where two negotiators are transmitting and receiving communication at the same time but are separated by physical distance. Telephone calls or video conferences allow create an atmosphere of proximity with the other party, though the richness of verbal cues suffers in this mode compared to face-to-face negotiation. In these negotiations, there is not enough distance for rational assessment of the situation and the deal, and at the same time, there is not enough personal contact to create a relationship of trust. In this mode of negotiation, therefore, both preparation and trust in the relationship play an important role. Prior familiarity between parties allows for faster progress. Negotiators who prefer a more personal touch in the negotiation process find negotiating through synchronous media insufficiently intimate. On the other hand, negotiators who prefer to negotiate through emails with a cold and calculated approach based purely on rational basis find synchronous media a bit interfering. For that reason, it's important to combine synchronous media with other channels of communication in the negotiation. Nevertheless, the use of these channels is increasing, and the styles are becoming more adaptable.

- **Different time, same place:** In these situations, negotiators interact in an asynchronous manner, though they have access to the same document or share the same physical space at consecutive times. An example could be the tendering of a public project that requires the participation of several companies, presenting their proposals in successive rounds, until the project is awarded to one of them. Another case could be that of two or more collaborators working on the same electronic document, negotiating and agreeing on their contributions depending on successive versions. It is an appropriate environment for contributing to the shared understanding phase of the negotiation object, the production of packages, the simultaneous consideration of equivalent offers, and the final drafting of the agreement, as far as special care is taken and recourses provided for a physical meeting if required by the degree of uncertainty or confrontation.

2. THE SOCIAL DISTANCE MODEL

COVID-19 made the whole world aware of the phrase *social distance*. Social distance is the third dimension that influences the negotiation process. As mentioned, if the distance is minimal or close, such as in a face-to-face negotiation, the use of language will be more expressive. Conversely, if the distance is long or remote, such as with shared files, the degree of communication will be much lower (see Table 14.2).

Table 14.2 shows the ascending model of this distance

Face-to-face	Video conference or video call	Telephone call	Instant messaging	Email	Shared files
Movement, environment, touch, tone of voice, appearance	Movement, environment, tone of voice, appearance	Tone of voice	Written signals, tone of voice (audio)	Written signals	Written signals
Close	Social Distance			Remote	

In one particular case of multilateral negotiation, numerous calls had to be made during the preparation phase and communications by email and chat were needed to obtain more information on the interests of the counterparts. Once they sat down to negotiate, they conducted the process face-to-face, but during one phase of the negotiation, they kept in contact with a department located in another city by video conference. When the time came to close the deal, they created a shared document which reflected all the points reached, editing successive versions that had to be revised until a final proposal was accepted. It can certainly be said that the chosen means of communication and interaction influence the quality of the process as well as its result. The success of the negotiations is ever more intricately linked to technology, and therefore, to the impact of digitalization.

3. THE ONLINE NEGOTIATION PROCESS

On average, an executive receives more than one hundred and fifty emails a day[3], covering everything from the most trivial to the most important issues. This constant updating in the face of a major data flow makes many feel that their emails are not read carefully, and they initially attribute less trust to the counterpart. As a result, compared to face-to-face negotiations, there is less trust both in the preparation phase of the negotiation and in the post-negotiation period, which means that long-term relations are less probable (Ebner, 2013). These lower expectations of collaboration are mainly due to the lack of non-verbal communication signals, characterized, according to the METTA model, by movement, environment, touch, tone of voice, and appearance (Thompson, 2015), which naturalize the relationship in the negotiation (see Table 14.3).

Table 14.3. METTA Model

Movement	Gestures, posture, body position, eye movement and visual contact, facial expressions, head movements, nervousness, and leaning the body
Environment	Location, distance between the people, design of the room, and atmosphere
Touch	Handshake, contact with objects (e.g., having a pen in your hand)
Tone of voice	Clarity of speech, pauses, volume, fluctuations, musicality of the voice
Appearance	Style of dress

In communication by email with shared files, contextual signals disappear. In calls, the only category from the model present is tone of voice, though in the video call option, movement, environment, and appearance are also relatively present. With instant messaging, written communication does not retain any of these signals, but a few additional functions, such as inserting an audio clip, a video, or an image, allow us to increase non-verbal communication in a selective (and, in certain cases, manipulative) manner, since we directly control what is shared and seen. In a video conference, all the signals except touch are retained, though they are significantly different than they would be in face-to-face negotiations depending on the quality of the software and the medium used.

The greater the social distance, the lesser the reach of communication and the greater the complexity in building a fluid relationship based on mutual trust. In the same way, the shorter the social distance from the counterpart with whom we are negotiating, the more easily information can flow with all its subtleties, increasing the probability of personal trust, which is an irreplaceable element in any type of negotiation. In the following section, the different phases of a negotiating process are reviewed in the light of the impact of digitalization and online tools in their broadest sense.

4. APPROACH

During the information exchange phase, when efforts are made to understand the interests driving the other party and reduce uncertainty, more and more negotiators are leaning toward telephone calls, video conferences, email, or services like WhatsApp for shorter information exchanges with the goal of streamlining the process. With written methods such as email, however, information is delivered asynchronously, providing more time for its analysis.

Those who write the message or make the calls have a greater or lesser degree of participation in the conversation. A study once showed that in a group of six, three people conducted more than 70% of the communication; in a group of eight, three conducted more than 70%. Even when participants were told that the success of the negotiation depended on collective contributions, the participation levels were far from equal (Thompson and Nadler, 2002).

However, by using technological media such as email to communicate, the party that theoretically has more power actually sacrifices the ability to establish leadership through different forms of communication (nonverbal, etc.). There is no direct visual contact, and the impact that relaxed and natural body language can have on an audience is lost.

On the other hand, virtual and digitalized relationships, with appropriate preparation, offer negotiators who represent a weaker position the chance to participate, since they can tilt the power, express themselves appropriately, and write in a clear and concise manner. The physical distance balances out analysis and persuasion.

If a negotiator expresses themselves in an abrupt manner (or is perceived to have done so), it tends impact the other party negatively (Brett et al., 2007), so opportunities to display warmth and a collaborative disposition in the negotiation are reduced, without necessarily increasing competitive tension, since there are fewer signals that are interpreted in a negative manner.

Depending on the strategy they want to use, the negotiator must choose the most suitable communication media and which, in turn, best suits each phase of the process. If the aim is to show greater cordiality and seek the trust of the counterpart, it is advisable to prioritize face-to-face or video conference negotiation, where social distance is minimized. If, on the other hand, a competitive negotiation is proposed, email may be a good way to present facts based purely on logical and analytical reasoning rather than emotion; in this way, attention falls on the message, responses may be managed more appropriately, negotiators may tend to make more ambitious proposals. When there is no personal contact, there is a certain degree of anonymity, and differences in power and status have a reduced effect.

5. EXPLORATORY PHASE

In this phase, negotiators seek to obtain missing or comparative information; the objective is to reduce uncertainty and lay the foundations for the personal relationship upon which the rest of the negotiation will be constructed. In the case of email, this phase is usually omitted, and it is common to open directly with offers, which introduces levels of risk that are difficult to control. Thus, it is advisable not to reject the opportunity to examine the counterpart's interests. The advantage of spatial-temporal distance is that it facilitates the comparison of information and the reviewing of calculations and weightings, and it eases potential tension via its inherent 'down time.' Contrarily, tensions and conflict have to carefully managed in face-to-face negotiations so that they do not cause mistrust or misunderstandings in terms of the power flow (the notion that, "If they ask for down time, it's because they feel cornered, unsure, etc.").

6. OPTIONS AND CONCESSIONS

During this phase, when the counterpart is not visible and there are no social norms regulating the conversation, some aspects of common courtesy may be perhaps disregarded and responses may become blunt, so special attention must be given to how the message is interpreted. It must be emphasized that the medium bears almost as much weight as the content of the message itself.

Another aspect that must be considered is the degree of privacy required during the negotiation. When one writes in a document, for example, one does not know who is receiving the message, or to whom it may be forwarded, or whether the message could be subsequently used for future negotiations, or even if it might be published. All these considerations seem self-evident, but they are not always taken into sufficient consideration.

Furthermore, any potential concern for the counterpart's subjective and personal outcome regarding the result of the negotiation can be set aside with more ease whenever there's a lack of face-to-face communication.

6.1. Closing

Once the closing of the negotiation is reached, the satisfaction with the result and the performance is lower among online negotiators (Thompson and Nadler, 2002), with experience indicating that the quality of the result and the possibilities of maximizing the benefits tend to be less than in a face-to-face negotiation.

In addition, the potential for a long-term relationship diminishes since the use of email or the telephone strengthens individual positioning, which promotes a more competitive nature. The virtualization of any relationship ultimately discourages inclusive communication and sets the stage for competitive tactics. It isn't difficult to counteract this factor; it would be enough to celebrate the closure of the agreement physically or for one of the parties to visit the other.

Since the use of electronic devices, such as tablets or the smartphones, eliminates non-verbal communication signals and weakens trust between parties during the negotiation process, these effects will be even more prominent at the end, which is generally in itself an eminently competitive phase. Both parties need to exercise self-control and find ways to reduce competitive tension when the time comes.

7. STRATEGIES FOR SUCCESSFUL ONLINE NEGOTIATIONS

7.1. Preparation

In this phase, a negotiator should identify expectations, analyze interests, assess power differences, and gain information about their counterpart—who they are, what they need, what they want, what their ambitions are (starting with personal ones), and what alternatives are open to them.

It would be advisable to consider an initial approach, striking up conversation without the explicit purpose of negotiating. As a result of this, information can be shared and obtained, while at the same time, the perception of distance is reduced. *A virtual relationship has to be created.*

In an experiment centered on negotiation by email, half the students that participated had the opportunity to make a five-minute call beforehand, provided they refrained from discussing the negotiation issues themselves. The students who made the call behaved in a more collaborative manner and reached better agreements than those who had not been given the option to do so (Thompson & Nadler, 2002).

If it is not possible to make this initial contact, it can be substituted with a video conference or a particularly friendly call in order to establish some kind of informal contact. One way to engender trust is to talk about something you have in common; a quick internet search should suffice to find topics of conversation. Another way of engendering trust is to display a profile photo in the email; it has been shown that replies to email requests to take part in a survey increase when a photograph of the sender is included, making the person more identifiable (Gueguen, Legoherel and Jacob, 2003).

Before initiating contact, a great help in fostering a good relationship is to ask about the most suitable time to call; this avoids circumstantial distractions or interruptions. Politeness always helps create a pleasant atmosphere, even in virtual relationships. Good digital manners are paramount for these communication methods.

Contact

Once the two parties have been introduced and acquainted, they establish negotiation bases. In the event that a strategy has a clearly competitive orientation, the emphasis should be placed on examining the requirements and actual power of the other party, while trying not to show one's own requirements. However, if the strategy has collaborative potential, the first interactions can be an opportunity to persuade the other party of any common interests. If the interaction is conducted over the telephone, it is necessary to listen actively to the other party, even remaining silent so as to allow them to reveal new information; given the awkwardness of remaining silent, the other party will be more ready to talk. In writing, on the other hand, the negotiator must rely on formality and good manners.

If you have prepared well for the negotiation, making the first call can place one party in an advantageous position if the other has not had time to prepare the process in the desired manner. If, on the other hand, the other party calls first and you do not feel prepared, you shouldn't hesitate to tell them that you are busy at that moment. However, you shouldn't wait long before returning the call once you have prepared yourself.

In video conferences, it is a good idea to maintain visual contact with your counterpart, looking at the camera and trying to avoid missing visual elements of non-verbal communication. Another possibility is to configure the screen so as to have both features. As for the surroundings, the most appropriate is a room equipped for meetings or video calls and free from any elements that could prove distracting. On a personal level, one should dress in keeping with the situation. One should take special care to not misinterpret the counterpart's pauses of the counterpart and accidentally talk over them. One should also bear in mind that free and low-cost video conference tools often have problems with the audio, reducing the resolution and quality of the call.

Approach

In this phase the, creation of value continues for both parties involved in the negotiation. If a competitive strategy is adopted, value is determined at the expense of the other party. If, on the other hand, a collaborative strategy is proposed, value is created together, which will subsequently be distributed. Steps should be taken to avoid attribution bias whereby negative intentions are identified in the counterpart.

In a collaborative negotiation, increasing the exchange of emails will help to collate information. This measure allows one party to send well-reasoned information and the other to process it carefully. Time is fundamental in order to understand the interests and options of the other party. Being careful with information, keeping communication brief and concise, using language that displays an interest and an intention to collaborate with the other party, defending proposals and motives, and, in a multilateral negotiation in which one of the parties is dominating the conversation, inviting other parties or potential allies to participate to a greater extent are usually effective strategies.

Remember not to fall into time synchronization bias, which involves negotiating as if in real time, making offers and counteroffers, with hardly any of the argumentations and clarifications that help to reach an agreement.

During online interaction, there are instances where it may be advisable to imitate the other party. In a study conducted in two different geographical areas, a group of negotiators imitated their opponent during an email negotiation: "When the other person uses emoticons in their message, such as ;), the other party should also do so. If they use a certain vocabulary, metaphors, grammar, specific words or abbreviations, such as "y'know" (you know), you should do the same. Both in the experiment conducted in Thailand and in the one conducted in the United States, the imitators that applied online mimicry during the first ten minutes reached more profitable agreements in their negotiations than those that applied them in the last ten minutes of negotiation." (Swaab, Maddux and Sinaceur, 2011). However, sending emoticons and abbreviated language seems a little unprofessional in certain negotiations, and it depends on the cultural context in which the negotiation is taking place.

One must take care not to fall into the *snowballing* effect. This consists of sending large quantities of information in justification of one of the underlying interests, since the other party may not read it carefully and instead respond right away with the same amount of information, which ultimately hinders communication. A study into this issue states that 70% of emails received by executives receive less than a minute's attention (Thomas *et al.*, 2006). Additionally, the recipient may interpret the build-up of emails as aggressive and impossible to reply appropriately. It's a good idea to establish clear arguments and lines of thought that can still be followed when read quickly, always respecting the message chain as it unfolds.

The appropriate course of action is to reply to the messages received during the process within a maximum period of twenty-four hours so as to avoid showing a lack of interest unless this is precisely the intention. Numerous studies have demonstrated that emails have the highest probability of being opened during the first hour of the day; subsequently, the opening ratio reduces by 5% and, after twenty-four hours, to 1%. However, the asynchronous nature of this particular tool can be turned to your advantage by reading the message carefully several times and checking the information. It has also been demonstrated how, in synchronous negotiation simulations, there was a greater competitive tendency than in asynchronous negotiations, principally due to the time available, which allowed the exchange of a greater quantity of information relevant to the process (Pesendorfer and Koeszigi, 2006).

When conversing via a call, impatient negotiators may be tempted to communicate a large amount of information in a short period of time to keep things moving quickly. They make the mistake of assuming a "reactive devaluation" by transmitting that the information is manipulative and serves only their own interests. However, it is also true that this method reduces uncertainty and clarifies interests. In this context, brevity and clarity work in your favor.

Generation of Options

In this phase of a negotiation by email, if there is no trust between the parties and the levels of uncertainty are high, the bargaining is more likely to intensify than in a face-to-face negotiation. In order to reduce this competitive tension and not fall into a confrontation bias, different offers must be proposed in an organized manner and in separate paragraphs, using multimedia tools such as charts, tables, presentations, and reports that elaborate on the information presented. Secondly, it is a good idea to present offers in packages, rather than variable by variable, with the aim of obtaining more information on the priorities of the counterpart and clearer responses while at the same time showing flexibility.

Each email must have its spelling and grammar checked and be properly edited before being sent to the recipient. When writing, you should include a greeting at the beginning and a sign-off or a signature footer at the end, except when it is part of a chain of instant messages. To avoid mistakes in the addressees of the message, whose possible recipients should be reviewed beforehand, it's a good idea to complete the "To" field after finishing writing the email and adding any attachments. Finally, it is advisable to fill out the subject line in an eye-catching manner so that the most important details stand out: instead of "Today's meeting", it is better to use "Next Meeting, Monday 11/5 at 12:00 hrs." or, rather than "Agenda for the negotiation process," it's better to use "Agenda for the [name] negotiation process for May: principal and secondary points."

Negotiators should respond in accordance with the urgency of the situation and in no more than twenty-four hours. Delays generate anxiety and a subsequent negative attribution. In a collaborative negotiation, if you need more time to answer, simply send a quick email requesting this time and create an alert that says when you will be in a position to respond. However, if the other party takes a long time to respond, two possibilities emerge:

- The offer is being studied and considered in expectation of other movements that may influence the negotiation.
- They want to foster an image of power: "If I take longer to respond, it's because I have the power to do so."

In a chain of sent and received messages, it is important to create an experience of uninterrupted contact that fosters a collaborative relationship, writing, for example, "As discussed earlier…" or copying a fragment of a previous message and, above all, maintaining a similar response time so as not to desynchronize the conversation. However, it is better not to send emails over the weekend since most people don't want their free time invaded. In this sense, waiting equates to moving forward.

In intercultural negotiations conducted by email, since the other person is not present, it becomes easier to forget certain markers, such as an accent or features that remind us of their origin, and as a consequence we make the mistake of employing certain cultural references specific to our own society. This is another reason why it is advisable to read each message several times before sending it.

Creating the Agreement

Once the parties have defined the topics to be addressed and the underlying interests and suggested certain options, the distributive phase begins, in which the created or integrative value is claimed and where an agreement that satisfies both parties is sought. In this phase, it is advisable to propose a previously prepared concession strategy and construct a specific and precise agreement.

There are two crucial elements to an agreement—the feasibility of the agreement, for which it helps to be clear about how the solution will be implemented, and the measurability of the agreement over time; for example, saying, "Let's meet in a week," is preferable to, "See you soon." Precise closures help avoid future conflict and confusion.

If you are negotiating by email, it is important to sort out any misunderstanding and request clarification when necessary. It also pays to be brief and concise and to end with a summary of the main points. Furthermore, it is particularly advisable to use the subject line in a purposeful manner in the final phases.

Once the message is sent, we accept the vulnerability that it may be read by strangers. Word documents that we send contain hidden saved data, such as comments, names of the people who have worked on the document, modification and revision dates, with the client's confidential or privileged information. For this reason, Word has the option to delete all hidden data.

This lack of privacy can be used in an advantageous and lawful manner by recording interactions or resending messages when any information is not clear or the offer and interests of the other party are inconsistent with new messages.

If, on the other hand, this situation arises over the telephone, staying silent is a powerful tactic during the concession phase. When one of the parties proposes a change to their position, if the counterpart does not say anything, they may be induced to make another concession. Furthermore, when the other party seems to have finished responding to one of the questions regarding their interests and objectives in the negotiation, a prolonged silence may prompt them to reveal more information.

Likewise, there are a considerable number of non-verbal communication signals that can be picked up during a telephone conversation, such as the rhythm, speed, inflexion, and volume of the speaker's voice.

- Most people find it easier to say "no" on the telephone or by email than face-to-face thanks to the feeling of distance. It is a good idea to propose alternative tools that provide a greater impression of closeness.
- Inflexion of the voice demonstrates a higher level of agitation and indicates greater satisfaction. To avoid this situation, prepare and modulate your voice to sound professional at all times and not give away your anxiousness to reach an agreement.
- An initial pause before rejecting the proposal on the table suggests that the person either has entered into the realm of acceptability or must articulate their reasons for rejecting the proposal.
- A significant pause may indicate that an offer is being seriously considered by somebody that did not hesitate to decline previous offers.

Closing and Follow up

The moment a potential agreement is reached, the closing phase begins. However, it is necessary to maintain confidence and avoid changing positions matched by the counterpart, since this could block the negotiation.

The action of withdrawing from the negotiating table is much easier in a negotiation by email or over the telephone, so the agreements that have been reached during the process must be respected at all times.

Once the negotiators believe they have reached a resolution, they should take the time to review all operational terms of the negotiation to avoid misunderstandings. Once confirmed, all points of the agreement should be confirmed by email. One of the most common biases in this situation is that of negotiation exit—viewing the negotiation as a done deal when there are still matters left on which to agree.

The application of different strategies will help us reduce the psychological distance from the counterpart. Depending on the phase and the device used, we can better develop our interests, achieve greater power without it becoming a competitive relationship, improve the relationship, and reduce uncertainty, all with the aim of obtaining valuable information to meet our expectations.

Biases are especially delicate during closure. Table 14.4 summarizes some of the main ones.

Table 14.4 Model of the biases we have when negotiating in a different place and time

Time synchronization bias	Negotiation exit bias
One negotiates as if in real time; offers and counteroffers are launched as if it were a game of tennis, with hardly any argumentations and clarifications that help reach an agreement.	The negotiation is considered finished too soon, when improvements could still be made. This is mainly due to the lack of visual information and the distance, reducing the ability to anticipate and retaliate.
Confrontation bias	**Fundamental attribution error**
The absence of social norms regulating negotiation at a distance and a feeling of remoteness and anonymity provoke greater confrontation on digital media.	Negative intentions and a tendency to exploit our interests tend to be attributed to others because of a lack of prior preparation.

Source: Compiled by the authors.

Concluding Note

Negotiation is a way to solve problems by creating value for the negotiating parties; it is not a zero-sum game. The parties decide to give and receive, to demand and to grant via a process in which they influence, convince, and counteract each other, proposing solutions and agreeing on how to implement them together. It makes sense to negotiate when both parties come out better off than before. This means a shift in mentality from *demanding* more from the counterpart to *exchanging* more, since the counterparts can solve their own problems only to the extent that they resolve those of others. Managed with expertise and common sense, technology can contribute effectively to this shift.

Final Remarks

The parties involved in a negotiation can create or demand value by adopting a competitive or collaborative style. By collaborating, the parties look to increase the size of the pie they are negotiating in a creative way. Through openness, clear communication, sharing information, an attitude that seeks to solve problems, and the cultivation of interests shared by both negotiators, the parties involved try to find a solution that allows them both to walk away under optimum conditions. At the other extreme, competitive negotiators tend to see this approach as ingenuous or a sign of weakness. They view negotiating as harsh, arduous haggling. They usually start high, give in gradually, exaggerate the value of the concessions they make, hide information, and try to outsmart the other party. They see negotiation as the process of demanding the largest possible piece of a fix-sized pie.

In the traditional view, negotiators act using one approach or the other. Nevertheless, neither a totally competitive approach nor a totally collaborative approach will be appropriate in all circumstances. Competitive or collaborative approaches coexist in all negotiations. That being said, the competitive approach predominates in situations in which winning is the overall goal (a type X agreement), while the collaborative approach will tend to prevail in win-win agreements (type Y). Therefore, a priori in any negotiation we can see the potential to collaborate or compete depending on the situation or problem to be solved. As the table below shows, the number of different needs involved in a negotiation, the relative power of the parties, the kind of relationship they have, and the characteristics of the information available to these parties can lead negotiators to adopt one approach or the other.

Situations that foster a competitive or collaborative approach

Competitive	<Tendency towards>	Collaborative
Opposite	Needs	Common
Unequal	Power	Equal
One-off	Relationship	Ongoing
High Uncertainty	Information	Low Uncertainty

However, despite the fact that all of these factors can initially slant a negotiation toward one side or the other, the negotiators' attitudes and arguments during the stages of strategy, generating options, and reaching an agreement are what will ultimately set the tone of the negotiation. They will decide whether or not to use their power and whether to enrich the negotiation by incorporating different levels of needs; they will determine whether the relationship will be a one-off agreement or ongoing, and they will determine whether to share a little or a lot of information. In that sense, despite greater or lesser potential for collaboration, the parties involved in solving the problem are the ones who will be more or less capable of generating value, depending on how they manage the negotiation process.

A PEEP INTO THE FUTURE: AUTOMATED NEGOTIATIONS

CHAPTER 15

1. INTRODUCTION

In general, entrepreneurs and executives spend more than 20% of their working time negotiating and resolving conflicts (Gettinger, Köszegi and Schoop, 2012); however, several studies have also shown that negotiators, when it comes to negotiating, bring significant value to the table. It has been demonstrated that collaborative potential maximizes the interests of the parties involved, though it's more complicated for the negotiators to reach *win-win* agreements, with both parties winning, due to the complexity of articulating multiple factors. The simpler course of action is to opt for a competitive, *win-lose* approach (one party gains what the other gives up, which is standard in transactions).

A lack of knowledge regarding the other party leads to negotiations with competitive frameworks. Not having information on the interests and intentions of the other party creates a degree of insecurity, causing us to fall into the temptation of holding our ground in the negotiation. In the end, fear and insecurity lead to a competitive approach.

The increase in interactions, possible coalitions, issues to be dealt with, and potential agreements make it more difficult to meet the expectations of each party. This complexity sometimes creates an agreement bias—the notion that not reaching an agreement is considered a failure. Negotiators who are too focused on reaching an agreement don't usually explore the value creation potential enough.

Finally, a negotiator's decision-making is affected by excessive concentration on their own requirements and weaknesses, ignoring those of others. This internal focus makes us weaker and more vulnerable to tricks and deception, since we don't take the appropriate measures to assess and process all the information presented during the negotiation. According to the Truth-Default Theory (Levine, 2014), human beings tend to assume that the other party (especially when unknown) is not providing us with true information.

Faced with these blocking situations caused by high levels of uncertainty and a lack of information, negotiation support systems and automated agents offer solutions to improve the analysis and the results of the agreement.

2. NEGOTIATION SUPPORT SYSTEMS

Negotiation support systems (NSS) are software that provide support in negotiations. In reality, an NSS is a type of *decision support system* (DSS) that helps with the decision-making process in complex situations. The objective of technological support is to make better decisions and negotiate in a more productive manner by reducing the negative effects of human interaction, some of which are caused by cognitive biases.

Negotiators tend to consider issues separately, ignoring possible synergies and potential concessions that help improve the result. They frequently "frame" the negotiation negatively, assessing their possible losses rather than considering the potential gains. They usually assume that the interests of the counterpart are opposed to their own.

NSS help the negotiator in four areas:

1. To understand all the factors and variables that affect their decision-making.
2. To examine the possible impact of the factors both on themselves and on their counterpart more effectively.
3. To interpret the expectations of both parties better.
4. To avoid or overcome emotional impact in a negotiation.

3. HOW DO NSS OPERATE TO COMPLEMENT AND IMPROVE THE NEGOTIATION?

The NSS can complement the process with different features: facilitation and communication, analysis of the negotiation, and analysis of decisions. It has been empirically demonstrated that their use improves the agreements reached in the negotiation. Negotiators that rely on an NSS display more collaborative behavior when compared to those that have access to the same information but lack this type of support. When the negotiators were provided with graphical displays of the negotiation history, they showed greater support, expressed fewer negative emotions, and talked more about impartiality. Additionally, they were more prepared to concede ground when dealing with highly conflictive issues and more satisfied with the results of the agreement (Gettinger, Köszegi and Schoop, 2012).

However, in potentially competitive negotiations, it has been demonstrated that the results are similar to those that do not rely on the support of NSS. In these situations, the negotiating parties tend to 'split the difference', reaching a reasonably effective and fair agreement (Goh, Teo, Wu and Wei, 2000). It can be said that if there is collaborative potential in a negotiation situation, the help of an NSS highlights this and helps the negotiator to avoid a mistaken competitive focus.

4. FACILITATION AND COMMUNICATION SUPPORT

This tool allows negotiators located in different places to exchange offers and counteroffers. It offers support features for communication, such as internal messaging or monitoring of the scope of negotiations. It can also be used as an automated mediator or advisor with the ability to suggest possible agreements.

Figure 15.1 Computer mediated negotiation

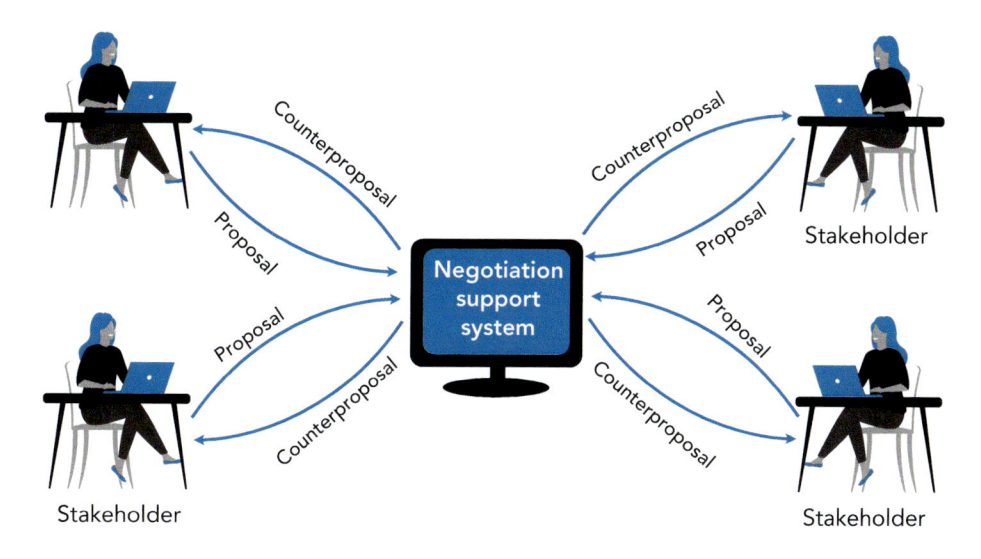

Source: Prepared by the authors.

For example, a pharmaceutical company wants to establish relations with a university so as to have better access to basic research, as well as to develop joint research projects. The R&D Department mentions a list of projects on which the company would like to work. The company will commit to a quantity of money after negotiating it with the university. The negotiation centers on the drug and the money. In the same negotiation, there are more stakeholders; for example, the Marketing Department, who would like to launch the products developed in a short time, introducing a new variable. The Human Resources Department, in turn, could leverage this agreement to give access to more young talent such as scientists or students from the university, which would introduce yet another variable: access to talent. The Finance Department would attempt to pay in such a way as to have reduced capital costs and thus greater liquidity, so now we also have the method of payment variable. The Accounts Department would be interested in the type of agreement to ensure compliance with all accounting regulations and to suffer the minimum impact in terms of taxes. Therefore, the more stakeholders are present, the more variables are introduced to the equation. An NSS would help prioritize and quantify the impact of the expectations and requirements of each stakeholder in order to reach a satisfactory agreement.

5. DECISION ANALYSIS SUPPORT

First of all, the negotiators specify their preferences regarding the attributes to be negotiated, and the system subsequently calculates a utility function. The system then evaluates offers and counteroffers based on the interests that they satisfy. The classification of these offers and their visualization allows the negotiator to decide on the best option.

As we've already demonstrated, the use of support systems improves the results of the negotiation; however, it is the human user that makes the final decision on whether to accept an offer, propose a counteroffer, or break off the negotiations. The result, therefore, does not always meet expectations. There are studies that reveal that negotiators behave in a manner inconsistent with their own interests, rejecting the support options of the NSS even when the options are shown during the negotiation process or the possibility of continuing with a subsequent negotiation to improve the agreement is proposed.

6. NEGOTIATION ANALYSIS SUPPORT

Support grants access to the analysis of the negotiation as well as the organization and the structuring of the processes. Additionally, it facilitates access to external information, negotiation records, experts, mediators, and facilitators that strengthen the arguments. Negotiating is a skill, and to improve a skill, it's important to identify the processes involved and to have certain criteria for measuring performance and identifying areas that need improvement. The challenge lies in the fact that it's difficult to analyze the quality of a negotiation based on the result. For example, if a person attending a job interview expects to have a salary of €40,000 a year, negotiates, and ends up obtaining it, one may ask whether they have conducted a successful negotiation. In theory, the answer is yes, because they got what they wanted. However, what this person may have not realized is that the company was prepared to pay €50,000; in that case, have they conducted a successful negotiation? Probably not as much. An NSS may help perform a more complete analysis of the situation, helping the negotiator control factors in the negotiation process, such as how much time was spent examining the information before making the offers, how the first offer was made, how the final result compares to the first offer, how the final result compares to the alternative, etc.

6.1. NSS and the Negotiation Process

This section describes how the NSS can help during the negotiation process. The structuring and the analysis of interests, the provision of external information, the negotiation records, or the suggestion of alternative solutions to the proposals are some of the features available during the different phases of negotiation.

6.2. Preparation of the Negotiation

During this phase, the object of the negotiation, your own expectations and interests (as well as those of the counterparty) are determined. Subsequently, the stakeholders, issues, and offers are identified, depending on their priority, as well as any possible combinations of offer packages.

The NSS provide a detailed description using analytical and visualization tools. They also serve as guides for the negotiator by means of the previous definition of parameters and constrictions, in which each problem is outlined, and the possible alternatives and consequences for each decision are suggested. The information obtained is saved and processed, providing support for the next phase of the negotiation.

Figure 15.2

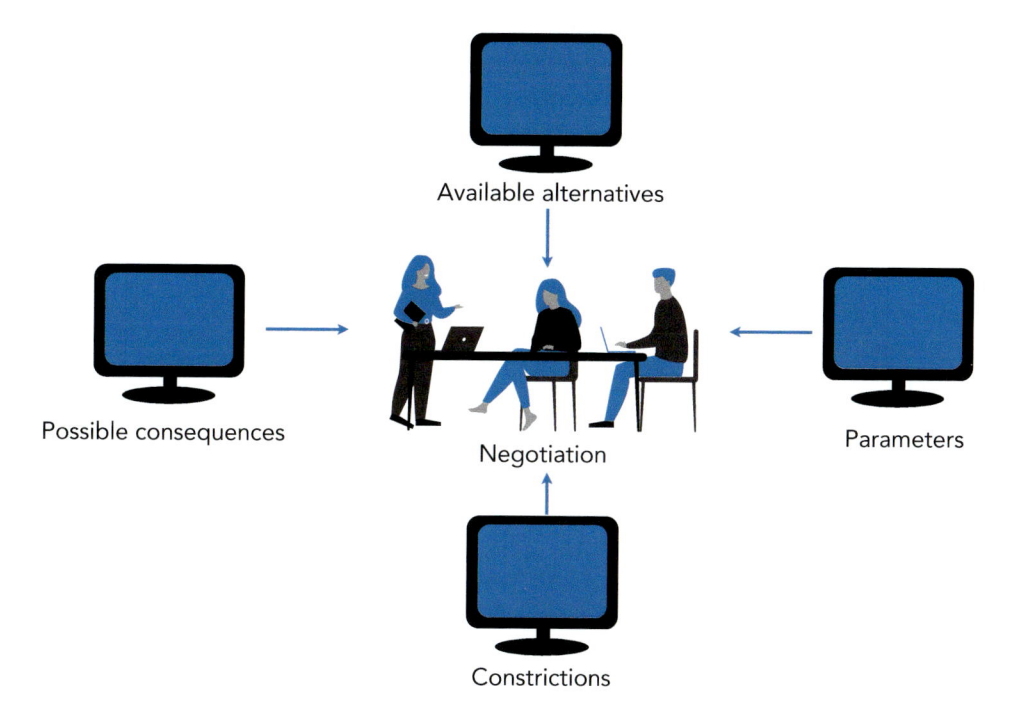

Source: Prepared by the authors.

6.3. Examination of the Information

In the case of a long negotiation, the NSS can help by providing a structure for collecting and saving information in such a way that facilitates its subsequent detailed analysis.

6.4. Offers and Concessions

In the negotiation process, the initial offer is proposed, and counteroffers and arguments are exchanged. NSS provide support in communication by means of message boxes, decision analysis, and the creation of new offers. Subsequently, priorities are reviewed and updated so as to overcome blocking situations. Also, charts are generated with the negotiation dynamics and, for each proposed offer, the interests that are satisfied are shown.

6.5. Post-Negotiation

During the post-negotiation phase, there is the option to evaluate and renegotiate an agreement. Based on information about the interests of the negotiating parties, the NSS determine whether the agreement reached is optimal in the sense that neither party can improve on it without loss to the other party (Pareto efficiency). Subsequently, they recommend certain offer packages, giving the option to continue the negotiation until another agreement is reached. In this way, satisfaction with the agreement is greater, and there is a greater probability of achieving a collaborative relationship.

As an example, in what is now a classic study, two scenarios were proposed on equal terms and with the same object of negotiation: one in which the negotiations were conducted face to face and by email, and another in which the negotiations were conducted with the help of NSS. In the first case, only 4 of the 34 negotiating pairs (11.1%) managed to reach a collaborative agreement. Meanwhile, in the second scenario, 29 of the 68 pairs (42.6%) managed to reach a comprehensive agreement (Rangaswamy and Shell, 1997).

7. THE AUTOMATION OF NEGOTIATION

Thanks to the development of artificial intelligence (AI), machine learning and deep learning, systems have been transformed into autonomous agents, capable of negotiating and taking decisions after being programmed.

Automated negotiation can be defined as the process in which the programmed software agents are automated according to the interests of the users and based on an interaction protocol. The principal objective is to maximize the benefits of the agreement, meeting the expectations of the negotiators. Automated agents are computer systems capable of acting in a flexible and autonomous manner within a defined environment and designed to meet a specific objective.

Their current application is developing exponentially in various business sectors and areas:

- Supply chains: In this area, there is a clear industrial tendency towards automated management. The agents that represent different business units negotiate the

conditions for the purchase of raw materials, decide and execute the programming, and negotiate the terms under which the products are delivered.
- Companies operating on the web, since they need automated agents to perform tasks such as mergers with small and agile companies with whom they can together take advantage of economies of scale.
- E-commerce, which offers automated processes that facilitate and improve interaction with suppliers and clients via the application of AI.

How does the automated agent work during the negotiation phases?

In automated negotiation, special attention should be paid to the following aspects: i) the analysis of the object and of the process, ii) an interaction protocol, and iii) the decision-making algorithms for the software agents.

- The object of the negotiation indicates the range of negotiation points that must be addressed. You can negotiate on just one point, like the price, or you can cover further issues related to the price, the quality, the timetable, and the terms and conditions.
- The interaction protocol covers the set of rules governing the interaction between agents. It also determines possible actions during the negotiation (acceptance or rejecting an offer, closing the negotiation, etc.), changes that may occur during the process (refusing or accepting further offers, etc.), and the regulation of the validity of any actions performed by the participants (what type of messages can be heard, by whom, for whom, and at what stage of the negotiation).
- Model algorithms vary depending on the range of decisions that can be taken, the protocol, the object of negotiation. and the range of operations that can be carried out.

8. NEGOTIATION PREPARATION

Depending on the state of the art, the object of the automated negotiation, the expectations and interests of the user are determined beforehand and remain constant throughout the negotiation. In most research, efforts have centered on predicting the counterpart's behavior. This research avenue can be divided into two categories:

- The first category starts from a lack of historical data on the behavior of the agent, and it is programmed with a series of previously defined strategies and functions.
- The second category uses agents with the ability to acquire experience from previous negotiations. The disadvantage of this approach is that the artificial neural network (deep learning) needs a large quantity of data during the training phase in order to identify the preferences of the counterpart correctly.

8.1. Negotiation Process

Negotiators can be people, software agents, or a combination of the two. In face-to-face or technologically mediated negotiations (video conferences, telephone calls, instant messages, or email), interaction protocols are not as strict or rigorous. The negotiators can easily deviate from protocol, interrupt each other, withdraw, or reach agreements after the termination of the negotiations. Therefore, the more automated the negotiation and the more actions delegated to the software, the less flexible the negotiation process is. When one of the protocol conditions is not met, the agent notifies the negotiator of their infraction.

After establishing the interaction protocol, algorithms or a decision-making strategy are used to define an agent's internal reasoning. The goal is to maximize value and reach the greatest possible achievement of interests. In the agent's decision-making process, the initial offer and subsequent offers are established according to a specific programmed strategy. It is established when it starts (initial offer), as the process continues (generation of options), and when it finishes (reaching an agreement or leaving the negotiation).

8.2. Post-Negotiation

In the last phase of closure and post-negotiation, the process is addressed again so as to analyze and improve the final agreement. It's often characterized by an exchange of decisive proposals accompanied by concessions as the parties converge on points of agreement. The majority of researchers in the AI field have developed models establishing unbreakable agreements, in which the commitments reached can neither be broken nor modified.

9. FINAL REFLECTION

Is it better for an automated agent or a human being to negotiate? There doesn't seem to be a single, definitive answer to this question. The conversation between two people and the conversation between a human being and a chatbot have apparent similarities, but also fundamental differences. In any case, it's a good idea to prepare for this phenomenon as it's here to stay. It is necessary to know how to handle, organize, and work with these *negobots,* and we must also know how to manage the negotiation when our opponent is one of these same *negobots* There is no valid alternative to recognizing the importance of automation processes and their impact on negotiation methods. These powerful tools multiply the capacity of negotiators but cannot replace their uniqueness, which relies on creativity when it comes to addressing value creation.

Automation becomes powerful through its commoditization, that is, equalizing us by the same standard. The key is to use these tools sensibly. Without them, the negotiations will suffer, but on their own they are 'blind.' Thus, they achieve their best results in the hands of a negotiator well-trained in negotiation and with well-developed criteria on the use of advanced AI media, for which non-artificial intelligence is required, at least for now.

SECTION III

CASES AND SELF - PRACTICE

In this section you are challenged with different negotiation cases. As first approach to each case, you should revisit the preparation sheet presented in chapter 9 (pp. 100-101) and consider how you would negotiate. As information relative to each party is available, you may well ask somebody else to play the role of one of the parts and conduct the negotiation exercise yourselves.

BAGHEERA

How many roles? – 2
Time for preparation – 15 minutes
Time for negotiation – 10 minutes

Instructions

There are two sides in this case, a buyer, and a seller. You can do this exercise in two ways. First, read one role. Ask a friend of yours to read the other (without you reading it) and conduct a negotiation exercise. Spend no more than 10 minutes in the negotiation. Once you finish the negotiation, exchange the exercises, and see what more you could have done. If you are working alone, then take one negotiation exercise. Prepare for the negotiation. Try to make a list of questions you would ask. Try to imagine for how much the deal would be closed. Read the next role and see whether your questions were effective or not. Reflect upon what important element of information you were not thinking about.

1. BAGHEERA BUYER

Since childhood you have been a big admirer of Rudyard Kipling's *The Jungle Book*. On your ninth birthday, your favorite aunt gifted you a set of ceramic statuettes of different characters from the book. However, there is one little problem with the set. You have all the important characters –Mowgli, Shere Khan, Kaa, Hathi and Tabiqui– except one of the most popular and iconic characters, Bagheera.

Today, while browsing in the local artisan fair, you spotted Bagheera at one of the stalls. You spent some time checking it and confirmed that this is your Bagheera. You even saw the mark under one of his claws that said "SCD (Sujo Ceramics, Dholka)" –the same mark you had seen carved under the statuettes that you have.

You had wanted a Bagheera during your childhood, but then preoccupations of the adult life distracted you, and the search for Bagheera faded away from your list of priorities. However, your interest was rekindled when a friend of yours, recently appointed curator of a newly constructed literary museum, visited you and showed interest in acquiring the collection. Your friend said that the value of the entire collection would be around $8,000 and with Bagheera the value could go up to between $10,500 and $11,000. The collection was valuable mainly due to its unique antique and nostalgic appeal. Your friend informed you that these ceramic statuettes were especially valuable because they were apparently produced in 1969, to celebrate the platinum (75th) anniversary of the release of *The Jungle Book*. Since Rudyard Kipling was born in India, the government of India had asked a family of prestigious ceramic craftsmen to make these statuettes. You could not verify the year of production, but from everything else –the look, structure, size, style and intensity of colors– you are sure that this is the piece you have been looking for.

Your friend added that his museum would like to acquire the entire collection and formally negotiate with you. You could not make up your mind immediately but at least the conversation got you interested in looking for the Bagheera statuette. After receiving the offer, you started looking for it and you saw some similar statuettes on websites that sold antiques and crafts. Similar-looking pieces were being sold for about $1,000 to $2,200. However, you could not buy those statuettes online because you could not confirm their authenticity.

On the basis of your friend's appraisal, you think that, as long as you pay less than $2,500, you will be in profit. However, this being an antique fair, the price should be negotiable. Moreover, you do not want to start at your limit straightaway but wish to leave a margin for negotiation in your first offer.

The seller, who until now was busy with another buyer, has seen you having a good time inspecting Bagheera and is approaching you.

2. BAGHEERA SELLER

You recently started an online auction business where you buy and sell a variety of items. You have gained good traction in the past 18 months and have been gaining a good reputation. However, you also participate in local artisan fairs, traditionally visited by good collectors and clients, and you find them a good opportunity to spread your name.

You are participating in one such artisan fair right now where you wish to get rid of the stock that you have been unable to sell online so that you can release some of the cash blocked in that inventory.

While you are trying to persuade a buyer, you notice that another potential customer is interested in a ceramic tiger statuette. You bought this from a supplier from India, and it cost you just $230 in one of your first big inventory purchases. You had to buy it because otherwise the supplier would not sell you very precious antique jewelry that you wanted to buy. After bargaining very hard, you managed to buy the entire set of jewelry (which is now selling pretty well on your website) along with this ceramic statuette. You paid only $230 for the statuette, compared with the $600 your supplier was asking. However, you have always maintained that, if you had more experience in the business, you would have managed to get it for free or would have avoided buying it altogether.

Some time ago, a collector at a similar artisan fair had shown willingness to buy the statuette but had said he would pay $700 at most. You closed the deal but, in the end, due to personal circumstances, the collector canceled the order. Then you tried to auction the statuette online but the highest bid you ever received was $250 out of three total bids you received. The bidding period will be over in about 3 days from now. You know very well that, in general, the prices of antiques vary widely but in online auctions if you haven't received many bids already, the probability of receiving very ambitious bids in the last few days was little.

The supplier had said that the statuette was Bagheera from Rudyard Kipling's famous book *The Jungle Book*. However, this made no difference as you did not have statuettes of any other characters from the book and statuettes that belong to a "family" do not have the same value individually as they would with the rest of the statuettes. Below the claws, the statuette has the mark of Sujo Ceramics, Dholka. Your research suggested that this used to be an important ceramics family in India, but the company is no longer in business. However, in their heyday, this family produced some wonderful ceramic pieces and some of its creations have bagged great prices as antiques.

You have not been doing very well today. So far you have sold just one product and you would love to get rid of the tiger, the supposed Bagheera. You would not mind selling it at a low price as long as it's equal to or higher than $250. You have not put any price tag on it, and everything is negotiable. You know you wish to approach this potential buyer who has been observing the statuette in detail to close the deal.

KUSHPHAL[1] CONUNDRUM

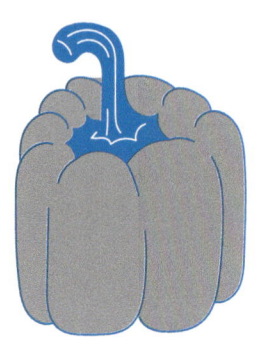

How many roles? – 2
Time for preparation – 20 minutes
Time for negotiation – 15 minutes

Instructions

There are two sides in this case, you can either be the representative of Nutrison or the representative of Brin University. For this exercise, we recommend you not to spend too much time between preparation and negotiation. The negotiation is happening in an unplanned and informal context. So, try to do the exercise in a similar setting. Once you finish the exercise, exchange the case with your partner and then collectively try to come up with the most appropriate solution.

---

1   An imaginary fruit – loosely based on fruits like Ramphal that belong to the Annona family of fruits

1. REPRESENTATIVE OF NUTRISON

1.1. About Nutrison

You work for Nutrison, a nutrition research program funded jointly by the Asian Development Bank and other governmental health agencies. The objective of the organization is to conduct research and come up with new products that can help alleviate malnutrition and starvation related diseases. The organization has various projects in pilot phase and continuation of its funding depends on the progress achieved in different projects. As per the constitution of the organization, during the current year, they should have at least one project in the trial runs to ensure renewal of the funding. The next review of the funding decision is due in 4 months' time.

1.2. About You

You are the Chief Procurement Officer of Nutrison. Your objective is to ensure timely procurement of food items and chemicals. Your function is of critical importance as your efficiency in managing requisite items on time ensures success of smooth progress of the projects. Quick progress of the project is a critical step in ensuring renovation of funding and hence continuation of the organization.

1.3. About Sanuter and Kushphal

'Sanuter' is the most ambitious project of Nutrison. Also, 'Sanuter' is the only project that has potential of entering the trial runs phase the earliest. Last year scientists of Nutrison were able to come up with an interesting formula which they titled 'Sanuter.' 'Sanuter' is a food paste based on the pulp and seeds of Kushphal, an Indian fruit. Despite belonging to *Annonaceae* family which flourishes in Latin and Central America, Kushphal is generally found in the Bhal Delta of the River Sabarmati in the region of Gujarat. The pulp of the fruit Kushphal has been found to be rich with thiamin and raboflavin (vitamin B compounds) (see Table Kushphal I). Deficiency of these elements is found to be critically scarce in pregnant women and children suffering from anemia and malnutrition in many underdeveloped nations.

Kushphal is not produced in huge quantity because of several reasons. The first being the irrigation technology used in Kushphal not to be very advanced. Moreover, Kushphal needs special natural conditions which are available in a very small geographic area. The total crop of Kushphal depends heavily on monsoon. Kushphal needs a very specific amount of water, and both very heavy rains as well as very little rain affect the produce negatively.

Table Kushphal I. Food value per 100 g of edible portion

Food value per 100 g of edible portion		Food value per 100 g of peel portion	
Element	Available quantity	Element	Available quantity
Calories	80-101	Quercetin	30-37.5 g
Moisture	45.3-55.1 g	Catechins	22.5-27 g
Protein	1.17-2.47 g	Proanthocyanidins	15-18.5 g
Fat	0.5-0.6 g		
Carbohydrates	20-25.2 g		
Crude fiber	0.9-6.6 g		
Ash	0.5-1.11 g		
Calcium	9.6-10 mg		
Phosphorus	6.7-12.1 mg		
Iron	0.42-1.14 mg		
Thiamine	5.75-7.119 mg		
Riboflavin	8.86-11.175 mg		
Niacin	0.428-0.90 mg		
Ascorbic acid	15.0-44.4 mg		
Nicotinic acid	0.5 mg		

1.4. The procurement procedure of Kushphal

The purchase process of Kushphal is regulated and also quite slow. Production of Kushphal is carried out by different small and marginal farmers, hence buying the fruit directly from the producer is virtually impossible. Generally, Kushphal may be bought from the Agricultural Producers Marketing Cooperative (APMC). Every year Kushphal is produced somewhere during late winter, around three months after the end of the monsoon. At the end of the monsoon, the potential buyer may approach the APMC and get information about estimated production and prices on the basis of total rainfall during monsoon. However, price is not confirmed unless an order is placed. The order can be placed only when the market is officially open. Every year, APMC announces in advance the day of market opening.

1.5. Post-Purchase Processing

Once Kushphal has been procured, it will be sent to an external company that is specialized in peeling. This peeling needs to be done in order to separate the skin of Kushphal, so the purchaser only receives the pulp and seeds. Peeling off requires special precision which should result in minimum loss of pulp. Peeling off by the special processor costs $0.80 per unit.

1.6. Estimates

When you enquired two months ago APMC told you that this year, because of an exceptionally heavy monsoon, Kushphal production will be limited to 30,000 units and the cost is likely to be $6 per unit. Since last year you needed only 2,000 units, you didn't worry too much about the availability. However, you informed the Chief Scientist and your immediate boss of "Sanuter" and asked for a prompt order. The expected purchase was 5,000 units. Accordingly, you put aside around $30,000 for purchase of Kushphal and went about buying other important materials for other projects.

1.7. Emergency

Ten days ago, you received a message from the Chief Executive Scientist that the renewal of the funding grant of the program depends heavily on trial runs of "Sanuter." Since "Sanuter" is the only project, which is in an advanced phase, not being able to start with trial runs might affect the funding renewal procedure. In order to prepare enough samples of the paste for studying its impact across different parts of the world, you need at least 25,000 units of Kushphal. In other words, you need to procure 20,000 units over and above what you already had budgeted for. Your sources in the APMC of India informed you that the final production of Kushphal is 28,766 units. However, the price of Kushphal will be $15 per unit. The sudden increase of price was due to interest shown by another international buyer. Despite your efforts, you could not get the name of the other international buyer who is also looking for Kushphal in huge quantity.

1.8. Meeting with the boss

In such an emergency situation, you went to speak with your boss yesterday. You put forth three important issues:

1. Of your annual procurement budget, what you have left is $300,000 (including $30,000 for Kushphal, which means in order to purchase 25,000 units you need an additional $75,000.

2. In case you do not manage to get all the required units how is it likely to affect the trial runs of "Sanuter" and, consequently, your own future in the organization?

3. Who could be the other international buyer who is equally interested in Kushphal?

Your boss told you that in case you can't get 25,000 units, get 'as many as you can' within the budget. Also, the boss said that, "In case we can't start with trial runs, it will be difficult to get a renewal of funding. All the scientists have affiliations with universities so we will go back to universities and Sanuter will probably carry on with collaboration between some university and other Non-Governmental Organizations. However, the executive staff, like Finance, Procurement (that means you) and administration will have to seek new jobs." Last but not the least, your boss was able to find out that the other potential buyer of Kushphal is Medicinal Research Laboratory of Brin University. Your boss further added, "I have no clue about why they want to buy it and how much. But they seem to have deep pockets, and the supplier has sensed it."

APMC is closed for the next two days and you can't really investigate with them. The market formally opens after two days, and the first thing in the morning you will do will be to place an order, and then keep your fingers crossed that they don't have any other order and, somehow, they agree to a reduction in price.

1.9. Today

Today you are attending a negotiation seminar at a prestigious international business school and suddenly you get to learn that a representative of Medicinal Research Lab of Brin University is also attending the seminar. You exchanged pleasantries with him/her over morning coffee but avoided any talk about the Kushphal issue. However, you requested a meeting after the sessions are over to see if you can persuade him/her to abandon the pursuit of Kushphal so that you can buy Kushphal comfortably, ensuring permanence of your organization as well as your job.

2. REPRESENTATIVE OF BRIN

2.1. About Medicinal Research Lab, Brin University

You work for the Medicinal Research Lab (MRL) at Brin University as a scientist in microbiology. You helped set up the Medicinal Research Lab three years ago to help garner a stronger relationship with pharmaceutical industry and manage greater public-private partnership for funding new clinical research in the area of skin care. Being a founder member of the MRL, you have also had the additional responsibility of attracting private sector corporations to start new research initiatives. In order to attract fresh talent for the research lab, it's important for you to keep getting new collaborations. Every research project of the Medicinal Research Lab is a joint collaboration between the University and one or more private sector partners. However, in case of absence of sufficient private sector participation, the University would discontinue the organization and re-organize its members into different academic positions.

2.2. About SkinShield

After a lot of efforts, you were able to bring together a young talented botanist, a micro-biologist and a major international pharmaceutical corporation to work on a new skincare product for MRL. The product was based on the peel of a tropical Indian fruit called Kushphal. The skin of Kushphal was found to be richly endowed with polyphenols like quercetin, catechins, and proanthocyanidins (see Appendix Cases.I). These elements are strong antioxidants, and they have a very positive impact on skin preservation and skin recovery especially in case of loss of skin caused by burns. Based on the peel of Kushphal, in the last two years you have been developing a cream titled, SkinShield. The project is supposed to complete its trials this year and then it will be transferred to the pharmaceutical corporation for commercialization for a big price. Being able to sell off the project during this year will be a big achievement for the project.

2.3. About You

You are the Chief Coordinator of the MRL and SkinShield which is like being the CEO of the organization. There are three important areas that you need to take care of. First, to ensure that MRL gets enough private sector participation so that it's easy to manage the financial feasibility of MRL. Second, attract the best of the talent to MRL to make MRL a name to reckon with in the field of skin care research. And third, once the projects have started, to make sure that they enter the clinical trials on time and can be soon transferred to the corporate partner for commercialization.

2.4. About SkinShield and Ramphal

SkinShield is the most ambitious project of MRL. SkinShield is likely to be positioned as an up-market medical treatment which can be highly beneficial in skin recuperation. SkinShield is the only project of MRL which is in an advanced phase and has the potential of getting transferred to the corporate partner. In other words, SkinShield is a major potential source for revenue for MRL which will ensure both survival and growth of the organization.

Kushphal is not produced in huge quantity because of several reasons, the first being the irrigation technology used in Kushphal is not advanced enough. Moreover, Kushphal needs special natural conditions which are fulfilled in a very small geographic area. The total crop of Kushphal depends heavily on monsoon. Kushphal needs a very specific amount of water and both, very heavy rains as well as very little rain affect the produce negatively.

2.5. The procurement procedure of Kushphal

The purchase process of Kushphal is regulated and also quite slow. Production of Kushphal is carried out by different small and marginal farmers, hence buying the fruit directly from the producer is virtually impossible. Generally, Kushphal may be bought from the Agricultural Producers Marketing Cooperative (APMC). Every year Kushphal is produced somewhere during late winter, around three months after the end of the monsoon. At the end of the monsoon, the potential buyer may approach the APMC and get information about estimated production and prices on the basis of total rainfall during monsoon. However, price is not confirmed unless an order is placed. The order can be placed only when the market is officially open. Every year, APMC announces in advance the day of market opening.

2.6. Post-Purchase Processing

Once Kushphal has been procured, it will be sent to an external company that is specialized in peeling. Since the paste depends heavily on the quality of the skin, it is really important to preserve all its antioxidants. Hence peeling is done in order to separate the skin of Kushphal and keep the pulp and seeds separate. Since pulp and seeds are of no use, they are generally disposed of by the processing company itself. Generally, the transportation cost, to and fro, is about $400 per 1,000 units while peeling and processing costs $1.20 per unit.

2.7. Emergency

The Pharmaceutical Corporation who collaborates with you sent you a message two months ago that the new CEO of the company is going to reshuffle the research portfolio. As a result, projects that have been dragging on for more than two years without a clear indication of entering completion phase will likely be cancelled. This puts the very existence of MRL as well as SkinShield in danger. After talking to the team of scientists you decided to accelerate the project. In order to ensure continuation of the project you need to produce a higher quantity of cream to speed up the test runs which will ensure a quicker passing on to the company and also will generate revenue for MRL. In the last couple of years, you had purchased a total of 3,200 units of Kushphal from APMC and have developed good relations with the chief commercial officer of the APMC. Last week you enquired with the APMC and mentioned that you needed to buy at least 20,000 to 25,000 units of Kushphal this year. Your budget for the entire process of purchase and peeling off the skin of Kushphal is about $300,000. The budget may increase but only after the review by the partner organization and the University, which is due in 3 months (see Table Kushphal II).

Table Kushphal II. Purchase of Kushphal during the past three years

Year	Phase of research	Quantity	Price	Total Kushphal production
1	Initial	50	$3.87	64,523
2	Experiment	1,000	$4.63	62,788
3	Experiment	3,000	$5.02	69,322

2.8. Decision

On enquiring with the Chief Commercial Officer of APMC about price and quantity you got to know that this year the production is likely to be 28,716 units and the market price will be $15 per unit. On asking why such a high price, after much persuasion the official of APMC informed you that some other international buyers are also interested in heavy import this year. On the other hand, due to a heavy monsoon the overall crop has been badly hit. Your scientists have asked you to get around 25,000 units to be safe. From other channels you found out that Nutrison, a research organization, is going to buy a significant quantity of Kushphal.

APMC is closed for the next two days and you can't contact them. The market formally opens after two days and the first thing in the morning you will do will be to place an order and then keep your fingers crossed that they don't have any other order, and that, somehow, they agree to a reduction in price.

2.9. Today

Today you are attending a negotiation seminar at a prestigious international business school and suddenly you get to learn that a representative of Nutrison is also attending the seminar. You exchanged pleasantries with him/her over morning coffee but avoided any talk about the Kushphal issue. You were really keen to talk further but he/she asked you to have a meeting when sessions are over in the evening. You are looking forward to this opportunity to see if you can persuade the Nutrison representative to abandon their pursuit of Kushphal and ensure continuity of MRL which you have set up with so much hope and aspiration.

THE APARTMENT

How many roles? – 2
Time for preparation – 20 minutes
Time for negotiation – 25 minutes

Instructions

There are two sides in this case, a potential tenant and the owner of the apartment. We recommend that you read the role of the tenant and ask a friend of yours to read the role of the proprietor and do the negotiation.

1. THE ROLE OF TENANT

Your company, a consumer multinational, has transferred you to a subsidiary in another country. For the last ten years, since you joined the company as a fresh university graduate, you had always been stationed at the headquarters. Recently, the national marketing director of a foreign subsidiary retired, and the Board of Directors decided to promote you to take charge of the said position. As you have no family responsibilities, this looked like a great opportunity, and you intend to make the most of it.

As soon as you took up your new position in the foreign city, you started looking for an apartment on various real estate websites and contacted several real estate agents in the town to let them know your preferences: you wanted a large, furnished, modern apartment with all the latest conveniences, with a parking space and, above all, proximity to your new office.

After a long search, you have found a 70 m^2 apartment furnished with designer furniture, on two floors, with the bedroom upstairs and quite a spacious living room downstairs, a parking space, polished stone floors, economical subfloor heating, and air conditioning, along with next-generation home appliances. As soon as you saw it, you called the advertiser, a private individual, to inquire about the terms and conditions and arrange a visit to the apartment. The owner told you that the price was high but that it was negotiable, although the minimum rental agreement was three years, non-negotiable, and three months' rent was placed as a deposit.

A few days after this conversation, you had to travel to the city to see the subsidiary's offices, so you took the opportunity to have a look at the apartment as well. The visit convinced you that this was where you wanted to live. There was no talk about price because, at the last minute, it was the caretaker who showed you the apartment, as the owner was unable to attend.

Your company pays for your accommodation, as well as various other expenses. However, the monthly allowance for rental and additional costs is decided based on different market factors and approved by the Human Resources Director. In your last conversation with the HR Director, he told you he would approve up to €2,000 for accommodation and expenses. The less you pay for rent, the more you would have at your disposal for other costs, which you have estimated at about €1,000 per month. However, you don't want to lower your living standard and feel that you wish to the apartment.

During the same trip, you took the opportunity to see if there was any other accommodation more economical, and one that would meet your demands. You found a furnished duplex in the same area, for which the landlord was asking €1,300. However, when you went to see it, you found it to be less attractive than the apartment, as it was not as elegantly decorated and did not have the home appliances. Buying your home appliances would cost anywhere from €750 (buying everything second-hand) to €1,800 (everything new). Also, the duplex was a bit farther from your office than the apartment (see Exhibit Apartment.1 and 2).

Three weeks later, you go back to sort out some final details about the subsidiary's initial work. You also want to get the issue of the accommodation sorted out on the same day. You called the apartment owner and were told it is still available, so you have arranged another visit.

After checking with several agencies and searching on the internet, you find nothing better, although you find several less attractive options. You will be meeting with the owner shortly.

Exhibit Apartment.1. Additional information

Average rental prices citywide in the last five years (20 x 5 being latest)					
Price per square meter					
Year	20 x 1	20 x 2	20 x 3	20 x 4	20 x 5
Furnished	21.52	24.84	27.18	26.14	24.04
Unfurnished	19.37	21.11	23.10	20.39	17.31

Average rental prices in the neighborhood of the apartment in the last five years					
Price per square meter					
Year	20 x 1	20 x 2	20 x 3	20 x 4	20 x 5
Furnished	25.32	29.22	30.2	29.04	25.31
Unfurnished	22.79	24.84	25.67	22.65	18.22

Source: Mehta & Stein own elaboration

Exhibit Apartment.2. Price per square meter over the last five years

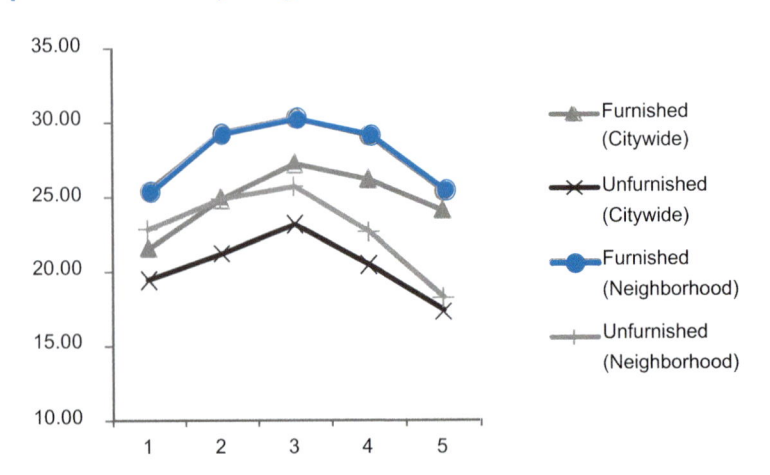

2. THE ROLE OF OWNER

You have taken up the job of renting your daughter's apartment. On the day of the negotiation, you wake up in the morning thinking about what you would say that afternoon to a prospective tenant, a foreign manager, who has already visited the apartment a few weeks ago during a visit to the city, where he is going to be living for a considerable future. On that occasion, it was the building's caretaker who showed the flat, as you had to accompany your wife to the **emergency ward of a hospital**. According to the caretaker, the manager seemed to be quite interested and satisfied with the visit, although they did not talk about rent.

The 70 m² apartments are situated in a high-end residential and office area. The price is not specified in the advertisement and is said to be "negotiable." The minimum rental period is three years, with the three month's rent as a deposit. However, you won't mind settling for just one month's deposit. You would like to have a bank guarantee during the rental agreement's life, but you know that asking for a bank guarantee will significantly limit the number of potential tenants. The apartment was built nine years ago and is furnished with designer furniture. It has two floors, a bedroom upstairs and a spacious living room downstairs, a parking space, polished stone floors, low-consumption subfloor heating with air conditioning, and next-generation home appliances. The property has had no major repair work done to it since it was built.

Your daughter has had to move to another country for family reasons. She has asked you to help her rent the apartment as soon as possible for a minimum of 1,000 net per month, that being the amount of her monthly mortgage payment, which she would not be able to afford otherwise. You know that a few hundred euros more would help cover other expenses associated with the apartment and would make your daughter happy.

As you are not an expert in this market and have other important things to do, you contacted a friend of yours who is a builder, who told you that similar apartments in that neighborhood used to fetch as much as €2,300 per month six months ago, however, the recent crisis had driven prices down. As of now, according to your friend, €1,900 per month was already considered to be a high rental amount (see Exhibit Apartment.1 and 2).

The person interested in the apartment is the new marketing director of a subsidiary of a multinational. You want to get the right person as the tenant to not burden your daughter with problems she will be unable to deal with effectively being half the world away from here.

On the other hand, yesterday, you showed the apartment to a young entrepreneur who has just started a software business in the area. He was very much interested, he but told you that, he could not pay at the moment more than €1,000 plus one month's deposit. He accepted all the other conditions without any problem. He also said that he could enter almost immediately. However, you are afraid that a tenant with an uncertain future may create complications for your daughter, and you wish to avoid them, so your priority is to reduce risks. You have agreed to give the young software entrepreneur a final answer tomorrow. After months of trying, these are the only two people who have shown a genuine interest.

In any case, whether this afternoon or tomorrow, you are determined to conclude the negotiation with the entrepreneur.

The marketing manager has just arrived and is waiting to meet you.

STYLE BIZ

How many roles? – 3
Time for preparation – 45 minutes
Time for negotiation – 75 minutes

Instructions

This is a three-party exercise that focuses on an internal disagreement in an organization between the director of Strategy and the digital director of the company. Operations Director mediates between the two in this conversation. We recommend that you read the role of the Digital Director and ask two of your friends to prepare the other two roles. When you finish the negotiation, read together the last document that explains the real outcome of the situation.

1. STYLE BIZ - GENERAL INFORMATION

Style Biz was a multinational company dedicated to manufacturing and distributing textiles with a presence in more than 60 countries. It operated as a family business group at the distribution level in small and large businesses and featured different brands aimed at different customer segments.

The company's 2018 turnover reached €300 million, placing it among the country's top 20 most profitable fashion companies, while worldwide it reached annual revenues of €2 billion with a presence in Europe, America, and the Middle East.

One of the main challenges the company faced involved digital transformation, not only for improving its channels, such as e-commerce (which represented 15% of online sales), but also for implementing and applying the new business strategies and smooth and efficient operations which in turn improve the speed and flexibility of project development. This new focus was not without its reasons; in a previous financial year, it had been estimated that at least 40% of the forecasted growth of the next three to five years would be driven by digital channels, although their distribution in the company's income statement was still less significant compared to off-line channels.

One of the main goals in 60% of fashion companies was the implementation of a digital strategy. In addition to having a strong social media presence and a commerce platform (which Style Biz already had), this also implied being able to transform the organization and the governance model by digitizing operations and the supply chain and by capturing new digital natives thanks to the transformation of customers' shopping experiences. It was estimated that if the Style Biz did not implement digital transformation strategies, it could lose between 30% and 50% of its expected growth.

The company's digital director, who had recently joined Style Biz after having worked in a multinational in the luxury sector, decided to contract the services of a consulting firm called Digital Strategy. The digital strategic plan included the creation and management of account plans for the company's main B2B customers in its digital channels, which up until that point had been neglected by the sales force. In order to achieve this mission, the company had to plan out its sales activities via digital channels of the selected customers' accounts as well as to launch new operational and oversight processes in order to monitor the activity on a weekly and monthly basis. Using key performance indicators (KPIs) that served to measure sales performance was necessary in order to achieve greater accuracy; the digital department wanted to obtain the sales data of the customers themselves, which the company had not previously used. Once the KPIs were obtained, they were grouped so that the Style Biz managers could make more effective decisions.

The company's oversight bodies fell under the scope of the Department of Strategy and Analytics and were supervised by the chief strategy officer; historically, they had been focused on the company's market share indicators (KPIs) and on the sales estimates of its main competitors within the sector. This information had been obtained through market panel data, provided by a specialized external company which periodically collected information on end consumers' purchases and consumption. It should be noted that a peculiarity of the Department of Strategy was that it generated and distributed follow-up tables only to the executive levels of the company in the central offices, not to Sales or other departments.

The operational requirements of the digital acceleration plan called for the implementation of customer account plans and end consumer sales, or *sell-out,* data. If this information were available, compliance with the Style Biz strategic plan goals could be measured with each customer. The ultimate goal of this approach was to highlight the deviations from the strategic plan, as well as the causes behind these deviations, in order to make faster and more effective sales and business decisions than had been carried out under the previous strategy. The digital team wanted to include the following KPIs in order to track the company's performance:

- The comparison between growth in consumer sales, or *sell out,* via digital and non-digital sales channels by using customer data.
- The growth of each Style Biz customer that was due to sales made via digital channels.
- The number of customers or end consumers registered in the Style Biz database thanks to digital channels' promotional campaigns.
- Employees' level of training and digital competencies, in the wake of having launched a digital education program within the company.
- A comparative index, with the company's main competitors, that measured and ranked the company's operational performance in digital channels.

In the context of the simmering conflict between the chief strategy officer and the digital director —in which a lack of communication predominated— the team of consultants that had been hired by the Digital Department decided to bring the issue to the director of operations, who was at the top tier of the company's organizational structure (see Figure Style Biz.1). The consultants wanted to convince him of how necessary it was to follow the push towards digital business not only in terms of using panel data, but also regarding the customer accounts' *sell out*.

Figure Style Biz.1. The Company's Organizational Chart

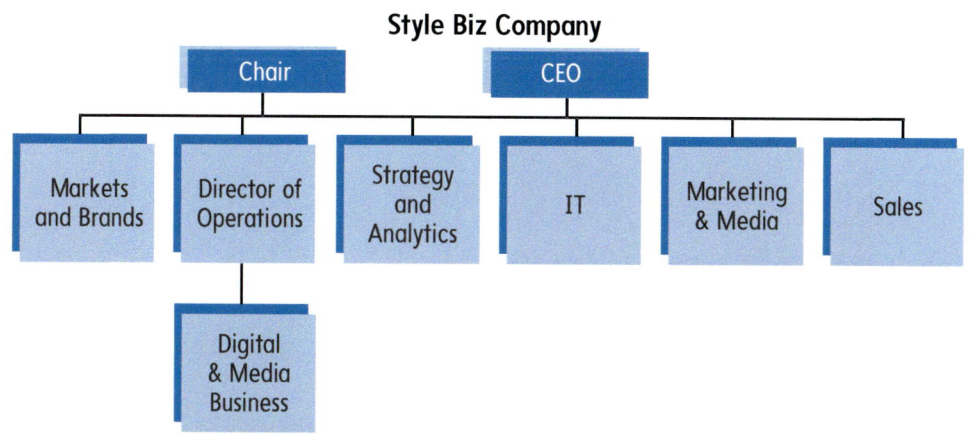

Style Biz Company

- Chair
- CEO
  - Markets and Brands
  - Director of Operations
    - Digital & Media Business
  - Strategy and Analytics
  - IT
  - Marketing & Media
  - Sales

Source: Prepared by the authors.

The director of operations sought to strengthen the relationship between the different stakeholders. He initially supported the decision to use the account plans in conjunction with the customers' sales data in order to evaluate the company's sales performance and, on the other hand, to use the Department of Strategy's panel data to evaluate the market share.

The problems that the new digital approach posed for the chief strategy officer were rooted in the incorporation of the main customers' account plans into the scorecard follow-up tables. These data were in the hands of the markets and the digital team and required, at that point in time, hours of manual work for processing and homogenization. The position of chief strategy officer would therefore lose its importance and the company's organizational structure could be altered in the short term.

2. STYLE BIZ COMPANY – ROLE OF DIGITAL DIRECTOR

The digital director had recently joined Style Biz. He had previous experience of more than 15 years as an account manager in companies in the luxury sector. Throughout his years of experience —in addition to getting involved in company processes, strategies, and decision-making— he had to directly monitor customer growth using key performance indicators (KPIs) in order to identify customer opportunities and perform sales. He had also occupied the role of director of digital business.

The digital director's transformative role within his former company, and his ability to implement digital solutions for the problems that arose there, had convinced Style Biz to hire him to carry out its digitization. His function was to transform the company's culture and to accelerate its digital business growth. He had moved from a multinational to a family company that had more limited resources. In order to achieve his goals, to the chief strategy officer's chagrin, the digital director had to lead the design and direction of the company's digital strategy.

The tension between the two directors was palpable from the get-go. Both were intent on winning but, as a new member to the team, the digital director wanted to lead the way and gain greater influence in the sphere of sales strategy. In order to do so, he had hired a team of consultants with the expectation that the Department of Strategy and the rest of the departments would recognize the importance of digital business and implement the necessary operational changes. This would allow the digital director and his team to reach more powerful positions and gain more importance in the company's governance model.

The most important KPIs were those related to sales, such as the incorporation of the account plans into the executive business scorecard follow-up table or the growth, measured in percentage, of digital sales contributions in proportion to total sales. Meanwhile, other KPIs were considered supplementary, such as the number of customers, employee training in digitization, and the benchmarking of digital operations (in comparison with competitors). The strategy for implementing the KPIs would be easier with a top-down approach —convincing the directors and senior management— than with a bottom-up one, which would be a slower process with greater obstacles posed from the business units, who held information on the company's profits and losses (P&L). These decisions brought transparency to the profits and losses that the sales team was obtaining in the customers' accounts as well as to their action plans; this had never before taken place at the company.

In case the indicators were implemented, the collaboration with the Department of Strategy and Analytics would be complete. In the absence —at least for the time being— of automated systems for collecting, aggregating, and distributing the information related to the KPIs, the digital team would be in charge of preparing, compiling, and sending the data.

Even without the approval of the Department of Strategy, the digital director could count on having the Markets & Brands, Marketing & Media, and IT departments as allies (see Figure Style Biz.2), seeing as the adoption of the new strategy would mean an increase in the company's digitization and greater involvement in decision-making in the medium and long term. However, Marketing & Media wanted them to have greater access to the Department of Strategy's analytics in order to optimize product sales.

The digital director wasn't sure if he should meet, together with the consultants, with the chief strategy officer, or whether the consultants should begin potential negotiations on their own.

Figure Style Biz.2. Affinity Diagram

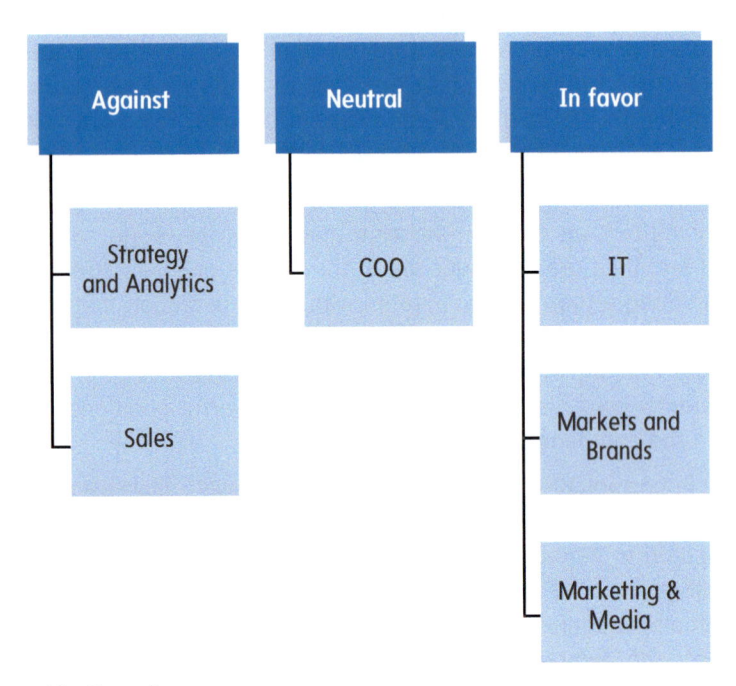

Against	Neutral	In favor
Strategy and Analytics	COO	IT
Sales		Markets and Brands
		Marketing & Media

Source: Prepared by the authors.

Letter From the Digital Director to the Director of Operations (A)

Digital Director, Style Biz Company

I'm sending you this letter in order to convey the company's need to implement a digital strategy, incorporating customer accounts and digital indicators. To this end, a meeting with the chief strategy officer must be arranged in order to specify how we will proceed with this strategic transformation.

Here at the Digital Department, we have estimated a 20% growth in online channel sales by 2020. We recommend that the design and implementation of the digital strategy be developed in under a year, with the aim of improving the company's performance and profitability. As digital director, I propose to lead the design and direction of the digital strategy. With the implementation of the indicators, the collaboration with the Department of Strategy and Analytics would be complete.

The chief strategy officer's refusal to meet with us has prevented us from moving forward with the strategy, thus greatly slowing the process. The chief strategy officer has agreed to meet with the team of consultants, who have been informed of the changes that will be made. However, a meeting between both departments is necessary.

Thank you in advance for your attention and for taking my comments into consideration. I am more than happy to respond to any questions or doubts you may have.

Sincerely,

Digital Director

The Digital Director's Goals for the Negotiation

Instructions

1. The student playing the role of digital director has a total of 100 points, which they can distribute as they see fit across the four main goals (indicated in bold) in the table by writing the assigned number in the *Total score* box.

2. Once the total score has been assigned, the student must allocate a specific score for each subpoint, on a scale of 1 to 100.

Digital Director			
Goals	Total score	Specific score	Score obtained
1. To lead the design and direction of the company's digital strategy			
• To implement the strategy with a top-down approach			
• To implement the new digital strategy in the short term			
• To get the chief strategy officer to collaborate			
• To get the Sales Department to collaborate			
2. To incorporate Account Plans into the business's scorecard follow-up table			
• Data on main customer sales via digital and traditional channels			
• Contribution (in percentages) of digital sales to the growth of each Style Biz customer			
3. To incorporate KPIs into the company's strategy			
• To add the number of end consumers and customers registered in the database			
• To raise the level of employee training on digital competencies			
• To incorporate benchmarking analysis of the company's digital operating capabilities as compared with the rest of the market			
4. To reestablish communication with the chief strategy officer			
• To gain access to information on the current strategy			
• To consider periodic meetings			

Source: Prepared by the authors.

3. STYLE BIZ – ROLE OF DIRECTOR OF OPERATIONS

You are the director of operations at Style Biz. The CEO trusts you and has authorized you to resolve the conflict at hand.

You have the authority to make a decision on this mediation. Through this mediation, you'd like to demonstrate your strong skills in managing department directors. The current CEO is due to retire in a few years and you are keen on presenting yourself as a candidate for his succession. One way to do this is by demonstrating your mediating capacity and your ability to lead. Both directors have written you an individual letter to express their feelings, which you will take into consideration during the mediation.

In the event that you see that cooperation between the two directors is not feasible, you may also recommend that one of them be dismissed. However, although your decision is highly influential, you yourself do not have the direct authority to dismiss either one of the directors.

4. LETTER FROM THE DIGITAL DIRECTOR TO THE DIRECTOR OF OPERATIONS (A)

Madrid

Digital Director

Style Biz Company

I'm sending you this letter in order to convey the company's need to implement a digital strategy, incorporating customer accounts and digital indicators. To this end, a meeting with the chief strategy officer must be arranged in order to specify how we will proceed with this strategic transformation.

Here at the Digital Department, we have estimated a 20% growth in online channel sales by 2020. We recommend that the design and implementation of the digital strategy be developed in under a year, with the aim of improving the company's performance and profitability. As digital director, I propose to lead the design and direction of the digital strategy. With the implementation of the indicators, the collaboration with the Department of Strategy and Analytics would be complete.

The chief strategy officer's refusal to meet with us has prevented us from moving forward with the strategy, thus greatly slowing the process. The chief strategy officer has agreed to meet with the team of consultants, who have been informed of the changes that will be made. However, a meeting between both departments is necessary.

Thank you in advance for your attention and for taking my comments into consideration. I am more than happy to respond to any questions or doubts you may have.

Sincerely,

Digital Director

5. LETTER FROM THE CHIEF STRATEGY OFFICER TO THE DIRECTOR OF OPERATIONS (B)

Chief Strategy Officer

Style Biz Company

I hereby state that on September 10, I met with the Digital Strategy team of consultants to learn about the changes they are proposing for the company's strategy. Having completed the meeting, I consider it essential that I see the viability of the proposed indicators for the medium and long term, in order to examine their possible incorporation into the company's strategy.

As chief strategy officer, my direction and execution of the strategic plan is crucial for fulfilling the company's goals. In recent months, the digital director has hindered this work, proposing a very different strategy from the current one, including the incorporation of the main customers' account plans in the scorecard follow-up table.

If immediate changes in the current strategy were to take place, it would slow down our strategical execution. Therefore, on behalf of the Department of Strategy and Analytics, I propose to manage the new KPIs myself over the coming months in order to monitor their performance. In order to communicate this decision, I would like to meet with the digital director.

Thank you in advance for your attention and for taking my comments into consideration. I am more than happy to respond to any questions or doubts that you may have.

Sincerely,

Chief Strategy Officer

Mediation Goals in the Director of Operations' Negotiation

Director of Operations		
Negotiation goals	Achieved	Not achieved
Meeting between both departments		
Consideration of all conceivable options		
Exploration of alternatives		
Concessions on both sides		
Both parties are satisfied.		
The relationship has improved.		
The problem has been resolved.		
The agreement is permanent and practical.		
The outcome satisfies the interests of third parties.		
The groundwork has been laid for future agreements.		

6. STYLE BIZ - ROLE OF DIRECTOR OF STRATEGY

You have been the chief strategy officer of Style Biz for 10 years. Until joining Style Biz 10 years ago, in 1999, you had held high-level positions in logistics companies in the area of corporate development. One of your biggest achievements was the strategy you implemented in order to diversify revenue flows and marketing channels, which had previously depended 100% on the wholesale trade of garments.

Within the company, strategies had to be proposed from the Department of Strategy and Analytics with the support of external consultants, prioritizing the traditional business. During the previous year, the Digital Department had hired a digital strategy team to accelerate the company's strategy concerning the industry's fastest-growing channels and to steer it towards digitization. This change brought with it more pressure to apply the digital KPIs in the reports that the team prepared, without first consulting the chief strategy officer and pressing the director of operations to implement the changes.

Your goal for the meeting with the consultants, who represented the Digital Department, was to find out what KPIs they wanted to incorporate in order to check their viability in the medium and long term. However, it was essential that you obtain this information first-hand and from sources with which you felt comfortable, in order to maintain control of the strategy and communication with the company's executive team. Opening up a debate around these issues would help you find out what KPIs could be useful to incorporate in the panel data, to understand (without damaging your image) how they are calculated, and to figure out if there really was a disconnect between the headquarters and different markets. Taking over control of the new strategy in the medium and long term would preserve your favorable position within the company.

One possible alternative was to convince the director of operations to manage the new KPIs, operating at a lower level, within his team over the coming months; you could grant them greater visibility and Strategy could take responsibility for the new plan. For this to work, avoiding subsequent meetings between the team of consultants, the Digital Department, and the director of operations would be crucial.

You could count on the Sales Department, which implemented the current KPIs in their strategies, as an ally within the company (see Figure Style Biz.3). A change in the company's approach would impact months of work and mean reconsidering, in terms of both the short and medium term, team members' functions. That said, the sales team ended up being willing to introduce the new digital strategy KPIs in the long term, with the consequent hiring and onboarding into Sales of candidates with digital expertise.

You thought that, after meeting with the consultants, meeting with the digital director would be inevitable.

Figure Style Biz.3. Affinity Diagram

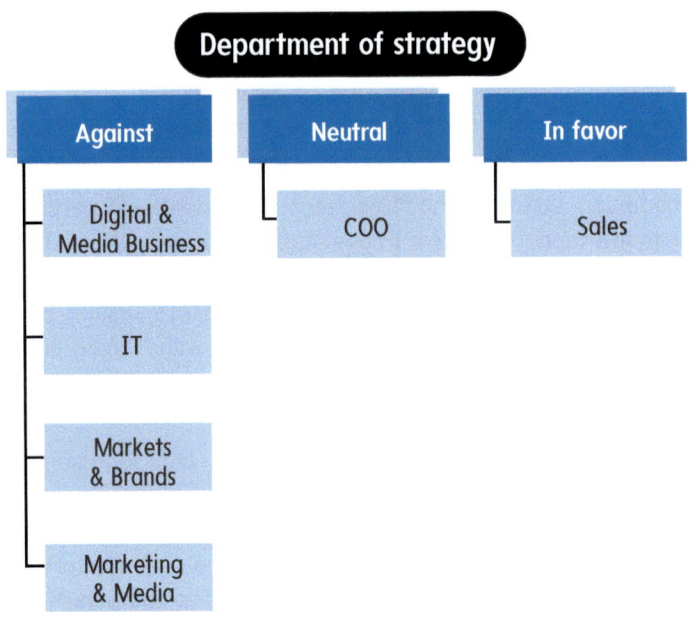

```
                    ┌─────────────────────────┐
                    │ Department of strategy  │
                    └─────────────────────────┘
        ┌───────────────────┬───────────────────┐
     Against              Neutral            In favor
        │                    │                   │
  Digital &                 COO               Sales
  Media Business
        │
       IT
        │
     Markets
     & Brands
        │
   Marketing
   & Media
```

Source: Prepared by the authors.

Letter From the Chief Strategy Officer to the Director of Operations (B)

> Chief Strategy Officer
>
> Style Biz Company
>
> I hereby state that on September 10, I met with the Digital Strategy team of consultants to learn about the changes they are proposing for the company's strategy. Having completed the meeting, I consider it essential that I see the viability of the proposed indicators for the medium and long term, in order to examine their possible incorporation into the company's strategy.
>
> As chief strategy officer, my direction and execution of the strategic plan is crucial for fulfilling the company's goals. In recent months, the digital director has hindered this work, proposing a very different strategy from the current one, including the incorporation of the main customers' Account Plans in the scorecard follow-up table.
>
> If immediate changes in the current strategy were to take place, it would slow down our strategical execution. Therefore, on behalf of the Department of Strategy and Analytics, I propose to manage the new KPIs myself over the coming months in order to monitor their performance. In order to communicate this decision, I would like to meet with the digital director.
>
> Thank you in advance for your attention and for taking my comments into consideration. I am more than happy to respond to any questions or doubts that you may have.
>
> Sincerely,
>
> Chief Strategy Officer

The Chief Strategy Officer's Goals for the Negotiation

Instructions

3. The student playing the role of the chief strategy officer has a total of 100 points, which they can distribute as they see fit across the three main goals (indicated in bold) in the table by writing the assigned number in the *Total score* box.

4. Once the total score has been assigned, the student must allocate a specific score for each subpoint, on a scale of 1 to 100.

Chief Strategy Officer			
Goals	Total score	Specific score	Score obtained
5. To lead the company in the direction of its strategy			
• To maintain current status and power in the company			
• To implement the digital strategy in the medium and long term			
• To ensure that the new KPIs that are proposed are under your control and supervision			
• To get the digital director to collaborate			
• To get the IT, Markets and Brands, and Marketing & Media departments to collaborate			
6. To preserve and incorporate the following KPIs			
• To maintain the market share value in the panel data			
• To keep the sales estimates of the main competitors in the panel data			
• To incorporate the market share comparison between brick and mortar (physical stores) and pure play (virtual stores) with the forecasts for the coming years			
7. To prevent communication between the digital director and senior management as well as persuasion on the part of the digital director			
• To prevent meetings from taking place between the digital director and the director of operations			
• To preserve the hierarchical structure of the company			

Source: Prepared by the authors.

7. STYLE BIZ – THE FINAL OUTCOME

The relationship between the Department of Strategy and the Digital Department continued to be troubled. Despite the meeting between the chief strategy officer and the digital strategy consultants, the outcomes of the negotiation had been meager. The KPIs with lower clout for the company were incorporated, including the following: registering in the database, the number of end consumers, and employees' level of training in digital competencies. On the other hand, the chief strategy officer had managed to incorporate his market share KPI for comparing brick and mortar (physical stores) and pure play (virtual stores) with the forecasts for the coming years. However, these indicators were not going to have any impact on sales for the coming years nor did they readjust the current strategy.

The chief strategy officer had achieved his desire to maintain control of company strategy and to convince the director of operations to relegate the digital team to a position below IT in the company's organizational structure. Meanwhile, the digital director, without his team under control, worked on upstream functions with the Department of Digital Media. Given this situation, the digital director considered resigning; he interpreted the situation as a clear movement to impinge on his authority in the company's decision-making processes. However, after reflecting on the matter for some time, he decided to remain in his new role, stating, "I know where I want to take this company's digital business and I will continue to carry out my mission."

He considered his job to be at risk because it depended on the outcome of the conflict; it was in greater danger than that of the chief strategy officer. That said, the digital director was confident that the implementation of the new strategy would be successful and encouraged his team to continue increasing their importance within the company with a bottom-up approach, integrating a new digital language and governance model in their work with other departments.

The digital team's next step, in conjunction with the chief strategy officer, would be to outline the guidelines for automating the KPIs that had been agreed upon during the meeting and to incorporate information gathered from customers' account plans. The company was considering changing the way that some of the departments functioned. It was necessary to implement these changes in the organization. Otherwise, sales from digital channels would not be boosted and losing that competitive edge would be irreversible.

CONTINENTAL INSURANCE VERSUS ALPACA HOTELS

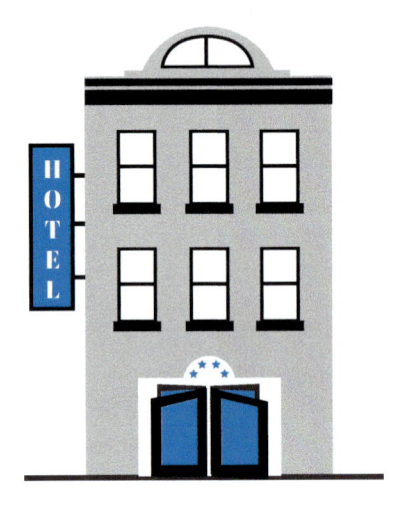

> This is a complex deal making exercise. The best way to use this exercise is to prepare both, the insurance, and the hotel side, one by one and then to think about a possible negotiation scenario. Try to put yourself in the situation of both sides and see which issues are likely to create tension. Also, think whether you would prefer to do this negotiation as a team or as an individual. If you are negotiating along with a team, what would your role in the negotiation be and who would be your ideal teammates?

1. THE CHIEF INVESTMENT OFFICER OF CONTINENTAL INSURANCE

Continental Insurance is a family business group with 70 years' experience as a leading provider of home and life insurance. It has 10 million clients throughout the country and an investment portfolio of €5 billion, of which approximately 10% is in real estate, including landmark properties and properties in the best areas of the capital and other major cities. The insurance firm distributes its products through numerous brokers and its own agencies, and through service providers and banks with which it has partnership agreements. The third generation has just joined the Board of Directors.

Six months ago, the Chief Investment Officer (CIO) presented the Board with several proposals for the commercial development of a building of 5,500 m^2, 4,000 of which are above ground floor, and which is located in the historic district of the country's second largest city. It is a historic building and the first property the firm acquired in that city, 40 years ago; it had been organized as a multitenant office building and was 50% occupied by tenants (lessees) who agreed to relocate, and by group companies, including the main agency, which had been there since "time immemorial." The historic district has been renovated and is now basically a tourist area with some hotels. There have been drastic reductions in the number of homes and offices, which have relocated to sites further from the historic district.

Aware that they were not maximizing the property's profitability as an asset, Continental Insurance considered commercial development to be the only solution. The insurance firm entertained the following options:

Total renovation of the building, keeping the ground floor as an office for the insurance agency (estimated investment of €4.3 million).

Renovation of the building, relocation of the agency, and commercial development of the ground floor (estimated investment of €4.75 million).

Conversion of the building for residential use, while leaving the ground floor for commercial use (no precise investment amount has been estimated, but in no case would it be less than €5.75 million to €6.75 million).

Conversion of the building for hotel use (estimated investment of €5.75 million to €6.5 million). The property had the Municipality's special permission for such a conversion, because such works in the historic district were no longer otherwise permitted.

Sale of the building (a recent appraisal valued it at €12.5 million, though the current selling price would have been around €10 million, due *inter alia* to the building's communal facilities and interior layout being outdated).

After having analyzed the business plans of the various options, the best long-term solution for the property, in view of the risk-return tradeoff, was deemed to be a conversion of the building for hotel use. The CIO was then appointed to prepare for the relevant negotiations. He has been expected to obtain at least a triple net yield[2] (excluding expenses) of 5% from the first year of the contract. Furthermore, he was instructed to conclude a lease agreement under Law 29/1994 of November 24 on Urban Leases, rather than a management agreement (with variable income based on hotel revenues), which is very common in the hotel industry, especially among the international chains. Continental Insurance does not want to assume any employment risk with the hotel staff that could give rise to a potential termination of the contract. This last condition, along with the converted hotel's potential size (64 rooms), according to Continental Insurance's consultants, drastically reduces the number of interested parties. All indicators suggest that they are able to create a four-star superior property.

The chief investment officer is aware that the building is outdated in terms of facilities and equipment and has not received any significant investment in the last 30 years; further, he is aware of the commercial department's sizable interest to push the main agency out of the building.

The Alpaca Hotels chain took interest in the property. It is a family chain that was founded in 1962 by a builder of very modest origins who grew the chain to its current four hotels within the city. While two of its hotels are three-star and the other two are four-star, none are located in the historic district. Lama's eldest son manages the hotels and the construction group, which no longer seems to generate the business it had during the country's recent general housing boom, and the city's in particular. The CIO met the CEO of Alpaca Hotels two years ago during a protracted negotiation for the lease of another building in the capital, which was already being operated as a hotel. Though the insurance firm ultimately decided to keep its original tenant, relations between the two sides have maintained a level of respect and trust.

After some careful calculations, the CIO decides to aim for a rental price of €14,000 per room annually. He knows that €15,000 would have been possible a few years back, even though the current crisis has raised prices for quite a few establishments (some similar) to €12,000 located in other areas. On the other hand, late last year he closed a renegotiation of €10,000 per room (having conceded €4,000 per room annually) in the only hotel within Continental Insurance's real estate portfolio, a somewhat dated four-star located on one of the capital's most famous streets.

After a few months of negotiations with Alpaca Hotels, the parties reached a gridlock. Alpaca Hotels agreed to carry out the necessary works to remodel the building in advance and on behalf of Continental Insurance, and bear all risks involved. The insurance firm would only accept a lease agreement containing a clause for the completion of works by the lessee (tenant). Further, Lama insisted on a minimum investment amount of €7.25 million. However, the insurance firm's technical consultants insisted that €5.5 million was sufficient to carry out the work, and that any difference was due to the builder's choice of higher quality materials and desire to secure higher

---

2   Yield: a measurement of future income from an investment, calculated annually as a percentage of an asset's cost or market value.

margins. The CIO has been explicitly authorized to go up to €6.25 million and would prefer to avoid requesting more. The hotel chain has requested advance payments, but the insurance firm would only accept such a condition after having obtained the relevant certifications. Financing is not a problem for the CIO, as he needs to make investments; he senses it's also not a problem for the chain.

The builder's blueprint envisions for a maximum of 64 rooms, which the parties both acknowledged. Alpaca Hotels claimed that they must invest an additional two million: one for refurbishment (kitchens, etc.) and another for furniture.

Both parties are in favor of a mutually binding long-term contract. The insurance firm and hotel chain respectively seek contractual terms of 20 and 10 years. The chain proposes a break option after 10 years, with subsequent annual renewal for a maximum 25-year term. This may trigger a breakdown of negotiations for the insurance firm. Any adjustments to annual rent will be made according to the CPI over the last 12 months. The insurance firm wishes to introduce the option to adjust for increases above the CPI over the life of the contract, in order for the rent to closely approximate market conditions. The chain does not want this clause. Other items at the negotiation's forefront are requests to secure the lease via a bank guarantee (which entails financial costs for the tenant) and a grace period for rent payments. The insurance firm pushes for a one-year bank guarantee without a grace period exceeding the licensing and construction periods.[3]

They have resolved to get the negotiations moving next week; otherwise, the CIO will have to look for alternatives. However, he believes that it is still possible to reach a mutually beneficial agreement with Lama. His goal is to obtain the returns expected on the property, and he considers that Alpaca Hotels has demonstrated its knowledge of the business with its similar assets. He further does not think that it is feasible to achieve the same outcome under which he is already negotiating with an alternative party, in terms of the property's characteristics as well as Continental Insurance's demands regarding the acceptable legal contract.

He just received a call from the firm's president, who inquired about the negotiation's progress and wondered if they were on track to permanently affix the Continental Insurance sign on the roof of the building once it became a hotel, so that it would form part of the historic district's urban landscape.

---

3   Six months are estimated for licensing and 12 for construction.

2. CONTINENTAL INSURANCE VS. ALPACA HOTELS

Alpaca Hotels is a family-owned hotel chain founded by a builder who migrated from the countryside to the city, where he remained and ultimately founded the chain in 1962, which has now grown to four hotels. The city is the second largest in the country and draws many tourists. Two of the hotels are three-star and the other two are four-star. Alpaca's construction group was profitable for years, achieving relatively standard 15% margins, and in some cases 20% margins, for the works it carried out. Things began to change a few years ago as the housing boom was followed by a deep crisis. At present, the family group's growth path depends on its hotels, all of which it built and fully owns, though none of which are located in the city's historic district. It is a standard hotel chain with good quality facilities in coastal areas, with an aim to establish its presence in major urban centers. Alpaca's eldest son is responsible for the active management of the hotels and construction group.

Two years ago, Alpaca Hotels bid to manage its first four-star hotel, which had 97 rooms and was somewhat dated but was located at one of the capital's busiest streets. The property belonged to Continental Insurance, a highly profitable insurance firm. The firm sought an alternative to its preexisting tenants, with whom its relations seem to have deteriorated due to continuous pressures for rent reductions. The CEO of Alpaca Hotels made contact with the CIO of Continental Insurance during this period and began discussions that took an interesting course for both sides. The company ultimately decided to keep its tenants. A sector analyst stated that the insurance firm's annual room rent of €14,000 was cut by almost 40%. The CIO and Alpaca Hotels were nonetheless able to establish a working relationship despite the outcome

A year and a half later, the CEO received news that this same insurance firm was considering renting a building in the city's historic district for hotel use. It was a landmark property known for housing the insurance firm's main agency on the ground floor and its large rooftop sign, which became a part of the quarter's landscape. The CEO consulted his father, and both agreed that they could not pass on this opportunity to seize what could be the chain's flagship property. The location was very attractive, as the area had gone from being residential to commercial and very touristy. Hotels were lacking and the Municipality was not granting permission to build any. In fact, the insurance firm had received authorization after much struggle and thanks to the property's location at the district's edge. International tourism displayed solid growth, and a similar trend was expected in the future. The city's position enabled 90%+ occupancy rates, leading to net margins of 15%.

Through an initial contact with Continental Insurance's chief investment officer, the CEO proposed a renovation project under a management agreement. The property had been half empty for some time and was mainly occupied by the insurance firm's affiliated companies, which the former was now relocating. No investments in the building had been made in decades, perhaps since it was acquired 34 years ago. The building was 5,500 m^2, 4,000 of which were above the ground floor. According to Alpaca Hotels, the building could house no more than 62 rooms.[4] Alpaca Hotels submitted a budget of €7.25 million for a four-star superior hotel, which included an acceptable margin for the construction group. Work could begin immediately. The CIO relied on the opinions of his technical consultants to counter that €5 million was sufficient, which Alpaca Hotels deemed unworkable, even if they were to negligently build with lower quality materials. It further meant spending the construction group's profit margin, and perhaps spending even more, which neither the CEO nor especially his father would accept. The CIO set a limit at €5.5 million, and at that point the negotiations stalled, despite the parties' agreement to a lease arrangement rather than a services management agreement, the latter being the industry norm and an absolute requirement by the major chains.

Both parties are in favor of a mutually binding long-term contract. The insurance firm and hotel chain respectively seek contractual terms of 20 and 10 years. The chain proposes a break option after 10 years, with subsequent annual renewal for a maximum 25-year term. This may trigger a breakdown of negotiations for the insurance firm. Any adjustments to annual rent will be made according to the CPI over the last 12 months. The insurance firm wishes to introduce the option to adjust for increases above the CPI over the life of the contract, in order for the rent to closely approximate market conditions. The chain does not want this clause. Other items at the negotiation's forefront are requests to secure the lease via a bank guarantee (which entails financial costs for the tenant) and a grace period for rent payments. The insurance firm pushes for a one-year bank guarantee without a grace period exceeding the licensing and construction periods.[5]

The CEO knew of three-star hotels on the city's coast that were paying €10,000 per room annually and four-star superior hotels that were paying €12,000. He also knew from the management industry that prices in the latter category could reach €14,000 for the newest hotels and that rent for ultra-luxury five-star hotels would exceed €16,000. The fact that Alpaca would only have 64 rooms, for which they could charge between €120 and €140 per night, rendered nonviable any offer above €13,250 per room annually. In addition to the insurance firm's investment, Alpaca Hotels would have to invest an extra €1 million to €1.5 million to finance additional facilities and furnishings, an amount it would need to recoup within five or six years. That period could be shortened with sufficient occupancy rates, since they were expecting a net margin of 15%. The chain would have problems if the yearly average were to fall below 60%, as had happened to one of its badly situated hotels during the two toughest years of the recession. However, this is an unlikely scenario.

Although the CIO had not opined on the matter, as the building was known in the city for locating the insurer's lead agency and the enormous sign on the roof, the CEO found that the proposal to give the hotel the same name might be a good idea. In any case, the sign was enough.

---

4   The hotel business produces significant economies of scale, given that common areas and services are not directly proportional to the number of rooms.

5   Six months are estimated for licensing and 12 for construction.

As the parties plan to resume negotiations in the coming days, the CEO prepares a summary of his offer. By setting the construction margin to 10% and carefully reviewing the project's qualities, he decides the work can be completed for €5.5 million; however, under no circumstances can the minimum investment in additional facilities and furnishings fall below €1.2 million, as the future hotel's image and preservation would otherwise be compromised. If the insurance company agrees to bear €300,000 of this investment, he would be willing to pay up to €13,000 per room annually.

YARIS VERSUS ZILAN

1. REPRESENTATIVE OF YARIS, FROM YARISTAN

Yaris Ltd. is a large, diversified electrical company based in the nation of Yaristan. The company has recently diversified into drone manufacturing and has been making small-sized micro-drones that have lot of applications in photography, agriculture, security, etc.

Yaris is the biggest electrical company in the nation of Yaristan and Yaristan is one of the strongest economies in the region.

A recent survey has suggested that Yaristan is growing rapidly in the manufacturing of electrical and electronic manufacturing. As of now, the total capacity of all the seven manufacturers in Yaristan is 40,000 (forty thousand) drones. The total capacity in the country for manufacturing micro-drones is about 10,000. Out of which, Yaris can produce about 2,000 drones a year. Yaris wants to double the capacity in the next three years. The application of drone technology and application of micro-drones is going to increase at the rate of almost 60% in the coming years.

Given the likely increase, you want to make sure that you capture the increasing market. While you have a very good network of dealers in the country, you do not trust other national manufacturers. That's why you want to import micro-drones from outside. You have identified a company that specializes in high quality micro-drones called Zilan plc. Zilan is a company that started as an R&D lab in the National University of Ziland. Ziland is a developed nation, about 6,000 kilometers from Yaristan. Zilan specializes in the manufacturing of high-quality micro-drones and your plan is to buy their drones and market them under your brand till you develop the capacity to manufacture enough micro-drones yourself, i.e., next five years.

1.1. Micro-Drones

Micro-drones are drones with the size of the tip of the thumb. Experts have said that these micro-drones will have applications in medicine, in pharmaceutical research, in security applications, etc. The Government of Ziland granted a huge research scholarship some seven years ago in the National University of Ziland's aviation laboratory to develop drone technology. Two years later its drone research project was spun off as a company owned by the Government of Ziland. Three years later the Government of Ziland divested forty percent of its ownership and passed it onto six private equity funds. Last year, the Government of Ziland completely privatized the company and now the company is owned by a consortium of two biggest technology companies of the country.

Demand for Micro-Drones in the Country

	Current	Year 1 (from now)	Year 2	Year 3	Year 4	Year 5
Demand of micro-drones	17,000	21,000	26,000	36,000	48,000	65,000
Production capacity of micro-drones (by Yaris) (without any collaboration)	2,000	2,800	4,000	6,000	9,000	15,000
Production of micro-drones in Yaristan	10,000	12,000	15,000	21,000	29,000	41,000
Deficit in the market	7,000	9,000	11,000	15,000	19,000	24,000

As of now there are three types of micro-drones, namely Palm-top, Dual-Wing and Helicopter. Palmtop is the simple drone with a four-blade fan. Dual-Wing are micro-drones with two separate wings on each side. While Helicopter is a special drone with four wings and space for attaching a camera below. Palmtop is considered to be very useful for meteorological research, agricultural research, geological and metallurgical applications. Dual-Wing is the most appropriate for gaming, while Helicopter model is considered to be a high-end product with applications in security and intelligence as well as in photography and movie production. As of now, the break-up of demand for all the three models is difficult to estimate, but experts suggest that all the three models will be in equal demand. At present, you can only make Palmtop micro-drones, and you need to wait for at least three years to be able to produce a good quality of micro-drones of the other two models.

You want to get all three products from Zilan Ltd. If they don't agree to provide the three you want, you can at least have two, one of which should be the Helicopter model, given that it is likely to sell at a very high price. Even if they do not agree to license Helicopter model immediately, you want to include it in the future, either from the second year or from the third year.

A few months ago, you got to know about the company and its capacity to produce high quality of micro-drones. Ziland is a country where the robotics and electronic gadgets manufacturers have flourished in recent years. At present in Ziland there are about 47 drone manufactures. However, Zilan has the best technology. Also given that it was started by scientists it has always been technologically perfect but in terms of commercialization they have been lacking. After not being able to commercialize on its own the company focused on technological licensing and knowledge transfer as its main business. Your plans currently suggest that if you continue to grow your capacity without any collaboration with a company with a better technology, at best you will reach 15,000 units by year 5. However, if you have a collaboration or a joint venture, this capacity could be doubled, and you can be capturing almost half of the micro-drones market on your own.

Your local representative in Ziland sent you a list of conditions from Zilan Ltd. and you have agreed to all of it. You in return had asked to have freedom to set prices yourself and Zilan agreed to it.

Primary issues already agreed.

1. Zilan will send micro-drones fully assembled for the first two years. In the third year, Zilan will start sending components and start assembling the micro-drones in Yaristan.
2. Zilan will help Yaris, develop capacity to develop an assembly production plant for the high-quality micro-drones.
3. The agreement will be for five years.
4. You will be free to set the price of the products in the market.

In this negotiation, you have five issues to contemplate.

1. Number of models Zilan would agree to license. Your target is to have all three and, in any case, you want to have the Helicopter model included in the deal.
2. The number of units to be imported from Zilan. Your target is to import as many as the current market deficit suggests. But you can go higher as well. However, based on your dealer network you cannot reach more than 60% of the market at any point. If you have more quantity than that, you may start accumulating inventory.
3. Initial price and quantity of each model.
4. Royalty: below you can see the price range and the target royalty that you want to pay from sales of micro-drones.

	Palmtop	Dual-Wing	Helicopter
Expected sales price	€200-350	€400-600	€650-950
Royalty	2-4%	3-5%	4-6%

Based on your calculations the distribution cost is fixed at €80 per unit across products.

5. License fees: this is the fixed payment of license fees. You only want to pay the license fees in the first year and from the second year onward you want to pay royalties only. Generally, license fees could be anywhere between €200,000 (two hundred thousand) and a €1,000,000 (one million). But you do not wish to pay a license fees that puts you in losses straightaway.

6. Exclusivity and lock-in: you do not mind if Zilan wants to enter the market on its own, after the second year. Also, you don't mind if they want to have a licensing agreement with some other company after the third year. However, you do not want to give up on this too easily. At the same time, you want to know if you will have the opportunity to collaborate with other technology partners with similar agreements in future. You do not mind a lock-in of 3 or even all the 5 years, where both the companies can only work with each other.

How is Yaristan?

- Yaristan is a sovereign nation for more than a hundred years and is known for its unique negotiation culture.
- When you negotiate, be direct.
- Be aggressive. Express your anger or frustration openly.
- Be informal. Treat people on first name basis. Use humor and jokes to make the other side feel relaxed.
- Show warmth.
- Outsiders think that you are a bit 'loud.' Don't be ashamed of it. Show off your loudness.
- In a negotiation, when the other side does not respond to questions properly or seems dodgy, you lose trust, and you express that clearly.
- You negotiate aggressively. You tend to start negotiations with high opening offers. You don't like beating around the bush too much.
- In your culture creating pressure on the other side during negotiation is considered appropriate.
- You are very proud of Yaristan, its culture and its heritage. Anyone, not respecting Yaristan enough, is given an appropriate answer on their face.
- You do not mind using threats in a negotiation against the other side if necessary.
- Yaristanis are known to use emotions as tactics. It is common to fake anger, sadness, happiness or pity to gain an advantage over the other side.
- You prefer to settle one issue at a time. You do not like people who do not close deals clearly and keep everything vague.

2. REPRESENTATIVE OF ZILAN LTD., FROM ZILAND

You are a representative of Zilan Ltd., and you are about to negotiate a licensing agreement with a company called Yaris from the country of Yaristan. The company wants to use micro-drones (drones of a very small size) manufactured by you. Yaris wants to buy your drones and sell them under their brand name for the next five years.

Zilan (your company) is located in the developed nation of Ziland. The government of Ziland granted a huge research scholarship some seven years ago in the National University of Ziland's aviation laboratory to develop drone technology. Two years later its drone research project was spun off as a company owned by the Government of Ziland. Three years later, the Government of Ziland divested forty percent of its ownership and passed it onto six private equity funds. Last year, the Government of Ziland completely privatized the company and now the company is owned by a consortium of the two biggest technology companies of the country.

In early years, Zilan Ltd. tried to commercialize its own product but it lacked expertise and experience. The main two reasons for the failure were, (i) it was a government-controlled organization and lacked a commercial perspective and (ii) it was mainly run by scientists whose primary focus was advancement of technological sophistication rather than market capitalization. Two years ago, the company decided to focus on export of technology as the main area for generating revenues and learn to commercialize in the process by partnering with other organizations.

Ziland is a paradise for technology companies. As of now there are 47 (forty-seven) companies that manufacture drones. However, Zilan was one of the first in this sector and its specialty is micro-drones. There are about five other companies that are coming up fast in the micro-drones but still their technology is much inferior to yours.

Your counterpart, Yaris Ltd., is a large, diversified electrical company based in the nation of Yaristan. It is the biggest electrical goods manufacturer in the country of Yaristan. Yaristan is an upcoming market, and it is growing quickly as one of the strongest economies in the region.

Yaris has recently diversified into drone manufacturing and has been making small-sized micro-drones that have a lot of applications in photography, agriculture, security, etc. However, their micro-drones are not really of a great quality, but they have a very good dealer network, and they can easily reach out to 50% (fifty percent) of the national market.

A recent survey has suggested that Yaristan is growing rapidly in the manufacturing of electrical and electronic manufacturing. As of now, the total capacity of the seven manufacturers in Yaristan is 40,000 (forty thousand) drones. The total capacity in the country for manufacturing micro-drones is about 10,000. However, you do not know precisely how much Yaris ltd. can produce. You also have the estimates of the demand of micro-drones in the country.

Demand for Micro-Drones in Yaristan

	Current	Year 1 (from now)	Year 2	Year 3	Year 4	Year 5
Demand of micro-drones in units	17,000	21,000	26,000	36,000	48,000	65,000

You want to capture this deal because of two reasons.

1. It will give you an entry into an interesting market like Yaristan.
2. It will give you an opportunity to learn distribution and commercialization of technology from an experienced company.

2.1. Micro-Drones

Micro-drones are drones with the size of the tip of the thumb. Experts have said that these micro-drones will have applications in medicine, in pharmaceutical research, in security applications, etc.

As of now, there are three types of micro-drones, namely Palm-top, Dual-Wing and Helicopter. Palmtop is a simple drone with a four-blade fan. Dual-Wing are micro-drones with two separate wings on each side. While Helicopter is a special drone with four wings and space for attaching a camera below. Palmtop is considered to be very useful for meteorological research, agricultural research, geological and metallurgical applications. Dual-Wing is the most appropriate for gaming while Helicopter model is considered to be a high-end product with applications in security and intelligence as well as in photography and movie production. As of now, the break-up of demand for all the three model is difficult to estimate but experts suggest that all three models will be in equal demand. On your own, you can only make Palmtop Micro-Drones at present, and you need to wait for at least three years to be able to produce a good quality of micro-drones of the other two models.

You only want to license the Palmtop model. At best, you would allow the Dual-Wing model. However, the Helicopter model is your star product, and you are not sure if you should license it easily. You would license Helicopter model only beyond the third year, by which time you will be ready to launch your own brand in the market too. Your objective is to have a license agreement, learn from the partner about distribution networks and commercialization and then launch your own brand in the Yaristani market after the third year when the demand is likely to pick up. That is the reason why you do not want a lock-in and exclusivity for all the five years.

When Yaris approached you, you sent a few pre-conditions for the negotiation to the company and they have accepted all the conditions. You were really enthused by their positive response to your conditions and are now looking forward to this negotiation. Yaris had only one condition and that was the freedom to set prices which you agreed to after internal discussions.

2.2. Primary issues already agreed

- Zilan will send micro-drones fully assembled for the first two years. In the third year, Zilan will start sending components and start assembling the micro-drones in Yaristan.
- Zilan will help Yaris, develop capacity to develop an assembly production plant for the high-quality micro-drones.
- The agreement will be for five years.
- Yaris will be free to set the price of the products in the market.

In this negotiation you have several issues to contemplate.

a) Number of models you would agree to license. Your target is to have just one model licensed now and not to grant the Helicopter model before the third year.

b) The number of units to be exported to Yaris. You have sufficient capacity, but you do not want to commit any number. Specially, in the first year you do not wish to commit for more than 4,000 units (across models).

c) Initial price and quantity of each model. Your objective is to have at least 10% margin over the unit cost. Here you have the unit cost information.

Cost of manufacturing and assembling of each unit:

Palmtop Model – €120

Dual-Wing Model – €230

Helicopter Model – €450

Your target is to have at least 10% margin on this unit costs.

d) Royalty: you also want a royalty of about 5-7%. In fact, if the price is satisfactory, you do not mind going down to 2% (in Helicopter model) or letting go of the royalty completely (in the other two models). However, you believe that if you sign an exclusivity contract, you should be rewarded with the royalty as well.

e) Based on your calculations the distribution cost is fixed at €80 per unit across products.

f) License fees: this is the fixed payment of license fees. You ideally want license payment for all the years. However, in an exceptional case you may let the license fee go for a particular year. License fees for such a product are not predictable. They can be anywhere between annually €20,000 (twenty thousand euros) and €1,500,000 (a million and a half euros). You may negotiate a reduction or increase in license fees over years. You definitely want a license fee for the first three years.

g) Exclusivity and lock-in: you do not mind if Yaris wants to collaborate with other companies because you are sure of your current technological superiority. At the same time, you also want the flexibility of seeking other partners or selling your product under your own brand beyond a particular period (especially after three years).

How is Ziland?

- Ziland is a developed nation that takes pride in its culture and heritage.
- The Zillish (people of Ziland) believe in harmony and they behave collectively as a group. They take decisions collectively and with consensus.
- The Zillish generally decide in advance who speaks when in a negotiation and they never talk over each other.
- The Zillish take pride in following their traditional culture, hierarchies and customs. You behave very formally and generally treat strangers only by their family names.
- You prefer to avoid eye-contacts and loud gestures. You prefer to speak in low-tone and use very formal language with outsiders.
- You always start the negotiation by highlighting how great your organization and your country is. You do not like to jump to make offers. You do not like to close one issue at a time. You never agree on a single issue and always agree on the complete agreement.
- The Zillish love to ask questions about the negotiation issues. You love to listen and to collect information, but you do not share information easily. After the other side has answered the question, the Zillish may respond by asking another question, repeating the question, or just remaining silent. They are unlikely to offer information in return. If you run out of questions, you often ask for information to be repeated. Your culture is a culture of consensus and you do not share positions unless you see a common position with the other side.
- In your culture, to say 'no' directly is considered to be arrogant and that's why you seldom say 'no.' instead of saying 'no,' you generally use expressions such as, 'we could look into it,' or 'we will think about it.' In a very unreasonable demand you may say, 'that is going to be a bit difficult.'
- Display of emotion is a very private and intimate issue for the Zillish. Showing emotions like anger, frustration, joy, etc. in a formal corporate setting is considered to be inappropriate and unacceptable. In corporate negotiations, you prefer to be rational and that's why your face is generally impassive and expressionless.

EPILOGUE: NEVER STOP LEARNING

As you set out for Ithaka
hope the voyage is a long one,
full of adventure, full of discovery.

...

Keep Ithaka always in your mind.
Arriving there is what you are destined for.
But do not hurry the journey at all.
Better if it lasts for years,
so you are old by the time you reach the island,
wealthy with all you have gained on the way,
not expecting Ithaka to make you rich.
Ithaka gave you the marvelous journey.

In 1911, Constantine Cavafy wrote his poem *Ithaca*. It is an allusion to the legendary Journey of the Greek hero Ulysses towards Ithaca. Reading a book is an adventure too, even more if it may have practical consequences in the reader´s life, which we authors were looking for.

Our aim is leaving a fruitful and lasting impact on you, that brings value of two kinds: an internal fruit in terms of personal growth because of the skills acquired and renewed; and an external one, in terms of getting more of what you need and want.

Wealthy with all you have gained on the way

Let us summarize some of the substantial gains:

It is up to you to negotiate good and negotiate well, to obtain more of what you want (effectiveness) while managing the process skillfully (efficiency).

Ambidexterity, negotiating with both hands to be competitive and collaborative, gives you the power to solve problems while making joint decisions with your counterpart, creating value.

If you take care of the process, the process will take care of you; therefore, there is no valid substitute to preparation. It is the only stage of the process you will have full command of.

Having a framework and using it in your daily life will provide you with a set of tools to improve your negotiating skills. It will discipline your rich experience and enhance your intuition.

Questioning is the essence, mainly of interpreting the information you receive in order to predict the likely behavior of your counterpart, because past behaviors drive future interpretations.

Learning is an attitude and a never-ending job: after each negotiation, stop for just a little while to think about how you performed, and use the given framework as the filter.

Be ambitious in setting the personal action plans after the self-examination. The name of the game is "trying again and again": whenever you say *enough,* you will stop winning.

Remember: **negotiation is always and fundamentally about human relations**.

You are only at the end of the book, but at the joyful beginning of your voyage as an ambidextrous negotiator, that we wish you good and well.

BIBLIOGRAPHY AND INTELLECTUAL INFLUENCES

Overall, in the development of this book, the following four sources have proven to be essential. The idea of the book originated from the first two technical notes developed by Prof. Juan Roure and Richard T. Pascale. Leigh Thompson's book, *The Mind and Heart of Negotiator* proved to be a critical resource with academic research, while *Getting to Yes,* by Fisher, Ury and Patton, is an essential reading for any scholar or practitioner in the field of negotiations and conflict resolution. For anyone interested in doing research in negotiation, Leigh Thompson's article co-authored with Jeanne Brett (2016) is a must read.

Chapter 1

Pascale, R. T. & Roure, J. (1995, May). *Negotiation: The Process of Solving Problems and Creating Value. Principles*. Barcelona, Spain: IESE Business School.

Pascale, R. T. & Roure, J. (1995, May). *Negotiation: The Process Of Solving Problems And Creating Value. Process*. Barcelona, Spain: IESE Business School.

Thompson, L. (2015). *The Mind and Heart of Negotiator.*

Fisher, R., Ury, W. & Patton, B. (2011). *Getting to Yes: Negotiating Agreement Without Giving In.* Boston: Houghton Mifflin.

Mehta, K. H. (2017). Negotiation Unit, Executive Program, International Nut & Dried Fruit Council.

Chapter 2

Galinsky, A. & Mussweiler, T. (2001). First offers as anchors: The role of perspective-taking and negotiator focus. *Journal of Personality and Social Psychology, 81*(4), 657-669.

Sabenius, J. K. (1992, January 1). Negotiation Analysis: A Characterization and Review. *Management Science, 38*(1), 18-38.

Chapter 3

Axelrod, R. (1984). *The Evolution of Cooperation.* New York: Basic Books.

Chapter 4

Gordon, T. (1975). *P.E.T. - Parent Effectiveness Training. The no-lose program for raising responsible children.* New American Library.

Rogers, C. R. (1951). *Client Centered Therapy.* Boston: Houghton-Mifflin.

Noesner, G. W. & Webster, M. (1997, August). Crisis Intervention : Usking Active Listening Skills in Negotiations. *FBI Law Enforcement Bulletin, 13.*

Malhotra, D. (2004). Trust and reciprocity decisions: The differing perspectives of trustors and trusted parties. *Organizational Behavior and Human Decision Processes, 94*(2), 61-73.

Malhotra, D. & Bazerman, M. (2007). *Negotiation genius: How to overcome obstacles and achieve brilliant results at the bargaining table and beyond.* New York: Bantam Books.

Chapter 5

Bonito, J. A. & Sanders, R. E. (2002). Speakers' footing in a collaborative writing task: A resource for addressing disagreement while avoiding conflict. *Research on language and social interaction, 35*(4), 481-514.

Donohue, W. A. (2001). Resolving Relational Paradox. *The language of conflict and resolution, 21.*

Putnam, L. L. & Holmer, M. (1992). Framing, reframing, and issue development. In L. L. Putnam, & M. E. Roloff, *Communication and Negotiation* (pp. 126-155). Sage Publications inc.

Bateson, G. (1972). *Steps to an ecology of mind.* Chandler Publishing.

Chapter 6

Lax, D. A. & Sabenius, J. K. (1985). The power of alternatives or the limits to negotiation. *Negotiation Journal, 1*, 163-179.

Brett, J. & Thompson, L. (2016, September). Negotiation. *Organizational Behavior and Human Decision Processes, 136*, 68-79.

About first offers, anchors and multiple equivalent simultaneous offers

Furnham, A. & Chu Boo, H. (2011, February). A literature review of the anchoring effect. *The Journal of Socio-Economics, 40*(1), 35-42.

Galinsky, A. (2004, July). Should You Make the First Offer? In *Negotiation*.

Magee, J. C., Galinsky, A. D. & Gruenfeld, D. H. (2007, February 1). Power, Propensity to Negotiate, and Moving First in Competitive Interactions. *Personality and Social Psychology Bulletin*.

McRuer, G., Gu, J. & Leonardelli, G. J. (2012, July). Multiple Equivalent Simultaneous Offers in Negotiations: Effects on Individual and Joint Gain. *Academy of Management Annual Meeting Proceedings, 1*.

Chapter 8

Ambidexterity in negotiations. About managing the competitive-collaborative tension in a negotiation

Mehta, K. H. (2012). Five Essential Strategies for Creative Negotiations. *IESE Insight*.

Galinsky, A. D. & Schweitzer, M. (2015). *Friend & foe: When to cooperate, when to compete, and how to succeed at both*.

Chapter 9

Brodt, S. & Thompson, L. (2001). Negotiating teams: A levels of analysis approach. *Group Dynamics: Theory, Research, and Practice, 5*(3), 208-219.

Thompson, L., Peterson, E. & Brodt, S. (1996). Team negotiation: An examination of integrative and distributive bargaining. *Journal of Personality and Social Psychology, 70*(1), 66-78.

Chapter 10

Thompson, L. (2015 6th ed). Multiple Parties, Coalitions and Teams (ch. 9). In *The Mind and Heart of Negotiator*. Pearson.

Michaud, P. (1988). The True Rule of the Marquis de Condorcet. In B. R. Munier, & M. F. Shakun, *Compromise, Negotiation and Group Decision* (pp. 83-100). Dordrecht, Boston, Lancaster, Tokyo: D. Reidel Publishing company.

Chapter 11

Weiss, J., Donigian, A. & Hughes, J. (2010). Extreme Negotiation. *Harvard Business Review*.

Voss, C. & Raz, T. (2016). *Never Split the Difference: Negotiating as if your life depends on it*. Harper business books.

Chapter 12

Brett, J. & Thompson, L. (2016). Negotiation. *Organizational Behavior and Human Decision Processes* (136), 68-79.

Malhotra, D. (2014, April). 15 Rules for Negotiating a Job Offer. *Harvard Business Review,* 92(4).

Chapter 13

Meyer, E. (2014). *The Culture Map: Breaking through the invisible boundaries of global business.*

Brett, J. (2011). *Negotiating Globally: How to negotiate deals, resolve disputes, and make decisions across cultural boundaries.* Jossey-Bass.

Chapter 14

Ames, D. & Parlamis, J. (2010, May 22). Face-to-Face and Email Negotiations: A Comparison of Emotions, Perceptions and Outcomes. IACM 23rd Annual Conference, Available at papers.ssrn.com/sol3/papers.cfm?abstract_id=1612871

Bernard, J. (February 2018). Escribiendo emails. In *Manual de escritura eficiente*, p. 24.

Bülow, A. M. (2011, August 1). The Double Monologue Principle: Argumentation in Email Negotiation. Available at papers.ssrn.com/sol3/papers.cfm?abstract_id=1899225

Bülow, A. M. (2010, December 13). Email Negotiation: Argument, Cognition and Deadlock in Email Negotiation. Available at research.cbs.dk/en/publications/email-negotiation-argument-cognition-and-deadlock-in-email-negoti

Craver, C. B. (2015, October 7). How to Conduct Effective Telephone and E-Mail Negotiations. Available at papers.ssrn.com/sol3/papers.cfm?abstract_id=2670011

DITRENDIA (2018). Todas las estadísticas sobre móviles que deberías conocer #MWC18". Available at mktefa.ditrendia.es/blog/todas-las-estadísticas-sobre-móviles-que-deberías-conocer-mwc18

Ebner, N. (2017). Negotiation via Videoconferencing. In Honeyman, C. & Schneider, A. K. (eds.) *The Negotiator's Desk Reference*. St Paul: DRI Press. Available at SSRN: https://ssrn.com/abstract=3029020

Ebner, N. (2017). Negotiation via email. In Honeyman, C. & Schneider, A. K. (eds.) *The Negotiator's Desk Reference*. St Paul: DRI Press, Available at SSRN: https://ssrn.com/abstract=2348111

Ebner, N. (2007). Trust-Building in E-Negotiation. In L. Brennan & V. Johnson (eds.) Computer-Mediated Relationships and Trust Managerial and Organizational Effects.

Hershey, PA: Information Science Publishing, 2007, Available at SSRN: https://ssrn.com/abstract=1722065

Ebner, N. et al. (2009). You've Got Agreement: Negoti@ting Via Email. Available at papers.ssrn.com/sol3/papers.cfm?abstract_id=1392474.

Frost, A. (2019). The Best Way to Reach Out to a Prospect for the First Time, According to 20 Sales Experts. Available at blog.hubspot.com/sales/the-best-way-to-reach-out-to-a-prospect-for-the-first-time

Guéguen, N., Legoherel P. & Jacob C. (2003). Solicitation of participation in an investigation by e-mail: Effects of the social presence of the physical attraction of the petitioner on the response rate.

IBM, Marketing Cloud (2016, January 13). Email Marketing Metrics Benchmark Study.

Lynett, M. (2016, October 12). The Advantages and Disadvantages of Shared Documents. Available at blog.mesltd.ca/the-advantages-and-disadvantages-of-shared-documents

McGinn, K. L. & Wilson E. (2004, March 1). How to Negotiate Successfully Online. Available at www.hbs.edu/faculty/Pages/item.aspx?num=16493

Nadler, J. & Shestowsky D. (2006). Negotiation, information technology, and the problem of the faceless other. In *Negotiation Theory and Research. Thompson, L. (ed.).* New York: Psychol. Press, pp. 145-72.

Naquin, C. E. & Paulson, G. D. (2003, February). Online Bargaining and Interpersonal Trust. Available at www.ncbi.nlm.nih.gov/pubmed/12675399

Nast, D. (2018, July 26). Negotiating for the Future. Available at www.raconteur.net/business- innovation/negotiating-for-the-future

Pascual, J. A. (2018, April 2). Cómo limpiar los datos ocultos de un documento de Word. Available at computerhoy.com/noticias/software/como-limpiar-datos-ocultos-documento-word-78409

Pesendorfer, E.-M. & Koeszegi, S. T. (2006). Hot versus cool behavioural styles in electronic negotiations: The impact of communication mode. Group Decision and Negotiation, 15.

Stuhlmacher, A. F. & Citera, M. (2005, September). Hostile Behavior and Profit in Virtual Negotiation: A Meta-Analysis. *Journal of Business and Psychology 20*, 69-93.

Swaab, R. I., Maddux, W. W. & Sinaceur, M. (2011). Early Words that Work: When and How Virtual Linguistic Mimicry Facilitates Negotiation Outcomes. *Journal of Experimental Social Psychology 47*(3), 616-621.

THOMPSON, L. & Nadler, J. (2002). Negotiating Via Information Technology: Theory and Application". Journal of Social Issues. https://doi.org/10.1111/1540-4560.00251

Chapter 15

Alsrheed, F., Rhalibi, A. E., Randles, M. & Merabti, M. (2014). Intelligent Agents for Automated Cloud Computing Negotiation. *International Conference on Multimedia Computing and Systems (ICMCS)*. doi:10.1109/icmcs.2014.6911305.

Asenador, S. H. (2018). El 'ecommerce' contiene su crecimiento en España este 2018. Taken from www.expansion.com/economia-digital/2018/10/14/5bc1e86ce5fde-a75428b45b4.html

Beam, C. & Segev, A. (1997). Automated Negotiations: A Survey of the State of the Art. *Wirtschaftsinformatik 39*(3), 263-268.

Bertino, E., Ferrari, E. & Squicciarini, A. C. (2004). Trust negotiations: Concepts, systems, and languages. *Computing in Science & Engineering 6,* 27-34.

Bevan, C. & Fraser, D. S. (2015). Shaking Hands and Cooperation in Tele-present Human-Robot Negotiation. Tenth Annual ACM/IEEE International Conference on Human-Robot Interaction. *HRI, 15,* pp. 247-254. doi:10.1145/2696454.2696490.

Cann, O. (2018). Las máquinas harán más tareas que los humanos para 2025, pero aun así la revolución robótica creará 58 millones de nuevos empleos en los próximos cinco años. Taken from reports.weforum.org/future-of-jobs-2018/files/2018/09/FoJ18_ES.pdf

Cao, M., Chi, R. & Liu, Y. (2009). Developing a multi-agent automated negotiation service based on service-oriented architecture. *Service Science, 1.* Taken from web.csulb.edu/~rchi/ssj/papers/20101/200944.pdf

Cao, M., Luo, X., Luo, X. R. & Dai X. (2015). Automated negotiation for e-commerce decision making: A goal deliberated agent architecture for multi-strategy selection. *Decision Support Systems 73,* 1-14. doi: 10.1016/j.dss.2015.02.012.

Cheng, C., Chan, C. & Lin, K. (2006). Intelligent agents for e-marketplace: Negotiation with issue trade-offs by fuzzy inference systems. *Decision Support Systems 42*(2), 626-638. doi: 10.1016/j.dss.2005.02.009.

Cruz-Maya, A. & Tapus, A. (2018). Negotiating with a robot: analysis of regulatory focus behavior. 2018 ACM/IEEE International Conference on Robotics and Automation (ICRA). doi: 10.1109/icra.2018.8460611.

Fatima, S., Kraus, S. & Wooldridge, M. (2014). *Principles of Automated Negotiation.* Cambridge University Press. doi: 10.1017/CBO9780511751691.

Filzmoser, M. (2010). *Simulation of Automated Negotiation.* Springer.

Foroughi, A. (1998). Minimizing Negotiation Process Losses with Computerized Negotiation Support Systems. *Journal of Applied Business Research 14*(4), 15-26. doi: 10.19030/jabr.v14i4.5648.

Gettinger, J., Köszegi S. T. & Schoop M. (2012). Shall we dance? - The effect of information presentations on negotiation processes and outcomes. *Decision Support Systems, 53*(1), 161-174. doi: 10.1016/j.dss.2012.01.001.

Goh, K., Teo, H., Wu, H. & Wei, K. (2000). Computer-supported negotiations: an experimental study of bargaining in electronic commerce. *Proceedings of the 21st Annual International Conference on Information Systems,* pp. 104-116. Taken from pdfs.semanticscholar.org/e319/7fdb9464582b79de5502aa4f322d547f4fec.pdf

Ennings, N. R., Faratin, P., Lomuscio, A. R., Parsons, S., Wooldridge, M. J. & Sierra, C. (2001). Automated Negotiation: Prospects, Methods and Challenges. *Group Decision and Negotiation, 10*(2), 199-215. doi: 10.1023/A:1008746126376.

Jonker, C. M., Aydoğan, R., Baarslag, T. Broekens, J., Detweiler, C. A., Hindriks, K. V., Pasman, & W. (2017). An Introduction to the Pocket Negotiator: A General Purpose Negotiation Support System. *Multi-Agent Systems and Agreement Technologies,* pp. 13-27. Springer. doi: 10.1007/978-3-319-59294-7_2.

Irfan, M. I. & Chishti, M. A. (2017). A model to incorporate automated negotiation in IoT. *IEEE International Conference on Advanced Networks and Telecommunications Systems (ANTS).* doi: 10.1109/ants.2017.8384094.

Irfan, M. I., Vij, S. & Mukhopadhyay, D. (2015). Automated negotiation with behavior prediction. *International Journal of Internet Protocol Technology, 9*(1), 44-50. doi: 10.1504/IJIPT.2015.074339.

Kersten, G. E. & Lo, G. (2001). Negotiation support systems and software agents in e-business negotiations. *The First International Conference on Electronic Business,* Hong Kong. Taken from iceb.johogo.com/proceedings/2001/pdf/252.PDF

Knight, W. (2017). Can Artificial Intelligence Master the Art of the Deal? *MIT Technology Review.* Taken from www.technologyreview.com/f/608850/can-artificial-intelligence-master-the-art-of-the-deal

Levine, T. R. (2014). Truth-Default Theory (TDT): A Theory of Human Deception and Deception Detection. *Journal of Language and Social Psychology, 33*(4), 378-392. doi: 10.1177/0261927x14535916.

Lewis, M., Yarats, D., Dauphin, Y. N., Parikh, D. & Batra, D. (2017). Deal or no deal? Training AI bots to negotiate. *Facebook Artificial Intelligence Research.* Taken from code.fb.com/ml- applications/deal-or-no-deal-training-ai-bots-to-negotiate

Lopes, F., Wooldridge, M. & Novais, A. Q. (2009). Negotiation among autonomous computational agents: Principles, analysis and challenges. *Artificial Intelligence Review 29*(1), 1-44. doi: 10.1007/s10462-009-9107-8.

Esteves, J. (2019, Jan 13) *Did You Know? 2019.* Taken from www.youtube.com/watch?v=bTM06NZOyDQ&feature=youtu.be

More, A., Vij, S. & Mukhopadhyay, D. (2016). An Efficient E-Negotiation Agent Using Rule-Based and Case-Based Approaches. *Leadership and Personnel Management: Concepts, Methodologies, Tools, and Applications,* 1003-1016. doi:10.4018/978-1-4666-9624-2.ch045.

Oliver, J. R. (1996). A Machine-Learning Approach to Automated Negotiation and Prospects for Electronic Commerce. *Journal of Management Information Systems 13*(3), 82-112. doi: 10.1080/07421222.1996.

Papaioannou, I., Roussaki, I. & Anagnostou, M. (2009) A Survey on Neural Networks in Automated Negotiations. *Encyclopedia of Artificial Intelligence,* 1524-1529. doi: 10.4018/9781599048499.ch223.

Rangaswamy, A. & Shell, G. R. (1997). Using computers to realize joint gains in negotiations: Toward an "electronic bargaining table". *Management Science 43*(8), 1147-1163. doi: 10.1287/mnsc.43.8.1147.